POLITICAL

AND SOCIAL
ECONOMY

Political and Social Economy
Edited by C. Addison Hickman and Michael P. Shields

Other Books in This Series:

Conglomerates and the Evolution of Capitalism
CHARLES R. SPRUILL

An Economic Analysis of Democracy
RANDALL G. HOLCOMBE

Economic Thought and Social Change
J. RON STANFIELD

Origins of Economic Thought and Justice
JOSEPH J. SPENGLER

The Political Economy of the Urban Ghetto
DANIEL R. FUSFELD
TIMOTHY BATES

Public Finance and the Political Process
RANDALL G. HOLCOMBE

Toward Social Economy
HOWARD R. BOWEN

The Social Economics

of Human Material Need

Edited by
John B. Davis and Edward J. O'Boyle

SOUTHERN ILLINOIS UNIVERSITY PRESS
CARBONDALE AND EDWARDSVILLE

Copyright © 1994 by the Board of Trustees,
   Southern Illinois University
All rights reserved
Printed in the United States of America
Designed by Jolene Faye Hamil
Production supervised by Natalia Nadraga
97 96 95 94   4 3 2 1

LIBRARY OF CONGRESS CATALOGING-IN-PUBLICATION DATA

The social economics of human material need / edited by John B. Davis
and Edward J. O'Boyle.
      p.   cm.—(Political and social economy)
   Includes bibliographical references and index.
   1. Basic needs.   I. Davis, John B.   II. O'Boyle, Edward J.
   III. Series.
   HC79.B38S63 1994
   302—dc20   93–8620
   ISBN 0-8093-1921-7   CIP

Chapter 6 is reprinted from *A Future for the American Economy: The Social
Market*, by Severyn T. Bruyn, with the permission of the publishers,
Stanford University Press. © 1991 by the Board of Trustees of the Leland
Stanford Junior University.

The paper used in this publication meets the minimum requirements of
American National Standard for Information Sciences—Permanence of
Paper for Printed Library Materials, ANSI Z39.48-1984. ∞

To the founders and the charter members of the
Association for Social Economics

Contents

vii

Figures

Tables

Editors' Preface

Undeniably, human material need is part and parcel of everyday human existence and yet, paradoxically, human material need is universally rejected as an authentic concept by mainstream economics. This paradox derives from the paradigm upon which mainstream economics is built and will be resolved only when a new paradigm emerges that is firmly and explicitly grounded in human material need under its two distinct aspects: physical need and the need for work as such. *The Social Economics of Human Material Need* presents such a new paradigm in a form that is more developed than an architect's rough sketch but less defined than a draftsman's blueprint.

In *The Social Economics of Human Material Need*, the emerging paradigm is identifiable by six main and unique characteristics. First, human material need is expanded to include not only physical need but also the need for work as such, a concept regarded by mainstream economists as outside the scope of the discipline.

Second, human material need is presented in the context of the three principles that organize economic affairs—competition, cooperation, and intervention—rather than just competition (which, according to the conventional paradigm, alone activates the four economic processes of production, distribution, exchange, and consumption). Competition and cooperation are represented as activating principles, while intervention is characterized as a limiting principle.

Third, underlying each of the three organizing principles

is a dominant social value. In the case of competition, the underlying social value is freedom. In the case of cooperation, the foundational social value is community. And in the case of intervention, the basic social value is equality.

Intervention organizes economic affairs by limiting competition and cooperation. For that reason, it limits not only the activating principles of competition and cooperation but their underlying social values of freedom and community as well. Hence, *The Social Economics of Human Material Need* is a more accurate rendering of how production, distribution, exchange, and consumption are organized in a market economy.

Fourth, a deliberate attempt is made to reconcile need and want by conserving what is sound in the conventional paradigm, especially individual freedom of choice, and by affirming the centrality of the principle of subsidiarity to the new paradigm.

Fifth, the duality of human nature—every human is at once an individual being and a social being—is explicitly acknowledged and linked to the task of defining and measuring both physical need and the need for work as such. To differentiate our view of human nature from the conventional economic view, we replace *Homo economicus* with *Homo socioeconomicus*. Affirming this duality helps reconcile the conflict between those who insist that poverty is an absolute concept and others who assert that it is a relative concept. Even though one or two of the contributors might not embrace personalism, *Homo socioeconomicus* springs directly from that ideology just as *Homo economicus* springs from individualism.

Sixth and last, human material need that individuals and their families are unable to meet alone is addressed through private-sector remedies as well as public-sector intervention. Broadly represented, the private-sector remedies for unmet physical need and for the unmet need for work as such include self-managed firms, interfirm and suprafirm cooperation, and neighborhood reconstruction.

Deliberately excluded from *The Social Economics of Human Material Need* is any account of the history of the debate in economics as to the nature and meaning of human material need. This debate, at least along the dimension of physical need, can be traced to Smith and Ricardo and subsequently has been taken up by other distinguished economists such as Marx and Veblen. We leave aside their works because, their best efforts notwithstanding, today's conventional paradigm takes no account of human material need and because starting anew offers greater promise. Such a historical account would add to the length of *The Social Economics of Human Material Need* and might deter a busy reader from getting directly to the substance of this book.

As the contributors affirm explicitly or otherwise, *unmet* human material need has profound and intertwined implications both for human dignity and resource (re)allocation. For that reason, the new paradigm must begin with and center principally on *unmet* human material need. So, too, for *The Social Economics of Human Material Need*.

All six contributors are second- or third-generation members of the Association for Social Economics. This collection of essays is an official fiftieth anniversary project of the Association and is dedicated respectfully and gratefully to the founding and charter members of the Association.

We wish to thank the publishers and individuals listed below for permission to quote from the following:

Toward a Philosophy of Praxis by Karol Wojtyla/Pope John Paul II. Copyright © 1980 by Alfred Block and George Czuczka. By permission of The Crossroad Publishing Company.

The Adequacy of the Benefit Amount in Unemployment Insurance by Joseph Becker, S.J. Copyright © 1961. By permission of the W. E. Upjohn Institute for Employment Research.

"The Changing Economy of Lincoln Park after World War II to 1980" by William Waters and Maurice Forkert. Unpublished manuscript. By permission of William Waters.

Portions of chapter 3 are revisions and extensions of Edward J. O'Boyle, "Poverty: A Concept That Is Both Absolute and Relative Because Human Beings Are at Once Individual and Social," *Review of Social Economy*, Spring 1990.

Introduction

John B. Davis

The concept of need, that is, human material need, is perhaps one of the most paradoxical of economic concepts. On the one hand, the idea of need seems an inescapable dimension of economic life. We can hardly begin to talk about the problems and concerns that drive economic thinking without speaking about those individuals, families, and communities whose needs go unmet and who are hoped to be the principal beneficiaries of economic growth and social policy. On the other hand, mainstream economic theory today—whose prominence and self-proclaimed scientific standing challenge the most dedicated of humanists—denies needs can be distinguished from wants and indeed denies that the concept of need has any legitimate standing in economics whatsoever. Need in the modern world, it thus results, is a matter of preeminent concern that nonetheless escapes formal recognition. Need is a real, inescapable dimension of contemporary economic life but is at the same time seemingly unworthy of the professional attentions of those who devote themselves to the systematic explanation of economic life. In short, the very concept of need escapes us, though in every day life we continually address our needs and respond to those of others in our ordinary practical affairs.

If nature abhors a vacuum, however, so we also seem ever driven to escape the paradoxes of the social world, if only because the social world is so much our own creation and responsibility. And though the paradox of need appears equally balanced upon the manifest reluctance of mainstream economists to acknowledge the concept of need and the continued genuine expression of need by persons in all domains of life, in fact the direction in which this paradox will ultimately be resolved is clear. Need *will* receive formal expression, because its character must be understood in order that individuals' real needs be clearly understood. Need, as so strikingly represented in the 1990 World Bank annual report, *World Development 1990*, devoted entirely to the question of world poverty, will ultimately command systematic attention, because its central place in economic life is inescapably evident even in the face of its sweeping neglect by most professional economists.

The essays collected in this volume make a contribution to this future understanding of need. Written together to form an integrated account of need and capturing some of the best insights of individuals who have for many years made the concept of need a key focus of their thinking about economic life as social economics, they lay important methodological and philosophical foundations for explaining the nature and concept of need. This brief introduction seeks to answer a question preliminary in nature to their concerns. Why does mainstream economic thinking not only ignore the concept of need but indeed also declare it unworthy of serious consideration? It seeks to answer this question because answering it tells us something valuable about how we must go about explaining the concept of need. It also seeks to answer this question because the paradox of need is in considerable degree the consequence of mainstream economists' adherence to a set of unexamined assumptions about economic life and the nature of economic reasoning that themselves require exposure and critique if the concept of need is to achieve the standing that attention to individuals' real needs demands.

Why is it, then, that conventional economists feel entitled to disregard the concept of need? In essence, the answer is that mainstream economics takes the concept of need to be value-laden, therefore unscientific in nature, where that which is value-laden or in any way touches upon normative concerns is subjective and unworthy of serious consideration. Pure science, the aspiration of contemporary mainstream economics, is widely believed to be positive and value-free, thereby objective. Accordingly, in place of the concept of need, conventional economists substitute the concept of individual wants, or tastes and preferences. Wants, it is assumed, may be identified, analyzed, and discussed without evaluation or judgment. They require no interpretation, are regarded as pure data, and are thought to be factual in nature. Moreover, wants manifestly exceed our means and as such are an important element in a science that seeks to understand itself as the scientific study of the allocation of scarce resources in the presence of unlimited wants.

From this perspective, the point of entry value judgments make in the characterization of need is straightforward to the mainstream economist. On the assumption that wants are the raw data of individual economic life, the identification of needs necessitates a ranking of wants that turns on comparing different individuals' wants. To say that such-and-such a want is in fact really a need requires saying that all individuals would have this want in certain standard circumstances, and that the general significance of this particular want then justifies our classifying it as a human need. Needs, that is, are not specific to any given individual but are generally shared by all individuals. In effect, needs are universal wants. However, in the eyes of the mainstream economist this comparability requirement—or, as it has been put in the utilitarian framework of mainstream economics, the requirement that we be able to make interpersonal comparisons of utility across individuals—simply lacks objective foundation. Since Lionel Robbins's influential *Essay on the Nature and Significance of Economic Science*, mainstream economists have insisted that interpersonal comparisons of utility are essentially value-laden and therefore subjective. How, it is typically argued, can one individual's wants be compared with another's without making value judgments about the relative importance of different wants to individuals generally? Since individuals are different from one another, each presumably has his or her own distinct scale or ranking of wants. Thus, from the neoclassical perspective, to say that some single ranking of wants applies across all individuals in order to identify a given need is to impose some single conception of this ranking out of the many possible such conceptions.

For conventional economists, wants and their rankings are

unique to each and every individual. This reflects their status as basic uninterpreted data, and as such is captured in conventional economists' customary insistence on characterizing wants or preferences as exogenous. Further, because each and every individual's wants, preferences, or tastes must be unique to the individual to whom they belong, it follows that each individual is a separate, autonomous identity with tastes known only to him or herself. Each individual, that is, is an atomistic being for whom the wants, preferences, or tastes of others are an impossible object of understanding and whose socioeconomic relations to others are necessarily secondary in significance to their own status as solitary individuals. Self-interest, it then follows, is necessarily the sole foundation for behavior in the economic world, since individuals' own wants and tastes can alone define their interest. All this, it should be emphasized, follows from the simple assertion that the concept of need lacks any place whatsoever in economics, since to allow the existence of an objective basis for comparing wants across individuals in society is tantamount to rejecting the notion that individuals are isolated atomistic beings who make their own wants their sole object of concern.

Unfortunately, in a world in which need is real, though in which economic science discourages its discussion, there are costs to those truly in need that might largely be avoided were the concept of need given formal recognition. In saying, as does mainstream economics, that wants alone explain the material transactions between people, one makes the ability to pay central to any explanation of demand and conceals the dilemma that those individuals in the marketplace who have the least ability to pay have the most unmet needs. The market understood solely in terms of wants, that is, effectively disguises one set of economic relations between people with another, since market exchange is said to reflect an agreement and harmony of interests between free and equal persons, though beneath the surface individuals in need are actually at risk and vulnerable as human beings. Worse than the concealment of this important reality, however, is the response of the market to the unacknowledged vulnerability of those in need. Since those whose needs have been fulfilled and who pursue inessential wants enjoy the luxury of being able to postpone their market transactions, while those in need are compelled to transact for their needs in the market in as short a time as possible, the former are able to exercise a bargaining power vis-à-vis the latter that puts the latter at an even greater disadvantage. When those trading for luxuries can wait to purchase and those trading for necessities cannot, market prices tend to be lower for luxuries and higher for necessities than would be the case were need given the sort of formal expression that would justify support for those genuinely in need. Moreover, because those in need lack the financial and material resources to express their needs in the marketplace, while those in pursuit of luxuries typically possess an abundance of such resources, the market tends to underproduce those goods that satisfy needs and overproduce luxury goods relative to what would likely be the case were need given formal expression and the reality of need to become widely apparent. These perverse results—which are at odds with the ordinary morality of our society—are the real costs of a science that rigidly defends itself as positive and value-free.

Yet is mainstream economics itself really free of value judgments, as it continually claims itself to be? Close examination of conventional economics' critique of the concept of need, it turns out, reveals important unexamined assumptions at the heart of the idea that interpersonal comparisons are value-laden and subjective. On the line of reasoning that flows from Robbins's argument, interpersonal comparisons of utility presuppose value judgments because they impose a common ranking or scale of wants upon the distinct rankings and scales of wants possessed by different individuals. Yet if one insists that ranking wants across individuals presupposes value judgments, doesn't it also (as Terence Hutchison wondered shortly after the appearance of Robbins's famous *Essay*) involve value judgments to say that single individuals can rank and scale their wants across different and distinct episodes of their lives? That is, if *inter*personal comparisons of utility and well-being presuppose value judgments, don't *intra*personal comparisons of utility and well-being presuppose them as well? And, if the latter are objective by the standards of mainstream economics, might it not be the case that interpersonal comparisons are also objective by those very same standards? Indeed, might it not even be possible that the very reason intrapersonal comparisons are objective is because interpersonal ones are?

Mainstream economics, not surprisingly, ignores these issues with the standard textbook declaration that economic science assumes that individuals can always identify and rank their own preferences. Perhaps the problem here is that mainstream economists, long wedded to the notion of the atomistic individual, cannot conceive of any other way of talking about preference and taste. This then becomes the natural way of understanding the matter, and any discussion of taste and preference across individuals, which requires the exercise of judgment and introduces the values of the analyst, by contrast appears arbitrary and subjective. As we will see, however, it is not difficult to demonstrate that value judgments are also involved in saying that individuals can make intrapersonal comparisons of utility. The real issues, rather, appear to concern the kinds of judgments and values we employ in making both interpersonal and intrapersonal comparisons of utility, and how these different kinds of judgments and values are related to one another.

Social economists, of course, do not deny that individuals identify and rank their own preferences and wants. Their argument is that in doing so we reason in much the same way and make much the same sorts of value judgments that speaking about a socially shared scale and ranking of preferences and wants requires. Their reasoning, moreover, begins with an implicit sensitivity to one of the traditionally overlooked presuppositions of discussing rational economic agents as real beings, namely, that since economic agents are thought capable of ranking their preferences and wants on any given occasion, then they must also be thought able to do this consistently over time. Real economic agents, that is, must be thought of as beings that survive through time and changes of experience, while carrying out programs of economic activity reflecting choices that are consistent through time and changes of experience. For this to be the case, individuals must be said to sustain personal identities amidst change in themselves and their surroundings, and this, social economists argue, necessarily presupposes a reliance on value judgments that permit us to explain what constitutes personal identity and what it means to be a person. From this perspective, intrapersonal comparisons of utility, because they presuppose an individual's personal identity, must themselves involve value judgments. Moreover, because our understanding of personal identity arguably depends in important respects upon our understanding of individuals as social beings, it is fair to suppose that those value judgments we make in speaking of intrapersonal utility comparisons are somehow linked to value judgments we make in speaking of interpersonal utility comparisons. Mainstream economics, however, ignores these manifest linkages between personal identity and social identity, and in the process fails to investigate the nature of the related value judgments underlying each.

Social economists accordingly argue that a dynamic view of intrapersonal comparisons of wants and preferences is bound up with the interpersonal comparison of wants and preferences. At the most rudimentary level this is manifest in an individual's linguistic system, in that an individual's own language of valuation is socially learned, so that the terms in which one keeps track of one's own preference rankings over time draw upon a public discourse concerning the ranking of wants and preferences. In the thinking of the philosopher Ludwig Wittgenstein, there is no such thing as a truly "private language," since individuals must always express their own thoughts, however private, in a shared language. On this understanding, the linguistic standards that individuals develop to rank their tastes and preferences are inevitably social standards. Peter Winch, in his influential extension of Wittgenstein's thinking to the social sciences, has argued that social standards operate in the sciences in establishing the accepted use of concepts and language to settle fundamental issues between scientists. Mainstream economists, we might then conclude, regard preferences as "like" only when they belong to the same individual, because the standards for preference analysis implicit in their discourse rule out judging different individuals' preferences as "like." In contrast, social economists, because they recognize the inevitable role value judgments play in science, are prepared to investigate how different individuals' preferences are "like" one another in the hope of making some progress toward explaining those shared wants we call needs.

How, then, might we properly look upon the concept of need in our theoretically more self-conscious investigation of wants and preferences? As a first caution, one would not want to say that, because individuals share a common language and discourse, there is but one system of ranking wants across individuals in society, and that all individuals implicitly make use of that same system of evaluation and analysis. Society clearly gives abundant evidence of competing and even incompatible views of wants and needs, and thus our investigation of need will not produce the overly neat and determinate results that often seem to be the goal of positive science. Indeed, an important message of the analysis developed in the essays collected here is that the necessary involvement of value judgments in any serious discussion of need requires that we address a variety of issues and considerations that relate to the nature of persons and their relations to one another in economic life. This inevitably makes the explanation of need complex and many-sided. Nonetheless, the essays collected here still share a common understanding of the nature of human material need. Need may be defined as *a condition of individual deprivation that threatens a person's livelihood and integrity as a human being*. Of course, the specific ways in which this might be true for different individuals vary across time and societies. But that needs are different at different times and different places does not change the fact that individuals find their very survival as human beings jeopardized when their needs go unmet. Recognizing that debates about the specific historical character of human material need are inevitable, this collection focuses on this single salient fact.

Warren J. Samuels, in "Need as a Mode of Discourse," opens the collection by arguing that because the economy is an institutional complex continually in a process of change, it is important to investigate the changing place and nature of the concept of need in Western civilization and the forces involved in and responsible for this changing conception. For Samuels, the meaning, role, and specific content of the concept of need are worked out in the total socioeconomic process in such a way as to make one or another particular normative argument in society at any one time. This constitutes what he terms the social construction of economic and social reality and is something that must generally defy sharp statement, being an ongoing matter. Accordingly, Samuels emphasizes need as a mode of discourse, in order to represent its conceptual framework in terms of the socioeconomic reality in which need is continually debated. Need as a mode of discourse, moreover, stands beside and interacts with other modes of discourse (e.g., those concerning rights, self-interest, divine will, and so on) and must thus also be understood in relation to the competing claims each of these modes makes upon us. Samuels's essay brings out complexities of the concept of need in a historically dynamic environment and in this way throws light on many of the debates over the nature of need.

Peter L. Danner's "The Person and the Social Economy: Needs, Values and Principles" begins by approaching need from the most basic perspective of the human person in economic life. Each of us has individual needs bound up with our physical, spiritual, and emotional requirements, yet each of us also possesses distinctively social needs that arise out of our personal, political, and economic relations to others. How these different dimensions of life get expressed and ordered in economic life is essentially a matter of the values people espouse, and here Danner investigates the three social values that dominate contemporary social thinking: liberty (or freedom), equality (or sharing), and fraternity (or community). These three fundamental social values themselves underlie and coordinate three main principles of organization in economic life, respectively, competitive self-interest, government involvement and intervention, and cooperative collaboration. Danner's portrayal well brings out the conflicts and harmonies in society's value structure, together with their impact on the dilemmas for decision making faced by both individuals and groups.

Edward J. O'Boyle, in "Human Physical Need: A Concept That Is Both Absolute and Relative," differentiates need and wants by approaching need from the perspective of a duality in human nature as both individual and social. In this line of reasoning, the *Homo economicus* of conventional economics is replaced by a *Homo socioeconomicus* of social economics, and the economist's investigation of instrumental rationality is replaced by an investigation of a rationality of ends. For O'Boyle, unmet material need undermines the very foundations of human dignity, and social economics and the social economy center principally on questions regarding the fulfillment of our material needs. He insists that there is no social economics or social economy without the principle of subsidiarity. The greater part of his discussion is devoted to careful technical definition and explanation of the problems associated with defining and measuring unmet physical needs. Distinguishing absolute and relative standards of physical needs in current social policy approaches to need, O'Boyle points out that the absolute standard approach implicitly defines human beings in only individual terms, while the relative standard approach implicitly defines human beings in only social terms. A comprehensive approach, which he then develops in detail, combines both approaches on the grounds that human beings are both individual and social. This entails a classification of unmet needs in terms of both income distribution and minimal living standards and permits an exhaustive treatment of need that is correlated with existing empirical evidence on need.

Anthony E. Scaperlanda's "Government Participation to Address Human Material Need" investigates whether government should address the material needs of individuals in society, what this participation might amount to, and how much of this participation might be required. Arguing that there is already a consensus in our society concerning the variety and level of unmet need in the United States and noting that the private sector is unable to fully alleviate this unmet need, Scaperlanda proposes a model of government participation in the economy in meeting minimal human material needs that is sensitive to the conventions of the American politico-economic process. Based on theoretical foundations influenced by Thorstein Veblen and Clarence Ayres, his analysis takes into account the historical interaction between technology and society's institutions and serves as a guide to a pragmatic policy making that is capable of combining the best from opposed viewpoints concerning the role of government in the economy. This is an especially valuable achievement in regard to any discussion of government policy aimed at reducing poverty, since recent studies have demonstrated a considerable diversity of reasons for poverty. Indeed, the importance of an imaginative and flexible approach to policy is especially clear in connection with the intractability of "underclass" poverty, which arguably demands a variety of strategies on different levels. Scaperlanda closes with a set of six general guidelines concerning the kind and extent of government participation in meeting human material need.

Edward J. O'Boyle's "The Need for Work as Such: Self-Expression and Belonging" extends the investigation of need in an often unappreciated direction by noting that physical need and the need for work are two equally fundamental dimensions of human material need. For O'Boyle, work is organized and performed through two main modes or channels, individual contribution and teamwork, that reflect the duality of human nature as both individual and social. Work also provides persons two main opportunities in life that also conform to the duality of human nature, namely, the opportunity for self-expression through individual contribution and the opportunity for belonging through one's involvement in work teams or groups. Within this framework, O'Boyle examines the character and significance of the need for work, providing in the process a large number of examples from actual work settings to illustrate the nature of work in the contemporary workplace. Allowing that there are special risks associated with the needs for self-expression and belonging, O'Boyle nonetheless emphasizes that these risks only demonstrate the great challenges the workplace presents in providing opportunities for personal development.

Severyn T. Bruyn, in "Social Management and the Self-Managed Firm," sees a long-range trend in the organization of corporations away from systems of command management and toward systems of mutual governance that enhance each worker's capacity for self-management. This transition, Bruyn argues, has most recently manifested itself in the emergence of increasing employee participation in managing work teams and in overseeing work systems. While early on corporations found these changes led to greater productivity and profits, social management in recent decades has also come to recognize the role of employee participation in making possible greater individual self-development. Bruyn provides an extensive and detailed account of the patterns of growth of self-managed firms and suggests that employee ownership and management are likely to become an integral part of corporate life in future years. He then speculates on new, more democratic forms of worker cooperatives and addresses arguments critical of cooperatives from conventional economists. On balance, it appears that worker self-managed firms are likely to experience fewer problems than traditional command management firms in future years.

In the concluding "Reconstruction of Mainstream Economics and the Market Economy," John B. Davis and Edward J. O'Boyle summarize the arguments of the previous chapters by arguing that a rethinking of market economics entails a rethinking of human nature and that the reconstruction of the market economy as a social economy involves devising strategies to help workers and consumers achieve greater personal security. In mainstream economics, the individual side of human nature is emphasized to the exclusion of our social side. Giving this latter dimension adequate emphasis changes our vision of the market economy and transforms our conception of the most basic objectives of economic science. Unmet human material need in the workplace and household manifests itself in the insecurity experienced by workers and consumers. Yet while mainstream economics gives little attention to these needs, the social forces afoot that do address them deserve study. Examples of private-sector and government initiatives to reform the workplace are presented. Also, special emphasis is placed on new concepts of the neighborhood in today's American cities that are beginning to play an important role in identifying and addressing the unmet needs of the household.

An understanding of the social economics of human material need involves a fundamental reorientation in thinking about economic life away from the accepted and customary approaches that characterize mainstream economics. That the magnitude of this task is only beginning to be appreciated by professional economists is disappointing. Yet at the same time, that significant progress has been made to reconstitute the foundations of an economic science cognizant of need gives us good reason to be optimistic. The essays in this book review and investigate these systematic foundations, elaborating upon their rationales and detailing their principles of analysis. We hope they will provide the impetus for further serious study of human material need in all its manifestations.

References

Hutchison, Terence W. *The Significance of the Basic Postulates of Economic Theory*. New York: A. M. Kelley, 1960.

Robbins, Lionel. *An Essay on the Nature and Significance of Economic Science*. 2d ed. London: Macmillan Press, 1935.

Winch, Peter. *The Idea of a Social Science*. London: Routledge, 1958.

Wittgenstein, Ludwig. *Philosophical Investigations*. 2d ed. Oxford: Basil Blackwell, 1953.

World Development Report 1990. Oxford: Oxford University Press, 1990.

The Social Economics
of Human Material Need

1

Need as a Mode of Discourse

Warren J. Samuels

The economy is the institutional complex concerned with the provision of goods and services to people. The economy includes more than the market, and the economic process encompasses more than the exchange of goods between individuals. The economy is comprised of the institutions that form and operate through it, but the social role of the economic process is the satisfying, through production and distribution, of the needs of people, needs whose satisfaction encompass more than material things. The crux of the process is the determination of needs and of whose needs count. This last point is important: to choose or to evolve an economic system is to determine or work out the structure and process by which it is determined whose interests and needs will count. Such counting is always in part system—and structure—specific. To discuss need is to penetrate to the very crux of the economic process, not to interject something otherwise exogenous and/or irrelevant.[1]

The objective of this essay is to explore certain facets of the economic process having to do with the concept of need. The essay will address the changing place of the concept of need in Western civilization, the forces that have generated and/or been involved in the changing conception, the larger significance of the changing concept for policy, and the problem of identifying substantive content to need.

The central argument is that the concept of need is rhetorical: the meaning, role, and specific content of need is worked out in the total socioeconomic process. It is used to make one or another normative argument (for example, more resources for poor people; more investment to have more production, which will benefit poor people). The identification of the content of need and of whose needs count constitutes a major element of the social construction of economic and social reality. It cannot be given by formula or wishful thinking. Attempts to render its definition positive represent blatant reification, a privileging device; whereas the concept of need, in addition to being both rhetorical and something that has to be worked out, is socially, culturally, normatively bound. Need is implicitly defined through the economic process and explicitly defined through discourse.

This essay focuses on both aspects of human material need: physical need and the need for work as such. Less explicit attention is given to the latter than the former, but the principal points made regarding physical need also apply to the need for work.[2] These points also apply to need putatively of a higher order than physical need. I distinguish among (*a*) physical need that is met through the economic order; (*b*) higher-order need that is met through the economic order; and (*c*) higher-order need that is met through other means. Clearly, *a* is within the scope of this essay, as is *b* (though less centrally), but *c* is not.

Inasmuch as the meaning of need is worked out by people within socioeconomic processes, it would be presumptuous to define it substantively here; any substantive definition would prejudice the argument. This makes the term impossible to use except as an undefined primitive term or category and that is how it will be used here.[3] Sometimes the term *need* will refer to the problem of definition of need and other times to the problem of need fulfillment or satisfaction. In practice, it should be pointed out, the two are connected; for example, experience with regard to fulfillment affects the definition of need.

Valuation

The economy is a process of valuation. This process of valuation encompasses not only commodity prices but the values, and the tradeoffs between values, that constitute the hallmarks of any given civilization. The valuation process includes both (1) the identification, juxtaposition, evaluation, and selection of values and (2) the interactions of values, experience, and reflection. Part of the valuation process is the determination of needs and of whose needs count. Markets, government budgets, central plans, and families are all arrangements through which such determinations are worked out.

End values typically are sought indirectly through the pursuit of intermediate values. Indeed, there is an endless values continuum in which values, pursued by certain means, that are themselves chosen in a valuational process, themselves become means to other values. Perhaps even more typically, values are sought in a manner not so much antecedent to experience as derived from experience. It is true both that our knowledge of values is derived, at least in part, from our reflections on our experiences and that our experiences are apprehended, at least in part, on the basis of our values: values and experience evolve to grow together in a process of cumulative causation.

Contemplation of human need in the present world is in part a mode of introducing, legitimizing, and reinforcing certain considerations that arguably would otherwise be neglected. More generally, consideration of need is both a product and a generator of a civilization: need and civilization are interdependent and evolutionary in nature, whether worked out through markets, budgets, plans, families, or as a matter of cumulative causation.

Need as a Mode of Discourse

Human beings have developed several quite different modes of discourse in the literal terms by which they consider questions of values, terms that are instrumental to the social (re)construction of social reality. These modes of discourse include the following: (a) rights, (b) natural law, (c) divine will, (d) social interest, (e) self-interest,[4] and (f) need. All are typically employed noncognitively; we are often not aware that we are in fact using a mode of discourse, believing instead that we are discussing something real in and of itself—a facet of the social construction of social reality through indirect processes and beliefs. Questions of policy are comprehended and debated in the terms of one or another of these modes of discourse.[5] The differences between these modes of discourse are enormous, and it is often the case that choice of the mode of discourse influences the treatment of substantive considerations and the determination of policy. There are overlaps and interrelations among these modes of discourse. Great hiatuses and conflicts arise both within and among modes of discourse. Nuances and implications for policy vary. Often the terms of conflictual discourse cannot be agreed upon. This essay is concerned with the historical evolution and processes of the need mode of discourse.[6]

Transformation of the Concept of Need

There have been two important historical transformations in Western civilization of the concept and role of human need; therefore there have been three epochs, each with its distinctive conception of need.[7] In the centuries prior to the development of the modern economy and polity, during which what Keith Tribe calls "the administrative state and economics" (or political economy) had the character of an administrative science, the identification of both individual human needs and social purposes were the province of ostensibly scientific state administrators. This was a society in which monarchs and their underlings did not believe that individuals could be responsible for their own lives. Consequently, need was to be determined by the proper authorities.

Eventually, with the development of the modern economy, there transpired the elevation of individual human needs over the social purposes identified and sought by state administrators (which, after all, were often the result of imperial ambitions). The modern economy is a mode of individual needs identification, pursuit, and fulfillment only because the premodern administrative state has been replaced with the modern state and the modern economy, in which individual, presumably self-chosen, preferences are given great weight. The transformation was from need determined and pursued by administrators to need determined and pursued by individuals.

However, the concept of need has now come to play a quite different role. In a world continuing to manifest hierarchy and inequality, the concept of need has increasingly become juxtaposed to individual self-determination within one's existing opportunity set. Given the fact of different opportunity sets, some small, some perhaps so small as to be vacuous, construing the economy as meeting individual needs means that the needs of many go unfulfilled, a condition anathema to conscience and also to the legitimation of the market economy itself. Considerations of distribution have come to confront the discourse of individualism. The concept of need, which helped to overthrow the administrative state, now implies for many the desirability if not necessity of collective, generally state, action to facilitate the wider provisioning of at least minimal needs, for both present adult generations and/or, and perhaps especially, for children. Which individuals? has become the central question, though also the object of ideological formulations directed to obfuscate the problem and prevent deliberate confrontation with it. The irony is that the discourse of the administrative state itself obscures the same question. Such is the fate of ideologies in the hands of ruling groups.

One further point: There is a difference between the freedom that one may have in determining one's own needs and the freedom one has in choosing the means by which those needs are to be satisfied. Modernity seems to have more to do with the latter than the former. Certainly the administrative state did not specially provide for the former. The modern economy seems to provide greater ambit for the former but also a dominating socialization. Still, individuals can resist status emulation and the like—which is the real meaning of the individuation that accompanies socialization.

Political Significance

In every society, therefore, attention to need is a political phenomenon and stratagem: it relates to the most fundamental social processes, which are processes of choice, and thereby of power, and which are engaged in the social (re)construction of social reality. Need as determined by the agents of the administrative state, need as determined by individual economic actors in a market economy, and need as contemplated by those who either are personally deprived or desire to act on behalf of those who are deprived is fundamentally related to the nature and structure of particular cultures and societies.

It is equally politically significant that the concept of need is often related to some notion of human nature, perhaps to some notion of an ideal or authentic human being. Indeed, theories or ideologies of the state, civil society, human nature, and human needs tend to correlate, as Tribe suggests. Similarly, perceived or expressed sensitivity to ethical concerns also give effect to the ethical content of such preconceptions.

The fact that one can discuss matters pertaining to need[8] in relatively objective and neutral terms should not obscure two critical considerations: first, that need is subjective—in at least the senses that it is historically relative and that the moral grounding of a set of needs is relative per se, that is, moral-system specific; and second, that distributional concerns—the question of which needs (which is really the question of whose needs)—are important. Indeed, as indicated above, the modern role of the concept of need derives in part from the combination of inequality and moral concern with the consequences of inequality. Its function is to help redress deficiencies and inequities—that is, deprivations in the conditions of life. The pain due to inequality and insecurity does exist for the persons who suffer, however much we may agree that need is subjective.

Discussions centering on the concept of need are thereby joined to other discussions, such as those predicated upon some definition of the past, to constitute the process of the social (re)construction of social reality. It also follows, however, that, as with often contrived definitions of the past, conceptions of the role and substance of need can be instrumentally manipulated politically to achieve reconstruction ends in the present and/or future.

The Economy as Selection and Incentive System

Every economy and social system is a selection system; the hierarchical structure of each society is both a continuing cause and consequence of that selection system. The distribution of success in an economy and a society is in part a function of such variables as the particular operative selection system, the distribution of talents and abilities relevant to the selection system, the differential motivation of individuals, luck, and so on. One can conceive of social systems in which rewards are distributed in terms of such criteria as: success in interpreting holy scriptures, discovering and taking advantage of opportunities to make money, accommodating either reigning monarch or party superiors, writing music appealing to teenagers, shooting three-point baskets, discovering new galaxies or mathematical theorems, and so on. The distributions of opportunity, income, wealth, and sacrifice, and the conditions of poverty, hunger, inadequate or nonexistent housing, and the vicious circles of the intergenerational production of dependency are, in a process of cumulative causation, both the result of and constitute the selection system. One function of the concept of need is to redress the suffering of those less gifted or accomplished in what contributes to success in the existing socially constructed selection system.

One may use the metaphor of the family to embrace all persons in a society, if not all humankind. Those who are successful in the lights of their particular society sometimes feel that, whatever the selection mechanism of their society, its operation inexorably has arbitrary and capricious consequences. These consequences may be seen as bearing no necessary relation to the worth as human beings of those who live in straightened and deprived circumstances. When all persons in a society (or on the planet) are understood to be members of the extended human family, the concept of need acquires and becomes viable in its modern role. The same discussion can occur, however, using the other modes of discourse—rights, for example, or social interests or divine will. In any case, this need not involve, or need not solely involve, simple redistribution. It could center on abbreviating if not terminating the use of the state and other institutions of collective action by and in favor of the interests and needs of the already privileged, and instead favoring the interests and needs of the presently disadvantaged.

Whatever the operative incentive and selection system, it does perform a motivational function; the problems are, first, that no single incentive and selection system can satisfy all putative values and, second, that every such system tends to produce hierarchical, that is, inegalitarian, results. Exclusive reliance on particular incentive and selection systems as a mechanism of social choice seems to lead inevitably to the circularity of defending the achieved valuational results on the basis of the particular incentive and selection system *and* defending the system on the basis of the results.

Consider, for example, the view that under capitalism production is for profit, rather than to satisfy human needs. There is a sense in which this is true, but also a sense in which it is false; indeed, the discursive construction (for that is what it is) is actually a code phrase, evocative of certain critical sentiments. Capitalism does contribute to the production of goods and does so through the pursuit of profit or other gain or advantage, at least insofar as the extant system tends to foreclose opportunities for making money which do not involve making goods. Capitalism has been very successful in producing high average per capita living conditions and has been so through the indirect process of seeking profit. A capitalist system gives effect to a certain definition or hierarchy of needs, which may or may not agree with the definition of need of any individual citizen. It can nonetheless be said that capitalism attends only to those needs that can be given effect in the market—that is, to those needs of others on which one can make a profit, and not to all needs—and that what capitalist systems produce indeed serves to *define* need for the society.

Parenthetically, profit-seeking activity within capitalism does more than create needs. It also generates both insecurity and particular distributions of the burden of insecurity. This is somewhat ironic in that capitalism historically has produced both high living standards and the circumstance that such standards are not assured for most human beings.

Consider also the idea of a tradeoff between equity and

efficiency, with equity connoting something like the provisioning of at least the minimum subsistence needs of people, or at least an acceptable set of initial entitlements (perhaps including welfare expenditures) and with efficiency connoting the maximum production of goods and services that people want (and therefore Pareto optimal as well). This idea is very misleading: efficient results are each specific to the set of entitlements that give rise to them; there is no unique wealth-production maximizing result, only entitlement-specific results. The satisfaction of needs other than by markets or by existing entitlements constitutes not a tradeoff between equity and efficiency but giving effect to certain other assumptions as to entitlements.

Every economy is an incentive and selection system. Pursuit and/or production of the rewards specific to a particular system can always be juxtaposed to the satisfaction of needs. Capitalism is not the only economic system about which the claim can be made that it does not function to satisfy human needs. The problems always concern the determination of need and of whose needs will count.

Finally, it should be obvious that the process in which the concept of need is worked out is extremely complex: the concept of need per se tends to counter the effects of a selection system. Individual selection systems generate or reinforce particular needs, certain selection systems give effect to certain needs, and so on, in a historical process characterized by extraordinary dynamism.

The Generation, or Recognition, of Needs

Both of the foregoing cases (production for profit versus need satisfaction, and the equity-efficiency conflict) are further complicated by the creation of needs in and through the market process itself. Many products satisfy desires for which no prior needs existed.[9] One of the features of capitalism is that it generates new needs and new demands for products whose existence is the occasion for efforts to create those needs and those demands. In the continuing quest for markets and profits, life becomes readily interpretable as essentially an ongoing frenzy of consumption.

In any case, the substantive content of human need varies among cultures and societies, and changes occur over time within particular societies. There are certain physical minimum requirements of food, clothing, and shelter that can be expressed in terms of nutritional and weather constraints. There also are both additional social needs and quasi-prescribed modes of satisfying the physical minimum needs that arise through the processes of socialization and individuation.

The important questions in the present stage of society are, first, what governs people's individual preferences? and, second, what governs our perception of need? (That is, what governs our perception of inhumane deprivation?) It is obvious that the two questions are related and may indeed be the obverse of each other. It should also be obvious that these questions neither negate nor are themselves negated by a further question, whether certain preferences and perceptions are morally praiseworthy. On the one hand, moral praiseworthiness is itself a matter of historical evolution and conflict; on the other, moral concerns and sensitivities influence the historical process.

The substance adduced need is the result of vast, complex, and changing social processes. Need formation and need satisfaction both take place through markets, social structure, and political learning. It may well be that status emulation is a critical force, but no less important is Smithian sympathy with regard to the predicaments of others. Need formation is influenced by the processes of socialization and individuation, which operate deeply in every society. Perceived needs have tended to be specific to particular cultural systems and to particular stages of economic development—the product, in part, of the processes of socialization and individuation operative therein. The growth of a world economy and of intercultural experience and learning have expanded the learning base. Perceived needs are also a matter of one's reference group, which is itself a matter of socialization and individuation.

An individual's sense of what life requires, either for one's self or for others, depends on the entire array of socialization and individuation processes operative in the relevant society, on one's place in social structure, and on the form(s) that status emulation and achievement motivation take. To penetrate the complexities and subtleties of these matters requires at least a comprehensive social psychology, consideration of which is beyond both the scope of this paper and the expertise of this writer. We do know, though, that one's conception of need is not absolute; it is a product of social forces operative on the individual.

In regard to social policy, need is a matter of a number of critical variables, including (1) the level of total output (that is, the degree to which natural resource constraints have been either taken advantage of or overcome); (2) the nature of the existing culture; (3) certain institutional and demographic variables; and, (4) the habits of the heart that mold ideas and goals concerning individual rights and responsibilities that are collective or social in both character and function. The latter includes, for example, the degree to which beliefs in individual responsibility are countered, or supplemented, by beliefs in collective responsibility. These, in turn, are in part derived from or related to the breakdown of both the extended and the nuclear family, which have historically been the principal modes of attending to individual problems of deprivation. In a world in which greater longevity is coupled with, first, the coming to "fruition" of the diseases of the aged and, second, the breakdown of the family, new social arrangements must be worked out, perhaps through government, to respond to the grievous needs of these people.

There is a complex interplay between the three chief sources by which substance is adduced to the concept of need: the ostensible social purposes of democratic politicians and political processes, the wants of individual self-choice within the process of economic development, and the moral concerns of those concerned with both the have-nots and the social values that otherwise would go unrepresented or underrepresented in the valuational process. The substance adduced to the concept of need at any time and place is both determined and determining in a process of cumulative causation.

Not to be neglected, however, is the place and roles of contemporary social economists, including both those who identify themselves as professional social economists and those activists who practice what the others often only largely preach, perhaps without even knowing that they are practicing social economists. They participate in social processes concerning social values, the formation and perception of individual needs, and questions of equitable distributions of income, wealth, and entitlements. Indeed, economists as a group, and not solely social economists, have played an instrumental role in conceptualizing what constitutes and generates happiness and, accordingly, need. In this and other ways, economists have joined the ranks of the secular high priests of modern society, though they do not all preach the same message.

The simple truth is that the machinations of the administrative state and the activities of nominally private economic actors, especially but not solely under conditions of inequality, exhaust neither the domain of the economic organization of society and the economic life of real people nor the attribution of content to need.

The combination of the total output of a society and the details of its composition are very important to the formation of one's sense of preference, need, and deprivation. The more goods that are available, the greater the per capita output, the higher the level of our perceived preferences and needs and the higher the level at which the sense of deprivation arises relevant to personal or family income.

Producing goods creates opportunities to satisfy needs; the question is whose needs are satisfied? This is, as already noted, complicated by the reality of system-generated needs. Profit-seeking activity under capitalism has produced many of the wants and needs that it has so effectively satisfied and has also, thereby, produced dissatisfaction based on the failure to achieve, at least distributionally, what the system has both induced people to want and led people to expect.

People's sense of need and deprivation depends very much, albeit not completely, on the lifestyle of their social peers as well as the lifestyles of persons above and below them in the social hierarchy. This does not, of course, mean that at certain terribly low levels of income, deprivation is not so physical as not to threaten survival. It means that need tends to be specific to cultural systems and operate through the processes of socialization and individual identity formation in which status emulation figures prominently.

For the great majority of humankind, the satisfaction of needs is contingent upon having a job. Economic policies to combat inflation and other problems, which necessarily and inexorably reduce the supply of jobs and increase the level of unemployment, are inconsistent with this requirement and, therefore, inhumane. Employment is both a means and a need; it is a means to livelihood and a source of identity. Employment helps form aspirations and expectations, both of which are seriously important to the recognition or formulation of need.

Psychology of Individuals

Much of the foregoing discussion is concerned with social processes and not with the individual qua individual. Of course, the individual is a social, or socialized, entity. There is a relation of cumulative causation between individual and social processes: each is both a cause and a consequence of the other. The normative identity of the choosing individual agent is a product of socialization, but socialization itself is the result of the action of individuals in various positions and roles. Still, analysis need not take the individual solely as either a given or a social product. One can analyze the individual qua individual human being. Abraham Maslow's (chapter 4) psychological analysis of individual needs has been very helpful to many people in this respect.

Maslow argues that human desires are means to ends and that behind both the desires and the ends are human needs. The study of human motivation is the study of ultimate human needs. These needs are thought not to differ much across cultures, although the daily activities of ordinary human lives do vary. Maslow constructs a theory of human motivation, a "holistic, dynamic theory," involving a hierarchy of basic human needs. These are, in ascending order: physiological needs, safety needs, belonging or love needs, esteem needs, and self-actualization needs. When lower needs are satisfied, higher needs appear; when these are satisfied, still higher needs appear. Maslow acknowledges that this hierarchy is not the same for all people; positions can be inverted and reversed. He also says that all needs are usually partially satisfied at any given time, with the lower needs generally achieving a higher degree of satisfaction than the higher. Finally, Maslow notes that not all human behavior is always related to basic needs; some behavior is due to external causes and circumstances.

Several important points need to be said about Maslow's list, if not hierarchy, of basic human needs. First, these needs obviously are very important, at least as general categories. One must only reflect upon one's own life to appreciate that. Second, Maslow's hierarchy of needs must be understood as being conceptualized at a fairly high level of abstraction and generality, seemingly dealing with the transhistorical or eternal. In practice, substantive content must be adduced to them through the processes whose existence and role are emphasized in this essay. Third, none of these needs, including the physiological, unequivocally require specific (commodity) means to their satisfaction. Fourth, specific means may satisfy multiple needs. Fifth, Maslow has not said the last word on human need. Other studies have suggested, for example, that the categories are not independent, that self-actualization is possibly not always present, that the sense of deprivation may be (variably) central for some but not all needs, that the status of needs may vary over developmental stages, that a changing mix of conscious and unconscious bases can have differential effects, and that different identifications of needs can have varying implications.[10] Sixth, one must beware of cultural egocentricity: very poor and/or very primitive people can have needs beyond the physiological satisfied. Seventh, the use of Maslow's list is not surprisingly demonstrably political, which of course does not denigrate either the list per se or its contents: Maslow's list is often employed to both legitimize and give substance to policies deemed necessary to provide at least minimal resources and opportunities to people. (This fact of politicization alone demonstrates that a need such as self-actualization involves more than a hypothesized drive and extends to individual choice as the direction and substance of self-actualization.)

It is this latter political consideration that is presently so important. Given the role of the concept of need in contemporary society, if policies and institutions are to be adopted (or adapted) to provide at least minimal resources and opportunities to people, then the subject of need ought to be discussed in a rational manner. Maslow's and others' analyses of basic needs have in fact both legitimized and provided substance, or at least a framework, for such a discussion. It must be recognized, however, that Maslow's hierarchy is neither transcendent nor absolute; it is a product of a specific time and culture. It can serve as a framework for discussing need generally to the extent that there is consensus concerning its basic validity. Caution must be urged against assuming the Maslow's or anyone else's hierarchy of needs is *fundamental*, that is, rooted in some unchanging human nature. Those who believe in and agree with Maslow's hierarchy will attempt to represent it as fundamental, as some piece of data discovered scientifically, because once they have done so they will already have won half the battle. They will have managed to reify their particular beliefs about needs, and then the discussion shifts to how to satisfy those needs or how well some system is satisfying them. Undoubtedly, their particular substantiations of the hierarchy are but individual contributions to the ongoing process of working out the meaning and content of need. The Maslow case is one of many examples, and a good one, of showing how people attempt to reify or privilege their definition of need by claiming some absolute (scientific, religious, etc.) basis for it.

Among the things that transpire in society and economy are the dual processes of socialization and individuation. In particular this means the perceptions of need are strongly environmentally conditioned—even determined, though not in any rigid sense. The needs that people come to have are nonetheless subjective. They are subjective in two respects: first, the environmentally conditioned perceptions of need are subjective by their very nature; and second, the individual forms that they take are also subjective by their very nature. Moreover, once one goes beyond stipulating that all people require food, clothing, and shelter, as well as a job, physical healing, and education, it is not clear that one can specify aspects of physical need that are common and invariant for all human beings and across all societies.[11] Nor, alas, can one confidently affirm unequivocal substance to need believed to derive from conceptions of human dignity. In all cases, institutions (what Thorstein Veblen called "habits of thought") play a major role in supplying specificity to both physical and nonphysical higher-order needs—say, those relating to human dignity—so that the definition of need varies from place to place and from one time period to another. The problems of freedom versus control, continuity versus change, and equality versus hierarchy can be understood in terms of conflicts over which needs and whose needs are not defined properly or met satisfactorily. Certainly one can readily feel, for example, that human dignity is diminished to the extent that physical need is unmet, but the conceptions of human dignity and physical need are variable, and are themselves the object of the manipulation of belief.

Working Out "Need"

It does say something about a society that meaningful human need is on the social agenda. Moreover, the substantive content of human needs is not purely, indeed not primarily, an empirical matter. Nor can it be dictated by some arid formula or by wishful thinking. It must be worked out through social processes. It is ultimately subjective and normative, and neither objective nor something given.

This latter is a major conclusion by John Galtung (55–126) concerning what has been called the "basic needs approach." Galtung points out that the idea of basic human needs is tied to both a sense of necessity and an image of what it is to be human. This implies a universal aspect but does not yield great specificity of content. The concept and substantive content of need relate to what is necessary for one to function as a human being, but which is, alas, both ambiguous and variable among societies and cultures. The idea of human need can enrich our image of human beings, but the substance of the enrichment is variable, though both it and its provision tell us much about the character of a culture. Needs are both material and nonmaterial and can be satisfied by both material and nonmaterial satisfiers and both needs and satisfiers are social- or cultural-context specific. Indeed, by emphasizing material need, other needs, such as mental health needs, may be neglected or even suppressed. Furthermore, what constitutes and satisfies human needs must be worked out. Need theory, or need discussion, constitutes a means of setting priorities, focusing on what is perceived as essential, watching out for problems and biases, serving as a measuring rod, and so on. Need analysis itself, however, probably cannot say much conclusively about the sources of deprivation and misery.

Otto Klineberg (19–35) indicates that human need is neither a historical nor a cultural phenomena alone but also a psychological or sociopsychological phenomena. Klineberg uses the work of Marie Jahoder to identify six positive personality characteristics that are instrumental to both the genesis and satisfaction (potential) of human need: attitudes toward self; growth development, self-actualization, and maturation; self-integration; autonomy; perception of reality; and environmental mastery. The form, or substantive content, that these characteristics take with regard to the fulfillment of human needs varies and is worked out through society. Self-actualization may be a drive, but it also involves individual choice and variation: the direction and substantive content of self-actualization has to be worked out. To have a society of achievement motivated persons does not specify what constitutes achievement and the same is true of other putative characteristics of human beings. To a very great degree, what governs the substance of achievement motivation also governs need. All this cannot be prescribed; it must be worked out.[12]

Do principles exist that properly instruct or channel the working out (determination and fulfillment) of need? Most people probably can articulate general propositions constituting such principles. Such propositions tend to be stated in terms of one of the other modes of discourse listed earlier: rights, natural law, divine will, social interest, or self-interest. Notions of freedom, justice, welfare, subsidiarity, and so on, readily suggest such propositions. Accordingly, such principles can be stated. However, four points must be made: first, it seems that no principle can be stated unambiguously; second, all seem to require additional, supplementary principles in order to be applied in practice; third, all principles need somehow to be balanced against each other; and fourth, no one principle seems conclusively to dispose of the issues to which it is addressed. At most, the aggregate of such principles constitutes a framework for discussion; at least, the principles are inputs into the process of working out needs.

Conclusion

The historical dynamics of the concept of human need involves both the role of the concept and the substantive content adduced to the needs themselves. The modern concern with human need is characteristic of a society of possessive individualists who have become concerned with certain consequences of inequality deemed to be inhumane and, through the conditions pertinent to children, even antagonistic to the future of the species. This role of the concept of human need is indeed very modern—though the practice of satisfying basic needs is, as noted above, characteristic of most if not all societies and cultures, the difference being that the modern concept (of the three described earlier) is now much more explicit. To affirm the necessity and desirability of provisioning material and nonmaterial needs is one thing. To determine, even to agree on, what those needs are and what will satisfy them as well as the mode of social organization best able to do so is ultimately what much of politics and social discourse is all about, including invocations of democracy, social interest, and rights, though these also constitute quite different modes of discourse. Social economists and others participate in this *process* of determining what substantive content is to be adduced to need and which means are most likely to provide the needs thus determined. Economic analysts of all kinds participate in this process, but it would be foolhardy to try to establish absolute definitions or formulas: such would be only a contribution to the process. We neither can nor should (if that were possible, which it is not) substitute our own preferences for those of all the economic actors as they constitute and operate through the process.[13]

Notes

The author is indebted to Todd Gustafson for helpful research assistance; to participants in the Association for Social Economics' session on "The Social Economist's Good Society and the Needs of Human Nature," Atlanta, December 28, 1989; and to Jeff Biddle, John B. Davis, Todd Gustafson, Edward J. O'Boyle, James D. Schaffer, and William R. Waters for comments on an earlier draft.

1. The basic needs approach is considered one of the basic competing paradigms of economics in Hunt (especially, 75ff and 259ff).

2. See Samuels and others (487–513).

3. Similarly, no precise relationships among needs, wants, preferences, demand, desire, happiness, and so on, are intended in what follows.

4. Wants may well constitute another mode of discourse. Although especially explicit in the case of young children, as we grow older and more subtle, most if not all wants become restated in terms of self-interest. See also note 8, below.

5. Moreover, both discourse and policy are each blends of deliberative and nondeliberative elements. To some extent, we simply are not aware that discussion and analysis are conducted within a mode of discourse that imposes a certain definition, including structure, or reality, though sometimes we do question the terms by which discourse is conducted. Similarly, much policy is made nondeliberatively or non-cognitively, in part through the invocation of linguistic, for example, ideological, formulas, though much policy also is made deliberatively and reflectively.

6. For development of these ideas, see Samuels (1988, 347–54); (1987, 113–29); (1990).

7. It is true, of course, that all or almost all societies and cultures, including the most traditional and primitive, have at least implicitly recognized the existence of human need for all people, typically through kinship institutions.

8. While the present discussion is concerned with need, many, perhaps most, economists reject the concept of need for that of wants, though even here the idea of wants generally is subordinated to the notion of self-interest. Indeed, the concept of need is in jeopardy when need is given an especially individualistic expression, so that for all practical purposes need is equated with individual wants.

9. There are many ways of modeling needs, desires, demands, and wants, and it is not necessary for present purposes to examine them. Clearly, desire does not equate with need. One can differentiate need and the other terms, as is done in the text, but one does not have to do so. One can postulate, for example, a universal need that is satisfied situationally (culturally) through various desires that reflect some broad need or class of need. It is not necessary that need be consciously

felt. Personal preferences (desires) likely will have both social and individual origins. Need may derive from some image of what it means to be human in the circumstance in which one finds oneself; which image also may have both universal aspects but is more clearly marked by local ones; and there may be considerable variety within a society based, for example, on occupational, ethnic, income class, and other differences. See the work of Galtung.

It is also possible to understand either that basic needs exist because humans have rights and that rights are prior to needs, at least in some cases, or that rights themselves should be predicated on (desirable) conceptions of human needs.

Apropos of the discussion later in this paragraph, one may normatively consider that modern materialist, consumption-oriented society consists of an extravagant waste of resources, a misplacement of satisfactions, and a distortion of the meaning of life, through the artificial creation of desires bearing no relation to human need, however much tied to the generation of markets and employment. On the other hand, there is no necessary reason to limit desires to those based on physiological needs. The irony of such considerations is evident, of course, when one considers the exigent plight of people in the less developed countries. For many people, even in the developed countries, provisioning of physiological needs is quite inadequate by objective (e.g., nutritional) standards. Finally, to take note of human potential well beyond physiological needs is to open up numerous subjective and normative notions (idealist philosophy, etc.).

10. See, for example, Porat (85–92), Goebel and Brown (809–15), and Samuels (1984).

11. The listed set of general needs effectively constitutes a specification of the conditions of survival. For the importance of this assumption in welfare economics and for marginalist analysis in general, see Samuels (1980, 528–40).

12. In my view, the resolution or combination of the functionalist analyses of Galtung and Klineberg with the idea of an always changing individual and social self also applies to Maslow.

13. See Samuels (1989a, 531–46); (1989b, 113–33).

References

Galtung, Johan. "The Basic Needs Approach." In *Human Needs: A Contribution to the Current Debate*, edited by Katrin Lederer, 55–126. Cambridge: Oelgeschlager, Gunn and Haim, 1980.

Goebel, Barbara L., and Delores R. Brown. "Age Differences in Motivation Related to Maslow's Need Hierarchy." *Developmental Psychology*. November 1981: 809–15.

Hunt, Diana. *Economic Theories of Development: An Analysis of Competing Paradigms*. Savage, Md: Barnes and Noble, 1989.

Klineberg, Otto. "Human Needs: A Social Psychological Approach." In *Human Needs: A Contribution to the Current Debate*, edited by Katrin Lederer, 19–35. Cambridge: Oelgeschlager, Gunn and Haim, 1980.

Maslow, Abraham. *Motivation and Personality*. New York: Harper and Row, 1970.

Porat, A. Ben. "Guttman Scale Test for Maslow Need Hierarchy." *Journal of Psychology* 97 (1977): 85–92.

Samuels, Frederick. *Human Needs and Behavior*. Cambridge: Schenkman, 1984.

Samuels, Warren J. "Determinate Solutions and Valuational Processes: Overcoming the Foreclosure of Process." *Journal of Post Keynesian Economics* 11 (1989a): 531–46.

——. "An Essay on the Nature and Significance of the Normative Approach of Economics." *Journal of Post Keynesian Economics* 10 (1988): 347–54.

——. "The Idea of the Corporation as a Person: On the Normative Significance of Judicial Language." In *Corporations and Society: Power and Responsibility*, edited by Warren J. Samuels and Arthur S. Miller, 113–29. Westport: Greenwood Press, 1987.

——. "Introduction." In *Economics as Discourse*, edited by Warren J. Samuels, 1–14. Boston: Kluwer Academic Publishing, 1990.

——. "The Methodology of Economics and the Case for Policy Diffidence and Restraint." *Review of Social Economy* 47 (1989b): 113–33.

——. "Survival and Pareto Optimality in Public Utility Rate Making." *Journal of Post Keynesian Economics* 2 (1980): 528–40.

—— and others. "Technology, Labor Interests, and the Law: Some Fundamental Points and Problems." *Nova Law Journal* 8 (1984): 487–513.

Tribe, Keith. *Governing Economy 1750–1840*. New York: Cambridge University Press, 1988.

2

The Person and the Social Economy

Needs, Values, and Principles

Peter L. Danner

Wants and needs pose problems not only for people in their daily living but for students of those disciplines dealing with right conduct. Too often what people want is not what they need and what they need they do not want. For the scholar there are two other terms, "lacking" and "being necessary," that so intertwine with "wanting" and "needing" that, unless disentangled, the four become a semantic mare's nest. This essay, therefore, begins by making clear how the interrelatedness of these terms is to be understood in the following chapter.

What people want are the goods and services they desire but are lacking. What people need are the goods and services they perceive as necessary for their survival and essential for their being and well-being. The substantive contents of wants and needs are, of course, culturally and economically determined and change as a person's life and circumstances change. They both reflect in some way, therefore, personal and social values. But statements about wants and wanting are more easily separated from value considerations, treating wants as value-free. Needs and needing, however, since they relate to a person's surviving and growing into the fullness of humanity, are more easily seen as value-laden.

Economics, therefore, as an objective science can concern itself solely with lacking and wanting in so far as these, implemented by material means, effect demand for scarce goods and services. But the economist must be at least aware that what people want and demand is subject to the higher criteria of what is needed and necessary. The social economist, in other words, must go beyond lacking and wanting.

While the study of human need is the task primarily of psychologists, anthropologists, philosophers and the like, social economists, because they perceive the economic process holistically as providing goods and services necessary or desirable for life and growth as human beings, must also address issues relating to human material need. Human need, in turn, depends upon what human persons are and what they hope to become and, since humans are complex beings, their specific needs are many and varied. A cursory review of what it means to be a person is helpful (and often sufficient) to set one's economic thinking into the larger context of life's meaning.[1]

Needs and the Human Person

The first and obvious fact about ourselves is that we are tangible, material, physical: we exist in time and space and have a bundle of material needs. While at each moment we must be somewhere, as mobile beings we need range and an area within which to move—some more, some less. Being biological, humans need air, water, food, clothing, shelter, medical care, tools for work, and safeguards against danger. As mammals, people need mates to reproduce, and their young need support and protection during infancy and pubescence. Blessed with five senses, the person needs a varied environment enchanting in its diversity, generous with its bounty, but awesome in its unpredictable destructiveness. Necessary for survival, the physical world challenges human management.

Human work, therefore, becomes an absolute necessity for satisfying people's constantly renewed physical and spiritual needs. The generally accepted rule is that people should share in the economy's output roughly proportionate to their contributions. (There are obvious exceptions: children, the infirm, the handicapped, even shirkers can claim sustenance appropriate to their needs and status.) Work, therefore, being necessary for survival, becomes a general obligation; as an obligation it becomes a universal right. Moreover, whatever a person does or however remunerated, work becomes a way of expressing and growing in personality, of relating the person to others, of maintaining public order, of caring for the human habitat, and of mastering and using the forces of nature for the benefit of all. For theists, fulfilling this need complements and completes divine creation.[2]

Though absolutely dependent on the material universe, the individual person is not confined to the here and now but can roam the past or dream of the future, and so in thought, desire, imagination, or intention can escape not only this place and time but the universe itself. Thus liberated to observe the world, to learn from others, to reason, to purpose, and to choose what they perceive for their own good, persons are in some fundamental sense responsible for what they do and intend to do. Moreover, being free to aspire and to hope, they can seek goods that transcend individual self-interest and can long for life beyond the present. Lastly, persons, in whom the physical and spiritual elements constantly interact, have emotions and fashion mental images. They need, therefore, to experience pleasure, joy, and bliss in what they do and to imagine, anticipate, and hope for what they intend. Such, in summary, are the person's *individual* needs.

Equally obvious, though often ignored, are *social* needs. For persons cannot come into existence, develop their humanity, or even survive except related to other persons in a tridimensional web of personal, political, and economic relations. Of the personal bonds, sexual ties can create the most intrinsic needs, like spouses' needs for intimacy and the child's need for bonding, guidance, and nurture. Cultural ties, however, generate the most comprehensive and varied needs, like the need for neighborliness and civility in everyday living, the need to share thoughts, feelings, and purposes informally with friends and others, and the mutual need for communion between author, artist, and actor and their audiences. Students are particularly dependent upon their teachers and masters to sharpen their learning skills. More importantly, such experts serve the need to organize civilization's accumulated knowledge, to develop categories and principles by which to acquire new knowledge, and to formulate criteria for separating the treasures from the trivial in the daily outpouring of literature, art, and thought.

Besides these strictly personal relations, people relate to each other politically and economically. These ties, of course, are personal: governor/governed, judge/defendant, manager/worker, buyer/seller, and the like—but both kinds have another element that differentiates them from each other and from strictly personal relations. Politically, people relate for the purpose of establishing and maintaining public peace and order; economically, to achieve efficiency in producing, exchanging, distributing, and using scarce material goods. It takes no particular perspicuity to conclude that practically every personal relation is both economic and political. Even the most intimate— the bond between mother and baby, for instance—is of concern to the state and certainly requires economic resources to survive.

Similarly, what we think of as economic or business dealings have their political and civil side because they pertain to public order. For the economy to function, property rights must be protected, dangers minimized, markets kept orderly, and credit and money kept trustworthy. On the other hand, the political order draws heavily upon the economic for the resources to keep its vast and complex operation going. Thus, however much we might try to consider the three kinds of relations separately, they never in fact work in isolation. Disturbances in the political order affect the most private relations. Events in the economy impact on both political and personal well-being. Changes in personal relations—births and deaths, marriages and divorces, feuds and fellowships—produce political and economic repercussions. Indeed they are the very stuff of the political and economic orders.

The dimensions of these relations are generally (but not necessarily) complementary and corroboratory. Personal relations flourish better in a peaceful, law-abiding public arena than in a crime-infested public arena and better in a modestly flourishing economy rather than in a depressed economy. The economy prospers when personal and factional disputes are minimal.

Political order thrives when people know, respect, and get along with each other. On the other hand, family ties can accentuate crime, business nepotism can sap profitability, corporate practices can disrupt neighborhoods, and government policies can break up families. In short, people are so linked personally, politically, and economically that anything occurring in one order has ramifications in the others. Keeping in mind how human relations are so intertwined, we will, nevertheless, examine individually the three general categories of that complex.

Roles and Relationships

Every person plays many more roles than Shakespeare's seven, and these simultaneously. A woman, for example, might be wife, mother, concerned neighbor, boutique manager, chairperson of the mission society, and so forth, all at the same time. Each role relates her to others and involves her in a complex set of conflicting priorities, interdependencies, and obligations. How people play their roles depends on the values they espouse. Specific to our interest here, the social values of liberty, equality, and community are most important in influencing people's actions as members of society, as citizens of the polity, and as participants in the economy and thus influence how they relate to each other personally, politically, and economically. This established, we will then examine how the same values harmonize the economy's organizing principles.

A note regarding the semantics of our study is in order here. While we shall tenaciously insist on the basic reality of people's simultaneous multidimensional complex of relations, we acknowledge both the clumsiness of constantly reiterating this relatedness and also the reality that each set has spawned a vast and complex set of institutions that can be treated as if autonomous of the personal, political, or economic relations by which they are constituted. When, therefore, we use the more convenient (as well as meaningful) society, polity, and economy, keep in mind we refer first and foremost to human relationships and only secondarily to the complex of institutions produced.

Society

Most basically and universally people relate to each other as human persons. Such ties are intrinsically natural, entirely spontaneous, and all-inclusive. All belong to society by birth, indeed, many would say, by conception. No one can be excluded entirely, either by happenstance, by personal choice, or by public banishment. Consequently, this encompassing web of personal relations, including bonds of family and kinship as well as many forms of cultural sharing (school, church, neighborhood, workplace, and artistic and civic assemblies), enjoys the highest priority as absolutely essential for the generation, survival, and growth of the human being into a fully developed and mature person. Since everyone is validly and equally human, society remains healthy as long as differences among people are not only tolerated but measurably integrated into the cultural mainstream. Achieving this good requires free expression and social intercourse, blended and articulated harmoniously.

While society enjoys absolute priority over the polity and economy, it needs both political peace and order and a moderately prosperous economy. A licentious and lawless society not only causes enmities and hatreds but breeds poverty and frustrates those social institutions that enhance human living. History is replete with examples of clan and tribal societies whose internecine warfare and ethnic hatreds impaired and sometimes destroyed their cultural achievement. Society also flourishes best with modest prosperity. An indulgent society dissipates its resources, encourages greed and envy, and denigrates work and saving. An ossified, rigidly structured society destroys initiative, because the rich and powerful are satisfied with the status quo and the masses are too cowed to change it.

Polity

While polity, strictly speaking, is the state, it emphasizes those relationships by which a people constitute themselves formally or de facto as a corporate body with a government empowered to maintain peace and order. Since even relatively small groups will find it necessary and rational to organize for their governance and protection, the state or polity is entirely natural. It is not, however, spontaneous and all-inclusive: participation in the state can be limited, revoked, or denied. Conversely, one can leave a state's territorial boundaries and even renounce citizenship. This simply affirms that the state is for the good of people and not vice versa. The state is *subsidiary* to the people: its purpose is to help people achieve their good and not to appropriate their good or goods for itself. A corollary is that the state should not arrogate to itself functions that individuals or private groups can do themselves.

On the other hand, the polity is vested in the duty of maintaining peace and order. This purpose is a true common good in that, if maintained, all can go about their business and engage in the ordinary give and take of the community's social and cultural life with a minimum of danger or exasperation. It means, of course, that the state has the right and authority to set and enforce laws to safeguard the common good. In this it may require people to sacrifice lesser private goods for the sake of the public good. Finally, it implies less tolerance of diversity and deviant (especially criminal) behavior.

Government's duty to maintain peace and order multiplies in the modern state into a vast network of institutions with a wide range of activities from national defense to protecting endangered species (not excluding humankind). The duty at times is interpreted as mandate to interfere not only in business affairs but in the most intimate personal relations. Totalitarianism and statism are the normal declension of unchecked political authority. The state dislikes the messiness of free markets and the espousal of values which deviate from the accepted. It is constantly tempted to substitute its laws for moral principles, its controls for business judgment, and its welfarism for personal responsibility. The state, if unchecked, inevitably creates a privileged class, who rule more and more for their own good at the expense of the general public. The antidote, of course, is an open society where diversity and, especially, minorities are protected, where the forum of public opinion is open to all, even to crackpots, and where the governors are periodically reviewed by the governed.

The economy obviously needs the polity. It needs the polity's power to protect property and the economic process, and the polity's courts to enforce contracts. Without legal justice, business operations would be chaotic, necessitating that the business community set up, as it did at medieval fairs, its own system of justice. By providing the means to render and enforce justice, the state has the right to define it and thereby to restrain business activity from harming the common good, from taking advantage of employees, and from defrauding customers. The state, by restraining such harmful conduct, will actually and often immediately benefit business just as much as by outright incentives to serve the public good.

At the same time the polity needs a prosperous, productive economy. Like society the state is dependent upon the wealth-generating capabilities of the economy for the revenue it needs to perform its multifarious functions. While its justice function is essential to keeping the economy going, an oppressive state by laying burdensome taxes, by cramping business with restrictive regulations, and by intervening in an otherwise orderly free market, can stifle the economy upon which it depends for survival.

Economy

While the economy, with its buildings, factories, machines, farms, fleets and forests, appears to be, much more so than society or polity, a physical thing, it is, nevertheless, primarily and most importantly a vast network of people related to each other in producing, exchanging, and distributing goods and services. As such it is coterminous with society and equally natural, necessary, and spontaneously generated. Economic activity arises inevitably from the facts of limited but differently possessed natural resources and of limited but differently endowed human skills. It can be as complex as a transnational corporation producing and selling worldwide and as simple as two boys trading baseball cards.

Since people associate in an economic way to provide the material means for existence, this aspect of relations among people is subsidiary to both polity and society. But it is derived from neither, and, consequently, functions by its own principles. These, while manifested differently in the many economic roles people play as workers, managers, owners, lenders, and consumers, can be reduced to two: self-interest and collaboration. Both are natural and spontaneous and, though similar to their social and political counterparts, are distinctively economic in application.

In short, economic self-interest requires collaboration and collaboration is motivated by self-interest. For no one can produce without associates nor exchange without correspondents. The result is a distinctive kind of competition in which one succeeds by sharing, and exploits an advantage by proffering something more or better. The seller gains by tendering a better product or lowering price; the buyer by paying more. The successful manager gets better work by paying higher wages; the successful employee by working for less or more productively. In sum, economic competition is inherently social.

Society and polity in their dependence on the material means for their own survival must respect these economic principles and the methodology by which workplaces operate, offices run, banks and financiers function, and free markets behave. In turn, the economy must accept society as it is, provide the goods and services it seeks, and employ the people—with all their diversities and shortcomings—it provides. At the same time in trying to get people with differing interests, abilities, and ambitions to cooperate, those who make the important economic decisions must accept and act on the other fundamental principle that all who participate in the process do so for one principal reason, to increase their own economic well-being.

While the stance of politicians and business leaders is, as we have seen, often adversarial, both orders need each other. The state needs a flourishing economy to support the programs it wishes to provide. No less, the economy needs the legal structure to protect property rights and to enforce contracts. Perhaps more so, it needs laws restraining selfish self-interest, which by impairing collaboration eventually frustrates the economic process itself. Furthermore, the more perceptive business leader will acknowledge that any government or private program that increases people's competence and skills, improves their quality of life, or enhances their dignity cannot be bad for business and the economy. Given the right attitude, harmonizing the three orders is possible.

Recapping the above, we can return to where we started: the individual person in his or her personal, political and economic relations to others. As such the individual is the focus of forces and tensions—self-interest, ideology, public opinion and the like—that pull one way or another as one dimension gains at the expense of the others. One's predominant interest—business, government, or householding—will usually determine which dimension will enjoy priority. While business, political, moral, and social leaders may dispute for turf among themselves and those with the most prestige, influence, and power may affect public policy to their liking, in an open, democratic society the masses of inconsequential people carry the most weight. The concerns they feel, the issues that affect their lives, and their instincts as to what constitutes the good life will determine the configuration of public order. These feelings and instincts, in turn, are largely governed by the values people espouse.

Social Values and the Public Order

Values are not simply feelings, although they may be deeply felt. Allport (126–27, 454) calls them "deeply propriate disposition(s)," imbedded convictions, "upon which a man acts by preference." According to Scruton (32), values are worth fighting for because "we learn to see and understand the world in terms of them . . . A value is characterized . . . by its depth, by the extent it brings order to experience."

Values and Social Values

For a more thorough analysis of values, the reader is directed to the German philosopher Max Scheler.[3] He defines values as the immediate perception (intuition) of the good of one's self or of another person, thing, or relation among persons and things and the simultaneous preference ranking of the good according to the four criteria of absoluteness: a good's duration, indivisibility, essentiality, and fullness. While some prefer to reserve the term only for values of some permanence and real significance in one's life, to what we call spiritual and sacred values, Scheler's definition is all-inclusive, applying equally to the ephemeral pleasure from a chocolate bar and to an experience as radical, transforming, and permanent as Saul's encountering Christ on the way to Damascus.

When people of the same class espouse, although individually and distinctively, a value derived from the same objective good, it is called a class value. When many, if not the majority, in a society espouse the same value it is called a social value. Love of country, patriotism, is a good example: each patriot cherishes his or her country uniquely, one willing to give his or her life for it, another disobeying laws in protest of injustices. Despite these differences, the individual's espousal is not only multiplied but the person's conviction is confirmed by others' affirmations. National events, the attack on Pearl Harbor for example, can spark a latent social value. Charismatic leaders can fan them into national movements. Whatever the influence individuals possess, a people's social values are the ultimate and most powerful forces for changing the social climate and, hence, the public order. Moreover as intimate to one's most basic convictions, a person's values, whether matched by others or not, produce harmony in his or her ties and dealings with others.

Becoming specific, we next examine how three social values, freedom, equality, and fraternity (community) interrelate and serve to balance a person's social, political, and economic dimensions. We also examine how the same three social values together steady the dynamics of society, polity, and economy. Our final task will be to apply these ideas and principles to the organization of the social economy.

Everyone, surely, is familiar with these values. All three can be found at the very fountainhead of Western thought. Achilles' tragedy involves his freedom as a warrior, his assertion of equality with Agamemnon, and his love for Patroclus. These values were carried to a new dimension in Christian beliefs that Christ freed humankind from sin and Satan's tyranny, that all are equally loved by the Creator and thus are children of God, brothers and sisters of Christ and of each other.

But manifested as a political creed they were formulated in the Enlightenment and found concrete expression first in our

Declaration of Independence when thirteen contentious colonies united to assert "that all men are created equal; that they are endowed by their Creator with certain inalienable rights; that among these are life, liberty and the pursuit of happiness." This triad of social values became the rallying cry of the French Revolution and inspired the Declaration of the Rights of Man and Citizens. Since then, every constitution of states choosing the democratic form of government has echoed its adherence in some way to the social values of liberty, equality, and fraternity.

This is not to say that stating these values as ideals is to realize them in practice. The great dilemma of American society throughout its history is to grant civil and effective freedom and equality to descendants of Negro slaves (Myrdal). Less soul-rending but persistent as a problem is the quandary of officially welcoming the world's poor and homeless, while the people have difficulties assimilating these ethnic and religious minorities.

That America is a marvelous rainbow of peoples and cultures attests to the efficacy, while not perfect, of liberty and equality. That it is a far cry from a totally united people is testimony to the relative weakness of the social values of community and fraternity. Since all these social values are rooted in human personality, both their failings and effectiveness gauge the state of social, political, and economic intercourse and the quality of public life. Further explication of each and their interplay, both complementing and conflicting, is required.

Liberty and Personal Freedom

Liberty and freedom are synonymous. But each emphasizes one of the two essential notes of the reality: liberty, exemption from restraint, and freedom, the right to seek one's good. Since the human person is subject to differing layers of restraint—from the very physical to the highly spiritual—and may seek many degrees of the good, human freedom is neither absolute nor uniform.

Time and space limit our moving about; needs for sustenance, rest, air, and the like restrict our efforts and activities; our procreative and most sexual actions require a partner; perceiving and sensing are limited by the efficiency of our senses; the imagination is conditioned by past experience and capacity for enjoyment by cultivation; even thoughts and aspirations will require words, numbers, or other methods of formulation. Contrasting the degrees of restraint are the gradations good people seek, from mainly material and physical things to the spiritual goods from learning, reasoning, willing, and aspiring, to the unuttered and unutterable yearnings of the heart.

Comparable degrees of freedom distinguish various relations between people, differing by the nearness of the relation and its import to the people related. Highest and most to be respected and safeguarded are the freedoms of family ties, the intimacy between spouses, the bonding between parents and child and of siblings with each other, and the relations with kinfolk in diminishing affinity. Beyond blood relationships, freedom of friendships is most to be protected as are, in varying degrees, other cultural ties such as counselor to client, teacher to pupil, and artist to audience. Even the freedom of simple contact, both constant and casual, between people requires protection. Thus personal freedom, whatever constraints, relations, and aspirations are considered, underlies everyone's right to seek one's good and to become one's true self.

Political freedom, of course, is the great achievement of modern democracies. The ingredients of this freedom are people's civil rights: freedom of religion, speech, press, and assembly; the rights to vote, to stand for office, to equality before the law, to protection of person and property, and to a fair and public trial. Not all, however, can claim all of these rights: noncitizens, resident aliens, the young, and the disenfranchised may possess some but not all civil rights.

Even more disparate in beneficence is economic freedom. Even though a free society and polity require (generally) free markets, private property, open competition, and the right to hire labor and to sell one's own, nevertheless economic wealth is unequally distributed and shared. Some people, consequently, have more market power, own more property, enjoy greater competitive advantage, and can hire more people to do their bidding. Economic freedom produces vast inequalities (and possibly inequities) and it is here the two social values, liberty and equality, most seriously conflict.

Equality and Individuality

Before addressing this conflict, we need to lay out the basic dichotomy in the concept of equality itself. Essentially all people are equally persons: in some way self-knowing, responsible, social, and transcendent. At the same time, everyone is equally an individual: uniquely existing here and now, differentiated from every other actual or possible human being in age, size, experience, talent, and biology. To be fully a person one must be fully individual and fully social. Equality, therefore, requires according everyone basic respect as social being while treating each differently as individual being. Thus the questions constantly surface: "When does equal treatment violate individuality and individual treatment violate equality?"

Every individual, of course, is a member of society and must be respected as a person who has the right to fulfill his or her needs as a physical, biological, social, and spiritual being, each in a unique way. Indeed it is generally acknowledged as fair that the disadvantaged should be accorded extra help precisely to compensate for their impairments. Theoretically every citizen stands as equal to everyone else before the law. But differential taxation according to wealth is a sacrosanct principle as are special programs to protect minorities. In the economic order, it is generally accepted that no one should be discriminated against or preferred on noneconomic criteria. But laws to protect the disadvantaged and efforts to equalize the opportunities of the poor are also universally approved.

Nevertheless, the freedom to be different prevents equal treatment. Society rewards the few with fame and honor while most live and die in obscurity. Many win respect and affection, others are lonely and abandoned. The rich, influential, and well-organized enjoy more political power than the poor and the disorganized masses. In seeking office incumbents have advantage over challengers. The wealthy can afford and withstand more costly litigation. The poor are more subject to military service and exconvicts more suspect of crimes. Economic freedom means that the wealthy, influential, talented, shrewd, and ambitious, not to say the dishonest and unscrupulous, can acquire property, capital, and power grossly above the average. All this suggests the need of another social value to mediate between freedom and equality.

Fraternity and Community

Of the three values, fraternity is probably the least appreciated and the most needed. Clarence Walton (28) is quite blunt: "To dwell on notions of justice, liberty, and fraternity is to recognize how much and how long Western man has talked of the first, more recently of the second, and almost never of the third . . . Indeed it is quite possible that contemporary liberal political thought which supports egalitarianism is essentially individualistic and unfraternal."

The value, fraternity, springs from perceiving our social nature not as just the ties which bind us to others but as alliances that complement our limitations. Fraternity, therefore, can permeate all of our relations to others from the most necessary to the most accidental. Fraternity engenders community, that sense of being one with others, of being accepted as a member of a group, of belonging. Fraternity is called solidarity in its effect of uniting different people with different interests and talents for a common goal or purpose. Fraternity, therefore, respects the other's personality, while accepting his or her uniqueness and individuality. In thus creating unity from differences, fraternity affirms the equal right of all to contribute to and to share in the common good but in a manner tailored to each. Fraternity preserves human personality by respecting both a person's individuality and social nature.

Fraternity, therefore, mediates freedom and equality by controlling freedom's tendency to selfishness and license and by neutralizing equality's disposition to envy and class animosity. People who are prompted by the values of fraternity, community, and solidarity highly respect personal freedom and individuality. They also help create a milieu of concern, caring, and support for everyone, especially for the most disadvantaged.

Beyond accepting everyone as citizen of the polity, fraternity leads people to share burdens, sacrifices, and benefits, respecting individual capabilities but avoiding privilege and partisanship. Regarding the economy, fraternity stresses cooperation, consisting of not only combining mechanically the productive factors (labor, resources, and capital) but also blending individuals' efforts, skills, risk-taking, and management with their own and others' property in producing something of use to others.

This mediation of fraternity between liberty and equality is not set once and for all. The three social values are dynamically interrelated in people's value hierarchies and their respective influences change as people's apprehensions, aspirations, and moral concerns change. An exaggerated freedom begets a me-first attitude in dealings with others, degrades many personal relations into cash connections, and by throttling the state encourages the worst kind of business license. When equality becomes the burning issue, society without fraternity is politicized: the poor incited by envy and the rich defending their niggardliness. Moreover, the state dominates the economy and its welfarism is more easily subverted into totalitarianism by unscrupulous and unconstrained leaders. In a society where a false fraternity prevails, either clannishness or tribalism renders the state impotent and the economy stagnant, or a sham solidarity bestows unlimited power on a ruling elite.

When, however, these social values are in overall balance, a general accord will prevail among personal attitudes, ordinary social intercourse, business practice, and public policy. In turn society, polity, and economy will manifest certain unifying characteristics: respect for everyone as a free and responsible person; toleration, even indulgence, of diversity; acceptance of all peoples—and in a special way the disadvantaged—as equally human with the obligation to contribute to and the right to share in the public good; and a sense of community as an overall social harmonizer in that all are respected both as persons and in their individuality and all belong, the contributions of each blending into the common effort. In this multifaceted dynamic, however, complacency is never in order. Social arbiters, moral critics, and political commentators, themselves possessing a sense of social balance, must be at the alert to maintain the symmetry and proportion among the personal, political, and economic dimensions of public life.

While we could apply the preceding analysis to both society and polity, we will, as the title suggests, apply these ideas to the social economy. There we will find that the principles that make the economy function require the orientation and coordination among the same three social values that keep society, polity, and economy in working order.

Organizing Principles and Social Values

The social economy, as that complex of people producing goods and services, distributing income and profits, exchanging product for money, consuming their collective output, and investing their savings back into the economy, is necessarily social. Its structure includes all manner of productive things, buildings, machinery, equipment, inventory, and the like, but mainly people organized into office forces, marketing staffs, production crews, and management teams in manufacturing firms, financial houses, services businesses, shopping malls, government bureaus, and nonprofit agencies.

What makes this vast, seething complex function is its three principles of organization: competitive self-interest, government involvement, and cooperative collaboration. Of these, competitive self-interest is the drive, the impelling force; government involvement is the safeguard, a guiding but mainly braking capacity; and cooperation is the manner and method of the economic process. The three social values that harmonize people's personal, political, and economic relations do double duty in keeping the social economy's organizational principles in order. Freedom prompts competition; equality justifies government intervention; fraternity fosters cooperation. We will discuss each in turn, beginning with what drives and initiates economic action, competitive self-interest.

Competitive Self-Interest

The rationality of addressing scarcity concludes to the necessity of both competition and self-interest. Because human material wants taken together exceed human abilities to satisfy them and because material resources and human skills are differently distributed, people must engage in the constant process of using material goods more efficiently. That is, they must try to improve their well-being by shifting, trading, or redesigning a good from a less to a more desired use. In short, people must seek their self-interest. By the same token, since scarcity is a condition affecting everybody, all must strive with each other to get what they want. Distasteful though this may seem to the more aesthetic kind of moralist, this is the way the world is even in their own case. In fact, people generally take this situation so much for granted that competing shoppers or competing workers can be quite friendly and helpful to each other. There is something different about both economic competition and self-interest.

Remember that economic competition is essentially social: one gains by offering more, so that while competitors may lose what they were seeking, they lost because others gave the buyers or sellers more of what they wanted. Self-interest also needs refinement. It expresses the basic rationality of getting the most return from effort and resources: that is, it dictates efficiency but does not prescribe the act's end, goal, or reason. In short, self-interest relates to economic efficiency, not to moral purpose. Applied to competition it affirms that competitors should seek to increase their economic return whether the material benefit accrues to themselves alone, to others, or to some combination of both. Self-interest applies whether the purpose is selfish or altruistic. Volunteers, for example, running a soup kitchen must be just as concerned for efficiency (stretching limited supplies as far as possible) as the manager of a supermarket for profits. (Maybe more so since their purpose is nobler.) It defies common sense to reduce all motivation to selfishness, rather than to accept the obvious fact that people act for a variety of and often mixed motives and to benefit others than themselves. The economist need not gag at this idea but simply take it as a given of human nature.

Competition in real life, the spur that makes businesses go, must also be distinguished from its pale, mechanistic abstraction in economic, especially neoclassical, analysis. Bernard W. Dempsey was a generation ahead of most contemporaries in assessing real-life competition as a constructive, vigorous innovative force even among huge commercial, financial, and manufacturing enterprises. "American competition," wrote Dempsey (336–43), "is a new thing in economics. It is itself an undigested innovation. It is not atomistic; it does not deal with small units. It is not impersonal: innovations come from persons; only people, not markets, have ideas."[4] It must be confessed that foreign competitors recognized and copied this force before economists acknowledged its importance.

Government Intervention

Being the aggressive thing it is, and its self-interest easily turned to selfish and greedy ends, competition needs control. Many firms have developed a strong corporate ethos that manages to keep self-interest and competition within their economic confines. Many industries police themselves, some quietly effective for years, others successful except when in the throes of crises. But just as both lawless and the law-abiding citizens need laws, police, and courts, so too all businesses can benefit from the restraining interventions of the state. Since it is the role of government to exercise prudent foresight regarding the proper order of matters for the public welfare, its proper activity can be "described in four functions: directing, watching, urging and restraining" (Dempsey, 56). Each of these implies that the state acts upon the economy as from without and must respect, therefore, "its proper principles of organization" (Dempsey, 283). But it has the authority to see that the people's needs and wants are provided to the extent natural resources, technology, and human skills and effort make this possible.

There is both a positive and negative side to government intervention. Negative would imply laws and their enforcement to prevent stealing, arson, dishonesty, fraud, extortion, and all advantage-taking by the powerful and/or unscrupulous against the poor and/or law-abiding. Positive relates first and foremost to protecting persons and private property, administering justice, effecting a more equitable distribution of income, providing needed public services for education and public health, taxing differentially, alleviating catastrophic losses, shoring up the poor's shortfall, and sustaining the hungry, homeless, and destitute.

The benefit, indeed necessity, of the state's involvement in the economy is too obvious to dispute. Any action that restrains evildoing and promotes honest dealing improves the climate of trust that is essential for business. Programs that enhance people's earning capacity, return them to the workforce, or renew hope after disaster increase the productivity of the economy. Any effort, private or governmental, that rescues a person from submerging into the permanent underclass has made a positive contribution to the economy. Conversely, policies that penalize self-interest (as distinct from guiding it), that favor monopoly over reasonable competition, that patronize people and lock them into dependency, such policies violate the economy's operating principles and thereby slow it down.

Cooperation

While self-interested competition drives the economy and state action guides it, collaboration is its mode of operation. Again, Dempsey (21–23): "Cooperation in the economic process is both implicit and explicit." Men and factors "working together on a job are obviously cooperating." But in intending to exchange their products with others similarly producing they are "also cooperating toward a common objective, namely, the provision of an improved standard of living for both." The necessity of collaboration and cooperation arises from the common sense of private property and especially specialization of labor. Neither labor nor property is productive without the other, and the more sophisticated the product the more diversified the skills and complex the resources that must be assembled to produce it.

Cooperation performs a further function in linking competition and state involvement together. It effects the same end as government: a larger population working at and sharing in greater economic output. More income and wealth is generated and spread more widely. At the same time cooperation preserves, indeed encourages, gain-seeking. By improving productivity, it heightens competition between firms. By offering more income, it spurs individuals to greater effort within their company.

Conflict and Coordination

The three organizing principles working together engender economic harmony. But spasmodic or disjointed emphasis of one principle at the expense of the other two provokes discord. Excessive and unrestrained competition tends to dissolve the social aspect of the ties that form the economy as a common good. Selfish aggrandizement, particularly by owners and managers, sours cooperation into coercion. A crude, heavy-handed, and selfish self-interest reduces the worker to a means and the buyer (or the seller) to a thing to be exploited. A more subtle selfishness will sire intimidation, fraud, and deception, all masked as vigorous competition. Both breed that alienation that Marx defines as intrinsic to capitalism, the dissolution of the workplace and marketplace into a cockpit of contending atoms (chapters 7, 25).

Elected government's egalitarianism (equality carried to excess) often motivates a damaging intrusion into the economy. While usually proposing to effect distributive justice, it may produce a statism emulating totalitarianism. Ideological egalitarianism (absolute equality) will inevitably create a governing elite whose political and economic privileges camouflage naked self- and class-interest: the pigs are more equal than others! A more pragmatic egalitarianism, often motivated by sincere desires to provide needed assistance, to redress disadvantages, or to protect the public from devious practices, tends, like the proverbial camel, to take over the economy. Governments subsidizing or providing housing, medical care, education, and basic maintenance run the risk of breeding dependency first among the very poor, but gradually infecting even the middle classes. In so doing they discriminate against private programs providing the same services. This illustrates that governments generally are uncomfortable with competition. They prefer legal prices to market prices, regulation and predictable prices and services to the capriciousness of economic rivalry, and franchising monopolies to many firms vying for the same business.

A cooperation, infected by complacency, collusion, or both, does not, despite appearances, resolve the competition/intervention conflict. Rather it skirts around it or covers it up. The complacent disdain competition, being superior to it and satisfied with the status quo (Detroit's attitude during the 1950s to the upstart Japanese automakers). An otiose management and a laggard labor force often will make common cause in seeking government protection, especially from foreign competition. Other kinds of collusion—rigged biddings, insider trading and dealing, sweetheart contracts between owners and union, follow-the-leader pricing—may actually be illegal or cut legal corners. In short, complacency and collusion tend to defuse competition and to blunt government intervention with the result not only of slowing the economy down but, worse, unraveling its social ties.

It should now be obvious that the three social values, liberty, equality, and fraternity, can coordinate the three organizing principles of the social economy. Just as the same people interact as social persons, as political citizens and as economic actors, so too in the social economy they are competitors, voters, and collaborators. The same espoused values will maintain the economy in balance and it in relation to society and polity.

Liberty inspires respect for everyone as a person in social intercourse, business practice, and public policy. It defends those rights essential to a healthy competition, the overall right to participate in the economy, including the right to benefit from economic opportunity, to engage in competition, and to exploit one's skills and advantages. Liberty also acknowledges the basic rightness that those whose effort, initiative, risk-taking, and skill produce a greater return should realize the benefit from their actions. Liberty would extend these rights as widely as possible and defend them vigorously. As to public policy it prefers private initiative to government undertakings and the market process to political fiat.

Equality, on the other hand, welcomes government intervention and involvement as not only necessary at times but also beneficial. In recognizing everyone's right to share in the output of the economy, equality supports laws and courts in suppressing injustice and sustaining justice and order in people's

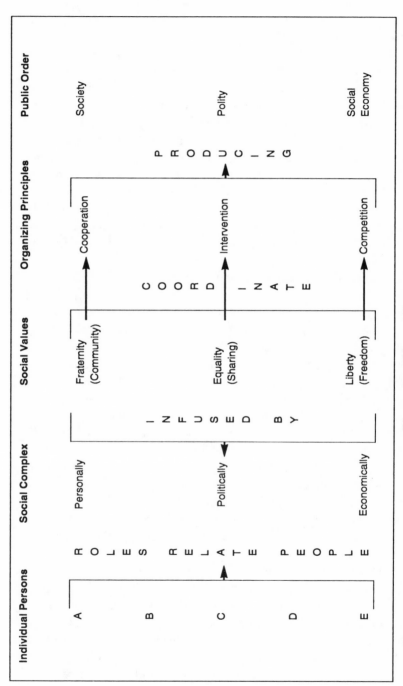

Figure 2.1. The social matrix

dealings with each other. It urges making certain public services available to all and not just to those who can afford them. Finally, it approves a range of government programs to assist the disadvantaged, however physically, socially, intellectually, or psychologically impaired, as a way of redistributing the benefits of the economy.

Finally, a sense of fraternity and community inspires all those considerations that highlight the social nature of business and the economic process. It sees cooperation and collaboration as of the very essence of that process. Without minimizing in any respect the motive force of self-interest, fraternity deplores the conflicts that inevitably arise and sees a disposition to share generously as the way to not only resolve conflicts but also avoid them. Moreover, it knows that such generosity both stimulates freedom and counteracts governments' itchings to intervene in the economy. (The interplay of human relations, social values, and the organizing principles of the economy are outlined in figure 2.1.)

We conclude with one final caution. There is no permanent solution to the inconsistencies, imbalances, and disharmonies among a person's and a people's roles and relationships. Their needs, relations to others, resources, technical abilities, and values are in constant change. All of these impact not only on society, polity, and economy but on the principles by which the economy is organized and run. There is, therefore, no definitive formula to correct and no lasting resolution of the economy's failures and of the shortcomings of the people who run it. What is available are guidelines on how policies, practices and attitude can produce a more reasonable and human life together.

Notes

I am particularly grateful for the helpful comments of the editors, Edward J. O'Boyle and John B. Davis, and two anonymous referees. The remaining faults are my own.

1. The following section relies heavily on the thought of the French philosopher and Resistance martyr, Emmanuel Mounier. See his *Personalism*.

2. One of the most forthright manifestos on the religious significance

of work is found in *On Human Work*, Pope John Paul II, St. Paul Editions, Boston, 1981, sections 9 and 10.

3. See Scheler (99–110).

4. It is appropriate in this anniversary book to highlight the thought of this founding father of the Association for Social Economics.

References

Allport, Gordon W. *Pattern and Growth in Personality*. New York: Holt, Rinehart and Winston, 1965.

Dempsey, Bernard W. *The Functional Economy*. Englewood Cliffs: Prentice-Hall, 1958.

John Paul II. *On Human Work*. Boston: St. Paul Editions, 1981.

Marx, Karl. *Capital I*. Edited by F. Engels and translated by Moor and Aveling. Chicago: Encyclopedia Britannica, 1952.

Mounier, Emmanuel. *Personalism*. South Bend: University of Notre Dame Press, 1952.

Myrdal, Gunnar. *An American Dilemma*. New York: Harper and Row, 1944.

Scheler, Max. *Formalism in Ethics and Non-formal Ethics of Value*. Translated by M. Frings and R. Funk. Evanston: Northwestern University Press, 1973.

Scruton, Roger. *The Aesthetics of Architecture*. Princeton: Princeton University Press, 1979.

Walton, Clarence. *The Ethics of Corporate Conduct*. Englewood Cliffs: Prentice-Hall, 1977.

3

Human Physical Need

A Concept That Is Both Absolute and Relative

Edward J. O'Boyle

> By necessaries I understand not only the com-
> modities which are indispensably necessary
> for the support of life but whatever the cus-
> tom of the country renders it indecent for cred-
> itable people, even of the lowest order, to be
> without.
>
> —Adam Smith, 821

Whether personally affirmed or denied, need is a requirement for human existence that derives from the materiality of human nature. A want is a thing that is desired, whether it is materially needed or not. In a market economy, consumers by virtue of their free will and intellect are able to choose, within the limits of the goods and services and economic means available, both the wants that are to be satisfied and the needs that are to be met. They use this freedom wisely and demonstrate the rationality of human beings whenever their free will follows their intellect, that is, whenever they want the things they need or, alternatively, whenever satisfying a want does not interfere with meeting need. Need, in other words, is an object of the intellect, a thing to be known. Want, in contrast, is an object of the will, a thing to be sought after.

The difference is real not only for consumers but also for

producers even if some producers are oblivious to it or disregard it entirely. For the producer, not meeting a need likely has greater consequences than not satisfying a want because needs typically run deeper and are less deferrable than wants. Wants include things that some persons might regard as frivolous, fickle, or fanciful. A fad or fashion is a want that is aroused by the behavior or influence of others and may even masquerade as a need. Genuine needs, on the other hand, include only those things that are consequential, constant, or commonplace and, for that reason, may reoccur more often than wants—a matter of some consequence to producers who depend on repeat business.

The individuality of all human beings means that, even though need proceeds from the materiality of human nature and in a general sense is the same for all, need in a specific sense is different from one person to another. What constitutes a need for one person may be a want for another, such as a whirlpool bath for a person with arthritis as opposed to a person in good health. Some persons do not want what others in the same circumstances regard as needed, as with automobile seatbelts and motorcycle helmets. There are even instances when a thing simultaneously meets a need and satisfies a want. A sweater may be needed for the warmth and protection that it provides and at the same time wanted for the attention that it attracts or the statement that it makes. Further, the needs and wants of any given human being change with age.

On occasion, consumers in a market economy will choose poorly in the sense that whatever they have chosen does not satisfy a want or meet a need. Others may mismanage their funds by satisfying a want at the expense of some need. Put differently, some choices made freely do not follow the direction of the intellect and consequently freedom of choice at times has outcomes that underscore the imperfection of human beings (i.e., they are not always able to achieve their potential fully).

A craving or obsession is a want over which the person has lost some freedom of choice. In some instances a craving becomes an addiction, that is, a want over which a person has no control. A dependency and an addiction are alike in that both signify a loss of control. They are different in that feeding an addiction, as with the cigarette-addicted smoker, is life-threatening while maintaining a dependency, as with the insulin-dependent diabetic, is life-enhancing (for more on need broadly construed, see Braybrooke and Griffin).

Conventional Economics and Physical Need

Conventional economics takes all of these things—wants, needs, whims, fads, fancies, fashions, cravings, addictions, and dependencies—and reduces them to human wants. Setting aside need and focusing instead on wants allow mainstream economics to sidestep the intellectual biases regarding the use of value-laden concepts such as need, to cast consumer behavior in a positive-economics mold, and to represent economics as an exact, value-free science.

Human wants, according to mainstream economics, are addressed through a market economy wherein the consumer is represented as commodity-acquiring, want-satisfying, and utility-maximizing, which concepts are taken from three core characteristics of human beings as individual beings—solitariness, autonomy, and self-centeredness—and reinforce those characteristics. *Homo economicus* is much more than a clever term, add-on, or afterthought. *Homo economicus* forms one of the foundations of mainstream economics.

By adding the "invisible hand" to individualism, conventional economics is able to argue that the well-being of everyone is served best when individuals singlemindedly pursue their own self-interest. Thus, in a market economy, the individual pursuit of one's own want satisfaction is the best means to the want satisfaction of one's neighbors. Further, conventional economics construes resource (re)allocation in terms of relative prices, thereby slipping away from the unmet need of resource holders that attends changes in relative prices and surplus resources, notably labor resources, that are not readily cleared by the market.

Strong advocates of libertarianism, such as are found among neoclassical economists, do not deny the existence of unmet physical need. Rather, they do not affirm an *obligation in justice* to help the needy. In addition, they argue that the practice of altruism or charity is a threat to private (market) control of resource (re)allocation and other economic decisions and to the incentive to produce and that state control of those decisions in order to meet human physical need is an unacceptable solution. Mainstream economists assert that only the softheaded would substitute the dubious good that follows from interfering with markets through the practice of justice and altruism for the much greater good that attends an unfettered market system. They look upon the needy as potential contributors to economic output, as threats to the incomes of others, or both.

Social Economics and Physical Need

Social economics rejects this ordering of priorities. The needy are seen primarily as persons,[1] not as objects, and economic systems are established ultimately to meet human material need so that human beings are not diminished as persons by their unmet physical need. Notwithstanding the centrality of price to the process of resource (re)allocation according to conventional economics, market economies in fact use the threat of unmet physical need to (re)allocate economic resources in the sense that, whenever a resource holder assigns a price that is too high, the resource becomes idle and no longer produces income (Becker and others, 292). The central dysfunction of the market economy and the dilemma of social economics is how to continue to (re)allocate resources on the basis of unmet physical need without diminishing the person of those whom the market renders redundant.

In what follows, the individualism and libertarianism that are characteristic of mainstream economics are replaced with personalism and humanism. The intent is not to deny the individuality of human nature that is captured in the term *Homo economicus*. Rather, it is to include sociality with individuality in order to represent human nature more accurately. This expanded understanding of human nature is conveyed by the replacement term *Homo socioeconomicus*.

The problem with conventional economics lies at its very foundations. Individualism asserts that *Homo economicus* has a one-dimensional nature—individual being. In *Homo economicus*, rationality as to means (but not ends) is emphasized to the near exclusion of materiality. In that sense, *Homo economicus* is disembodied, is rational only in a narrow sense, and is essentially unknowable as to ends. *Homo economicus* knows what he or she wants, though economists cannot posit any ends, and given his or her income uses the market wisely to achieve the maximum satisfaction possible.

Personalism insists that *Homo economicus* is a half-person because overlooked by individualism is the second dimension of human nature—social being. The duality of human nature means that being self-centered, solitary, autonomous, unique, and self-made are not the only personal characteristics of consumers that matter much. At the same time, by virtue of the social dimension, *Homo socioeconomicus* characteristically is other-centered, communal, dependent, alike, and culture-bound. In terms of behavior *Homo socioeconomicus* is want-satisfying and need-fulfilling, utility-maximizing and utility-satisficing, privacy-protecting and companion-seeking, and commodity-acquiring and gift-giving.

The personalist view in social economics argues that the individual dimension of human nature means that specific goods and services are selected by individual consumers acting autonomously and looking inward at times to determine and serve their own self-interest. From the personalist perspective, the social dimension of human nature means that specific goods and services are chosen by individual consumers who are constrained more or less by the social environment, looking outward at times to determine and serve their own self-interest and at other times to determine and meet the needs and satisfy the wants of others, especially family members, neighbors, and peers.

The individuality of *Homo socioeconomicus* enables him or her to make intrapersonal comparisons of wants and needs over time. The sociality of *Homo socioeconomicus* enables him or her to make interpersonal comparisons at any point in time. Trend-setting is evidence of individuality. Protecting the environment through recycling is evidence of sociality.

Along both dimensions, whenever free will follows an intellect that is property informed, choices are made rationally and wisely. Otherwise, they may be irrational, unwise, or both. The pure rationality of *Homo economicus* is a claim that does not stand close examination.

If an individual's needs are fully met even when that individual has made some unwise choices, one does not have to differentiate needs from wants unless using a specific good or service to satisfy a given want is dangerous or harmful. The consumer routinely will attempt to maximize both want satisfaction and need fulfillment. Simply put, with one general exception, there is no social question.

On the other hand, if an individual's needs are not fully met even when that person's financial resources have been applied wisely and even when none of the wants satisfied are dangerous or harmful, one must differentiate want from need. Under these circumstances, it is necessary to determine the extent to which society should intervene, by private or public means, to help meet the needs the individual is not able to meet alone. In this regard, the principle of subsidiarity is instructive.

Subsidiarity and Unmet Physical Need

Some social economists favor discarding the market economy entirely and replacing it with a command economy where human material need, it is argued, is better provisioned.[2] This writer rejects that remedy for the United States on grounds that the market economy for some time has been provisioning human material need reasonably well[3] and that, following the principle of subsidiarity,[4] the state should intervene and provide help for only that portion of need that the private sector is unable to provision by itself. It is subsidiarity—which reinforces the democratic principle by placing control of decision making as close to the individual as possible—not sociality that transforms unmet human physical need from an individual question into a social question.

This mixed-economy remedy has two main advantages and two main disadvantages. As to advantage, it allows considerable individual freedom of choice and it encourages personal responsibility for one's own need, thereby preserving a powerful incentive to produce. As to disadvantage, by permitting a wide exercise of personal freedom of choice it runs the risk that individuals will use their financial resources unwisely, choosing to satisfy whims, fads, fancies, and fashion, and to feed obsessions and addictions, at the expense of meeting needs and dependencies. Additionally, it opens the possibility that the strong might use the state not to help the weak but to enhance their own economic standing. The mixed-economy solution is viable only as long as (1) the market economy continues to produce in abundance the goods and services required to meet human physical need, (2) individuals use their freedom wisely, putting needs and dependencies ahead of wants and obsessions, and (3) the strong truly care about the weak.

In personalism, truly caring about the weak means resisting the tendency to reduce them to mere objects. Le Troquer warns that this tendency is *ever-present*: "There is evidently in human society an inherent state of tension. Of course, society should be naturally directed to the good of the human person, but it bears within it the seed of conflict owing to its tendency to regard the person only as a mere part, an objective element in the whole social body. By so doing society loses its own nature, since it loses and oppresses its centre, the person" (Le Troquer, 54–55). Resisting objectification may be likened to preserving freedom. Both demand eternal vigilance.

For social economists who accept the mixed-economy solution, there is additional work to be done regarding the determinants of consumer behavior in a market economy. In general, this means incorporating emotions such as whimsy, obsession, fear, impulsiveness, and peer pressure into an understanding of consumer behavior (which is grounded too narrowly in rationality alone). That task is not within the scope of this volume (for examples of work in this area, see Etzioni, and Lutz and Lux).

Seen from the perspective of the principle of subsidiarity, the market economy is a set of complex economic institutions to help individuals meet those needs, satisfy those wants, and indulge those whims, fancies, and obsessions that they cannot meet, satisfy, or indulge alone, at the same time preserving the widest possible exercise of personal freedom. If the market economy were able to provide for all of these demands, there would be no unmet need and therefore no role for the state. As observed previously, however, the market economy uses the threat of unmet physical need to (re)allocate resources and for that reason there always will be a social question.

Unmet physical need is regarded as a social question, while unsatisfied wants, fancies, and cravings and unfed addictions[5] are not, because unmet physical need threatens existence and routine daily functioning whereas the others do not. Failure on the part of the state to respond to the physical need that is unmet by the private sector has profound implications for the three central social values of freedom, equality, and community and thus for the personhood of those in need.

To illustrate, an addiction that is left untreated destroys the personal freedom of choice of the addict whether that person acquired the addiction more or less voluntarily, as with a mother, or involuntarily, as with her newborn baby. Hunger destroys equality because begging for one's food subordinates the beggar to the provider. Illiteracy destroys community because it interrupts the communication that draws people together.

Unmet physical need attacks the foundations of human dignity. By failing or refusing to provide help to needy persons, the state denies that freedom, equality, and community are central social values. Further, the state would be casting aside the principle of subsidiarity as a requirement of the good society. Under those circumstances, any help that the state provides to the needy would be for instrumental purposes only, that is, not for the well-being of the needy person but for the benefit of the rest of society. Addicts, for instance, would be treated not to free them from their addiction but to reduce the probability that they will engage in criminal activity to support their addiction.[6]

Subsidiarity is consistent with a humanism that sees humans as unique beings of infinite worth. Any help that is provided under subsidiarity is intended principally for the purpose of protecting and preserving the dignity of the person. Instrumentalism is not consistent with that kind of humanism because human beings in need are seen as threats to the rest of society and the help that is provided is intended to remove that threat.[7]

Just as the Bill of Rights guarantees government provisioning of the political goods that are demanded by the fundamental dignity of human beings, so too the safety net guarantees government provisioning of the economic goods required for the same purpose. The exact content of the economic goods in the safety net are redefined continuously by the legislature just as the specific dimensions of the political goods in the Bill of Rights are continuously reinterpreted by the judiciary.

Social economics and the social economy begin with and center principally on *unmet* human material need. Even so, the need fulfillment of social economics is not a replacement for the want satisfaction of conventional economics. Indeed, it is necessary in general to preserve want satisfaction in the new paradigm because removing it means restricting freedom of choice and diminishing the individuality of *Homo socioeconomicus* as consumer. Want satisfaction is the corollary of voluntary unemployment that is preserved in order to assure the freedom and protect the individuality of *Homo socioeconomicus* as worker.

There is no authentic social economics of unmet human material need without the principle of subsidiarity because without that principle the needy who are helped are seen as instruments or threats and thereby are diminished as persons. See figure 3.1 for a brief summary of the person of the consumer. In the section that follows, the task of defining and measuring unmet physical need is addressed.

Defining and Measuring Unmet Physical Need

There are two ways to address the problem of defining and measuring unmet physical need. One is by demonstrated need, the other is by presumed need. By demonstrated need, a set of physical needs is defined beforehand and persons are determined to be needy (more or less) if they are able to demonstrate that their financial resources are inadequate to provide (more or less) for those needs. This method is used in the social assistance form of direct aid to the needy, such as Aid to Families with Dependent Children, Medicaid, and Public Assistance. By presumed need, a person is presumed to be needy if a certain reasonably predictable life event occurs that is indicative of need such as being unemployed, being elderly and sick, or being orphaned. This method is used in social insurance programs

THE DUALITY OF THE CONSUMER, NEED FULFILLMENT, WANT SATISFACTION, AND UNMET NEED	
Individual Being	Social Being

as a being who is both individual and social, consumer is both:

unique . . . . and . . . . alike
solitary . . . . and . . . . communal
autonomous . . . . and . . . . dependent
self-centered . . . . and . . . . other-centered
self-made . . . . and . . . . culture-bound

Individual Being	Social Being
individuality means that at various times the consumer makes intrapersonal comparisons	sociality means that at any point in time the consumer makes interpersonal comparisons

may be   trendsetter+
              conformist++
              traditionalist+
	may be do-gooder*
	              free-rider**
	              environmentalist*

apart from individuality and sociality, the consumer as person is:
free to act and therefore morally accountable
rational (whenever will follows intellect)
emotional (whenever will does not follow intellect)
capable, more or less, of achieving full potential
foresighted and hindsighted

consequently, in terms of behavior, consumer is both:
want-satisfying and need-fulfilling
utility-maximizing and utility-satisficing
privacy-protecting and company-seeking
commodity-acquiring and gift-giving

if individual need is met even when choices are made unwisely, no reason to differentiate needs from wants: there is no social question

if individual need is not met even when choices are made wisely, wants are to be differentiated from needs: there is a social question

principle of subsidiarity asserts that to some extent state should provision goods and services not for unsatisfied wants but for unmet need and only insofar as private sector is unable to provision that need

+ much individuality ++ little individuality	* much sociality ** little sociality

Figure 3.1. *Homo socioeconomicus*: The person of the consumer

such as Unemployment Insurance, Medicare, and Survivors Insurance. Presumption scrutinizes personal and family financial circumstances less intrusively than demonstration.

All of the programs just enumerated have macroeconomic effects but each one was established mainly for microeconomic purposes, that is, to provide aid to a particular type of needy person or family. The task that this writer has set for himself in this essay is to develop a general measure of unmet physical need for macroeconomic purposes, that is, to determine how well the mixed economy is performing in terms of meeting the physical need of individual persons and families. Such a measure is a macroeconomic diagnostic tool quite similar to other diagnostic tools for the macroeconomy, such as the national income accounts, the various price indices, and national employment and unemployment data.

Over the years, two types of general measures of unmet physical need have emerged. One defines and measures physical need in an absolute sense. The other defines and measures it in a relative sense. Of the two, the absolute measure is the more widely accepted in the U.S. However, both standards are based on personal and family income and both therefore incorporate aspects of demonstrated need. Even so, neither one determines unmet physical need with the specificity of demonstrated need. Rather, both presume that if income is below some particular level, unmet physical need in general is indicated.[8] Thus, both the relative standard and the absolute standard of unmet physical need incorporate elements of demonstrated need and presumed need, and both standards are indicators of unmet physical need in a general sense. Neither one can be used to indicate a specific unmet physical need because neither one actually probes the specific physical needs of persons or families.

A general measure of unmet physical need is useful in determining macro-economic performance. It does not, however, define or measure the number of persons or families with a specific type of unmet physical need such as health care. Even so, at times a general measure may be used at the microeconomic level to determine a person's eligibility for a specific program of assistance.

Absolute vs. Relative Standards of Physical Need:
The Conceptual Issue

An absolute standard of physical need is built around the cost of the goods and services required to meet that need in some fashion, either minimally, adequately, abundantly, or superabundantly. The most widely used absolute standard of minimal physical need, the poverty standard, originated in 1964 at the Social Security Administration (see Orshansky, 3–29). A minimum standard may be defined by expert opinion, as with the official U.S. poverty standard, or by public opinion, as in Mack and Lansley's study of poverty in Britain (see Mack and Lansley, 45–48).

In the past the U.S. Bureau of Labor Statistics estimated three other family budgets: the lower budget, the intermediate budget, and the higher budget. These three budgets are absolute standards of human physical need that can be characterized as specifying the cost of the goods and services required to meet that need adequately, abundantly, or superabundantly. However, the program that provided estimates for these three BLS budgets was eliminated in 1982 in compliance with overall budget reduction requirements (*Monthly Labor Review*, 44).

In what follows, this writer is concerned with the standard of minimal physical need because any minimal need that is unmet likely will have more serious implications for existence and functioning than unmet need at the adequate level or higher. The social question at the minimal level of physical need, in other words, is more compelling.

The official U.S. poverty standard is based on the current cost of the Department of Agriculture's 1961 Economy Food Plan. The cost of the other goods and services to satisfy physical need minimally is estimated on the basis of the Department of Agriculture's 1955 Survey of Food Consumption, which found that families, on average, spend almost one-third of their income on food. Thus, the total cost of the goods and services required to meet physical need minimally or at the poverty level is fixed officially at three times the current cost of the Economy Food Plan. Critics of the official poverty standard point to this aspect of its construction as one of its main weaknesses as an accurate measure of subsistence (see Congressional Budget Office for a discussion of this and other criticisms of this standard). For a family of four persons in 1988, the poverty standard or poverty threshold was $12,092. For a person living alone, the threshold was $6,024 (Series P–60, No. 166, p. 88).

A relative standard of minimal physical need or poverty is built around the economic resources that a person possesses in relation to the resources of others. To illustrate, people whose income puts them in the lowest quintile of an income distribution might be classified as needy. Or, minimal physical need might be defined as having an income that is less than one-half of the median income for the entire population. According to the relative standard, a person who does not have what others typically possess, however much or little that may be, is needy.

Sawhill notes an important difference between types of relative standards. Unmet physical need can be eliminated, theoretically, when need is defined in terms of some percentage of the median. It cannot be eliminated when the standard is defined in terms of the bottom fractile of the income distribution (Sawhill, 1076).

Ruggles (20–23) identifies a third type—"subjective"—that utilizes householder assessments as to the amounts of income or consumption needed by persons who are like the respondents. She suggests that "subjective" could resolve the differences between the relative standard and the absolute standard. In my judgment, subjective is not a third type but rather is a public-opinion approach to defining either a relative standard or an absolute standard. Consequently, "subjective" cannot resolve the fundamental differences between the relative standard and the absolute standard.

Townsend (1979, 31) insists that poverty is definable only in relative terms of inequality and deprivation. Additionally, he asserts that poverty can be defined objectively.

Townsend's rejection of any validity to an absolute standard reduces poverty to a one-dimensional concept by implicitly asserting that humans are social beings only (more about this shortly). Even though he affirms that the measurement of poverty is not value-free (1974, 36–37), Townsend's insistence that poverty can be defined objectively gives the impression that it is possible to address poverty in a value-free context. Definitions of poverty or unmet physical need invariably reflect the values of the person(s) using the concept and for that reason it is virtually impossible to devise a standard that is objective.

For my purposes, there are two main problems with the conventional wisdom regarding absolute and relative standards. The first is a matter of semantics. The second is more substantial.

Even though one standard is called absolute and the other relative, both in fact are relative. The relative standard defines physical need relative to the economic resources that people typically have at their disposal as compared to what others have. The absolute standard defines physical need relative to the cost of the required goods and services. I suggest and employ hereafter two other terms: "minimal-living standard" in place of absolute minimal standard and "income-distribution standard" for relative minimal standard.

The second problem is that, conventionally, physical need is defined from two different perspectives and students of minimal physical need or poverty do not agree as to which type of general standard to use. Those students who use the minimal-living standard in effect ignore income distribution. Those who employ the income-distribution standard disregard the critical minimum.

This controversy, which has persisted for twenty-five years, calls to mind Marshall's famous insight as to whether it is supply or demand that determines market price.

> We might as reasonably dispute whether it is the upper or the under blade of a pair of scissors that cuts a piece of paper, as whether value is governed by utility or cost of production. It is true that when one blade is held still, the cutting is effected by moving the other, we may say with careless brevity that the cutting is done by the second; but the statement is not strictly accurate, and is to be excused only so long as it claims to be merely a popular and not a strictly scientific account of what happens. (Marshall, 348)

The solution is the same now as then: properly understood physical need is *both* a minimal-living concept *and* an income-distribution concept.

Physical need is two-dimensional because, as argued previously, humans are two-dimensional: individual being and social being. Physical need, therefore, incorporates both minimal living *and* income distribution. Thus, persons are needy if (1) they cannot afford the minimum market basket of goods and services or (2) they are separated from the company of others by a wide gap in income. The needy person is one who is physically depleted or socioeconomically segregated. The more severe the segregation or depletion, the greater the unmet personal need.

This controversy has persisted because students who use the absolute standard are not aware that they implicitly define human beings one-dimensionally as individuals alone. Similarly, those who use the relative standard are unaware that they implicitly construe human beings as only social beings. To my knowledge, Halladay (46–47) alone ties the absolute standard to individuality and only Zimbalist (421) connects the relative standard to sociality. Even so, among sociologists who address the problem of poverty, there is an awareness of the linkage between the relative standard and human sociality, no doubt because sociology disciplines its students to see humans as social beings. Mainstream economics, in contrast, disciplines its students to see humans as individual beings.

Defining physical need one dimensionally misleads because it suggests that unmet physical need deals just one blow. Defining it two-dimensionally is a reminder that poverty delivers two blows: too little food for one's table and too much distancing from one's neighbor. Figure 3.2 summarizes the foregoing remarks about standards of human physical need.

Criteria of Unmet Need

In 1969, the U.S. President's Commission on Income Maintenance Programs affirmed the dual nature of poverty: "As society becomes more affluent it defines poverty as not only the lack of the components of a subsistence level of living, but also the lack of opportunity for persons with limited resources to achieve the quality of life enjoyed by persons with an average amount of resources. The definition of poverty progresses from

Absolute Standard = Minimal-Living Standard

Absolute standard is based on cost of goods and services required to meet need minimally. Reflects human individuality. Specifies unmet physical need in relation to cost of required goods and services. Required goods and services may be defined by experts, as with official U.S. poverty standard, or by public opinion. Official U.S. standard is absolute standard which has been defined by experts such as Mollie Orshansky.

Criticized as arbitrary. However, "arbitrary"often is used when "value-laden" is more appropriate. To elaborate, since human physical need is normative concept which reflects values of person(s) using it, all standards of need are value-laden. "Arbitrary" is appropriate only when, in applying specific standard to given data base, some persons/families are classified as needy while others in same circumstances are not.

Relative Standard = Income-Distribution Standard

Relative standard is based on economic resources a person/family has in relation to resources of others, for example, income < 50 percent of median income for entire population is relative (minimum) standard. Reflects human sociality.

Criticized on grounds that, since there always are some persons/families classified as needy, government's task of assisting needy is never ending. The principle of subsidiarity, however, resolves this problem. To extent that persons/families are capable of meeting their own need without government help, there is no reason for the government to intervene.

"Subjective" Standard, "Objective" Standard

"Subjective" is identified by some as a third type of standard but, properly understood, is public-opinion approach to specify either relative or absolute standard.

"Objective" is characteristic of standard which is thought to be value-free. However, "objective" cannot inhere in standard of human physical need because need is normative concept and reflects values of person(s) using it. Specific standard mistakenly may be called "objective" because it has been specified by experts who are regarded as free of values.

Figure 3.2. Standards of human physical need

one based on absolute standards to one based on relative standards" (8). Zimbalist in 1977 asserted that "the general public as well as authorities in the field have favored the inclusion of a social dimension as well as a 'subsistence floor' in defining basic needs" (421). Three years later, Korpi concluded from the debate between the proponents of the absolute standard and the advocates of the relative standard that "there are not two definitions of poverty, between which we can choose according to taste, but instead two different aspects of poverty" (291). Howard (6) in 1982 stated that a study on poverty measurement of the Australian Social Welfare Policy Secretariat made the claim that popular conceptions of poverty usually include both relative and absolute components but the study did not set forth what such a hybrid would look like. No one, it seems, has proposed a definition incorporating both standards in a single measure that can be expressed in measurable form and applied to preexisting data. That is the task to be undertaken in the following sections.

Before either a minimal-living standard or income-distribution standard can be used empirically, it is necessary to express physical need in measurable form. A criterion of unmet need expresses physical need in measurable form by assigning a critical value to the amount of unmet need that is incompatible with physical well-being. When "criterion" is used in this fashion, the standard may be seen as a set of critical values ("thresholds" is the word used in the official U.S. poverty standard) that express physical need in measurable form. Whenever economic resources fall short of the critical value, unmet need is said to exist and the person is classified as needy.

Given the widespread acceptance of the official U.S. poverty standard, it is reasonable to begin the construction of such a criterion of unmet need with the official poverty index, using for example $12,092 as the critical value of minimal living for a family of four in 1988. The official standard, however, incorporates a two-way classification scheme—poor/nonpoor—that operates according to a hard-and-fast rule: a family of four is poor if annual income is $12,092 but not poor if annual income is $12,093. To help reduce this built-in stringency, a three-way classification scheme is employed as follows.

Suggested Need Classification	Established Poverty Classification[9]
needy	poor
marginally needy	
not needy	not poor

The suggested scheme demands a much larger difference in annual income for a family or a person to pass back and forth between the status of needy and not needy.

The next step in the construction of a satisfactory criterion of need is to fit the two-dimensional character of physical need—minimal living and income distribution—into the three-part classification scheme. In this regard, three criteria are suggested, all three of which are identical in terms of minimal living but different in terms of income distribution. For that reason, the three are identified on figure 3.3 as Criterion 1.1, Criterion 1.2, and Criterion 1.3.

The minimal-living portion of each of these criteria employs the poverty thresholds from the official standard that are higher for larger families and households. The income-distribution portion defines needy in terms of the lowest and the second lowest deciles in the income distribution.[10]

In constructing these three criteria, minimal living and income distribution are combined in such a way that, as regards Criterion 1.1, a person or a family to be classified as needy must have income below the poverty threshold *and* in the lowest decile of the income distribution. To be classified as needy under Criterion 1.2, income must be below the poverty threshold *and* in the lowest or next lowest decile. Criteria 1.3 sets forth a different set of conditions: a needy person or family is one with income below the poverty cutoff *or* in the lowest decile.

It is easier to be counted as needy under Criterion 1.3 than under the other two. To illustrate, large families with multiple wage earners may meet the minimal-living requirement but not the income-distribution requirement. Under Criterion 1.1 and Criterion 1.2, those families would not be classified as needy because they do not meet *both* requirements. Under Criterion

Need Classification	Physical Need Expressed Two-Dimensionally	
	Minimal Living	Income Distribution
	Criterion 1.1	
Needy	below poverty and	in lowest decile
Marginally needy	I. below poverty and	above lowest decile
	II. above poverty and	in lowest decile
Not needy	above poverty and	above lowest decile
	Criterion 1.2	
Needy	below poverty and	in first or second decile
Marginally needy	I. below poverty and	above second decile
	II. above poverty and	in first or second decile
Not needy	above poverty and	above second decile
	Criterion 1.3	
Needy	below poverty or	in lowest decile
Marginally needy	above poverty and	in second decile
Not needy	above poverty and	above second decile

Figure 3.3. Three criteria of unmet need that express physical need in terms of income distribution and minimal living

1.3, however, such families would be counted as needy because to qualify *only one* requirement must be met.

The income-distribution data are national in scope, which means in effect that persons and families are ranked against all other persons and families in the U.S. In a nation where information is so widely and quickly shared and upward socio-economic mobility is so valued and still achievable, a good case can be made that a criterion of need that is fully national in scope is less arbitrary than any other.[11]

There is nothing compelling about *three* criteria as opposed to a larger or smaller number. Three criteria, for sure, provide more data than one and should help us decide how the official standard might be improved. Even so, that decision turns no less on human judgment than on empirical evidence because need or poverty is a concept that is unavoidably normative. Thus, there is a point of diminishing returns in proposing additional criteria and amassing more data in order to address the question, What is the proper definition of need?—a question that is quite distinct from others such as How many persons are needy? and What are the origins of unmet need? which have wholly different data requirements. In this task, it is not clear, a priori, where diminishing returns begin, but it is clear that improvements in the standard of unmet physical need cannot be made without demonstrating how that criterion actually operates. This means estimating the numbers of persons and families classified as needy under the proposed criterion and comparing those estimates with the official poverty figures.

Empirical Evidence

Table 3.1 provides estimates of the number of needy persons and families in the U.S. for 1985 and for 1988 based on Criterion 1.1, Criterion 1.2, and Criterion 1.3. All of the data reported in this section derive from the microdata files of the March 1986 and March 1989 Current Population Surveys.[12] In-kind transfers or noncash benefits and taxes are not included in the data because my purpose here is to compare the suggested criteria of need with the official poverty figures. While including that kind of information would improve the *estimates* of the number of poor or needy persons and families, it would not improve the *comparison* because virtually the same adjustments would be made to the various items being compared.[13]

The poverty data and the income-distribution data used here were extracted directly from the CPS files without modification. Separate estimates are shown in table 3.1 for (1) persons in families where income distribution is specified in terms of family income and for (2) persons in households where income distribution is specified in terms of household income.[14] Strictly speaking, estimates of persons in families are not to be compared directly with estimates of persons in households. Table 3.1 presents separate estimates for families where income distribution is specified in terms of (1) family income and (2) household income.

All three criteria were applied to the weighted estimates from both Current Population Surveys in a way that left the income-distribution data unadjusted for size of family and size of household. Thus, all three criteria are one part family/household

Table 3.1
Persons in Families and in Households, and Families, by
Need Classification and Criterion of Unmet Need

(thousands)

	Criterion 1.1		Criterion 1.2		Criterion 1.3	
	1985	1988	1985	1988	1985	1988
Income Distribution Specified in Terms of Family Income						
Persons in Families (Total)	203,963	208,056	203,963	208,056	203,963	208,056
Needy	17,896	17,939	24,375	23,250	27,035	25,794
Marginally needy	9,139	7,855	14,958	16,382	12,298	13,838
Not needy	176,928	182,262	164,630	168,424	164,630	168,424
Income Distribution Specified in Terms of Household Income						
Persons in Households (Total)	236,130	243,362	236,130	243,362	236,130	243,362
Needy	16,007	16,324	25,376	25,598	33,635	32,769
Marginally needy	17,628	16,446	16,901	16,816	8,642	9,645
Not needy	202,495	210,592	193,853	200,948	193,853	200,948
Income Distribution Specified in Terms of Family Income						
Families (Total)	63,558	65,837	63,558	65,837	63,558	65,837
Needy	5,717	5,724	7,044	6,773	7,861	7,733
Marginally needy	2,144	2,009	5,846	6,494	5,029	5,534
Not needy	55,697	58,104	50,668	52,570	50,668	52,570
Income Distribution Specified in Terms of Household Income						
Families (Total)	63,558	65,837	63,558	65,837	63,558	65,837
Needy	3,769	3,831	6,195	6,127	7,223	6,874
Marginally needy	3,454	3,044	3,019	3,060	1,991	2,313
Not needy	56,335	58,962	54,344	56,650	54,344	56,650

Sources: March 1986 and March 1989 Current Population Surveys (microdata files).

size adjusted and one part unadjusted. The minimal-living portion is adjusted because that adjustment is directly built into the official poverty standard. There is no other way to properly construct an absolute standard. At the same time, the income-distribution data are unadjusted because this writer senses that human beings whether they live in large families/households or small, compare their own economic resources with the resources of others across a wide spectrum of families and households of different sizes and not narrowly against families and households of the same size.

For 1985 and 1988, Criterion 1.3 produced the highest estimates of needy persons (in households as well as in families) and of needy families. Criterion 1.1 produced the lowest estimates. Criterion 1.3 yielded the lowest number of marginally needy persons (in households) and marginally needy families (using household income in specifying income distribution). Criterion 1.1 gave the lowest estimate of the number of marginally needy persons (in families) and of marginally needy families (based on family income). At the same time, Criterion 1.1 gave the highest number of marginally needy persons (in households) and families (using household income to specify income distribution).

Table 3.2 supplies estimates of the number of needy and marginally needy persons in families and in households by poverty level (100 percent and 125 percent[15]) using Criterion 1.1, Criterion 1.2, and Criterion 1.3. Under the three criteria of unmet need all of the persons classified as poor at the 100 percent poverty level, by definition, are counted as needy or marginally needy.

In ten of the twelve comparison sets for both 1985[16] and for 1988, all of the persons classified as needy also were classified as poor by the official poverty standard whether family income or household income is used and whether the 100 percent standard or 125 percent standard is applied. However, large numbers of the marginally needy are not included in the official poverty population. The number excluded in 1985 is estimated under Criterion 1.2 as high as 13.6 million persons in families (15.6 million in 1988) and 9.4 million persons in households (10.7 million in 1988). Large numbers of the marginally needy are excluded from the poor population even when poverty is defined at the 125 percent level. At the same time, millions of persons (as high as 10.3 million in 1985 and 9.7 million in 1988) who are officially classified as poor under the 125 percent standard are counted as not needy under Criterion 1.1, Criterion 1.2, and Criterion 1.3.

Table 3.3 presents comparable data for families where in-

Table 3.2
Persons in Families and in Households, by Poverty Status, Need Classification, and Criterion of Unmet Need
(thousands)

	100 Percent Poverty				125 Percent Poverty			
	Poor		Not Poor		Poor		Not Poor	
	1985	1988	1985	1988	1985	1988	1985	1988
Persons in Families	*Income Distribution Specified in Terms of Family Income*							
Criterion 1.1								
Needy	17,896	17,939	0	0	17,896	17,939	0	0
Marginally needy	7,833	6,109	1,306	1,746	9,139	7,615	0	240
Not needy	0	0	176,928	182,262	7,359	6,718	169,569	175,544
Criterion 1.2								
Needy	24,375	23,250	0	0	24,375	23,250	0	0
Marginally needy	1,354	798	13,604	15,584	6,687	6,616	8,271	9,766
Not needy	0	0	164,630	168,424	3,332	2,406	161,298	166,018
Criterion 1.3								
Needy	25,729	24,048	1,306	1,746	27,035	25,553	0	240
Marginally needy	0	0	12,298	13,838	4,027	4,313	8,271	9,526
Not needy	0	0	164,630	168,424	3,332	2,406	161,298	166,018
Persons in Households	*Income Distribution Specified in Terms of Household Income*							
Criterion 1.1								
Needy	16,007	16,324	0	0	16,007	16,324	0	0
Marginally needy	16,840	15,421	788	1,025	17,625	16,445	3	0
Not needy	0	0	202,495	210,593	10,280	9,740	192,215	200,854
Criterion 1.2								
Needy	25,376	25,598	0	0	25,376	25,598	0	0
Marginally needy	7,471	6,147	9,430	10,669	12,099	10,963	4,802	5,853
Not needy	0	0	193,853	200,949	6,437	5,948	187,416	195,001
Criterion 1.3								
Needy	32,847	31,745	788	1,025	33,632	32,769	3	0
Marginally needy	0	0	8,642	9,645	3,843	3,792	4,799	5,853
Not needy	0	0	193,853	200,948	6,437	5,948	187,416	195,001

Sources: March 1986 and March 1989 Current Population Surveys (microdata files).

Table 3.3
Families, by Poverty Status, Need Classification, and Criterion of Unmet Need
(thousands)

	100 Percent Poverty				125 Percent Poverty			
	Poor		Not Poor		Poor		Not Poor	
	1985	1988	1985	1988	1985	1988	1985	1988
Families	*Income Distribution Specified in Terms of Family Income*							
Criterion 1.1								
Needy	5,717	5,724	0	0	5,717	5,724	0	0
Marginally needy	1,506	1,150	638	859	2,144	1,891	0	119
Not needy	0	0	55,697	58,104	1,892	1,669	53,805	56,434
Criterion 1.2								
Needy	7,044	6,773	0	0	7,044	6,773	0	0
Marginally needy	179	101	5,667	6,393	2,101	2,094	3,745	4,400
Not needy	0	0	50,668	52,570	608	417	50,060	52,153
Criterion 1.3								
Needy	7,223	6,874	638	859	7,861	7,615	0	118
Marginally needy	0	0	5,029	5,534	1,284	1,253	3,745	4,281
Not needy	0	0	50,668	52,570	608	417	50,060	52,153
Families	*Income Distribution Specified in Terms of Household Income*							
Criterion 1.1								
Needy	3,769	3,831	0	0	3,769	3,831	0	0
Marginally needy	3,454	3,043	0	0	3,454	3,043	0	0
Not needy	0	0	56,335	58,963	2,530	2,410	53,805	56,553
Criterion 1.2								
Needy	6,195	6,127	0	0	6,195	6,127	0	0
Marginally needy	1,028	747	1,991	2,313	2,244	1,987	775	1,074
Not needy	0	0	54,344	56,650	1,314	1,170	53,030	55,479
Criterion 1.3								
Needy	7,223	6,874	0	0	7,223	6,874	0	0
Marginally needy	0	0	1,991	2,313	1,216	1,240	775	1,074
Not needy	0	0	54,344	56,650	1,314	1,170	53,030	55,479

Sources: March 1986 and March 1989 Current Population Surveys (microdata files).

come distribution is specified in terms of (1) family income and (2) household income. In eleven of the twelve comparison sets for both 1985 and 1988, the families classified as needy under the three suggested criteria also were classified as poor by the official standard, whether family income is used or household income and whether the 100 percent standard or the 125 percent standard is applied. Yet, large numbers of marginally needy families under Criterion 1.2 and Criterion 1.3 are classified as not poor at the 100 percent level especially when income distribution is specified in terms of family income. Even when poverty is defined at the 125 percent level, a substantial number of marginally needy families are classified as not poor. Further, based on 1985 household income, as many as 2.5 million poor families (2.4 million in 1988) are classified as not needy.

Table 3.4 shows that in 1985 almost one million of the 32.8 million persons (almost one million of the 31.7 million in 1988) living in households officially classified as poor at the 100 percent level are in the upper half of the household income distribution. At the 125 percent poverty level in 1985, 1.3 million persons (1.3 million in 1988) classified as poor are in the upper half of the household income distribution. In contrast, for both 1985 and 1988, all of the poor persons living in families are in the lower half of the family income distribution, whether poverty is defined at the 100 percent level or the 125 percent level.

The data on persons that are displayed in table 3.4 reflect the fact that the official poverty standard operates differently for persons living in families as opposed to persons in nonfamily households. In the case of persons in families the income of all family members is regarded as pooled. Thus, if total annual income of all family members puts the family above the poverty threshold, every person in that family is regarded as nonpoor. In contrast, the total annual income of all persons living in a nonfamily household routinely is regarded as not pooled and for individuals in this situation to be classified as nonpoor it is necessary that their personal income be greater than the poverty threshold for one person (Series P–60, No. 163, p. 158). These data strongly suggest that there would be a substantial decrease in the official estimate of the number of persons in poverty if the incomes of persons living in nonfamily households were

Table 3.4

Poor Persons in Households and in Families, and Poor Families,
by Income Distribution and by Poverty Level

(thousands)

Income Distribution	100 Percent Poverty Level				125 Percent Poverty Level			
	Poor Persons in:				Poor Persons in:			
	Households[1]		Families[2]		Households[1]		Families[2]	
	1985	1988	1985	1988	1985	1988	1985	1988
Total	32,847	31,745	25,729	24,048	43,912	42,509	34,394	32,272
lowest decile	16,007	16,324	17,896	17,939	16,792	17,348	19,202	19,445
second	9,369	9,274	6,479	5,311	13,212	13,066	10,505	9,624
third	4,608	3,739	1,199	584	7,922	7,140	3,969	2,573
fourth	1,395	938	155	214	3,655	2,701	538	525
fifth	545	538			1,001	935	180	105
sixth	306	290			540	481		
seventh	242	246			311	321		
eighth	137	137			182	180		
ninth	110	123			151	168		
highest decile	128	136			146	169		

923 poor persons in hshlds w/ 1985 income > national median
932 poor persons in hshlds w/ 1988 income > national median

1,330 poor persons in hshlds w/ 1985 income > national median
1,319 poor persons in hshlds w/ 1988 income > national median

Income Distribution	100 Percent Poverty Level				125 Percent Poverty Level			
	Poor Families with Income Distribution Specified in Terms of:							
	Household Income		Family Income		Household Income		Family Income	
	1985	1988	1985	1988	1985	1988	1985	1988
Total	7,223	6,874	7,223	6,874	9,753	9,284	9,753	9,284
lowest decile	3,769	3,831	5,717	5,724	3,769	3,831	6,355	6,465
second	2,426	2,296	1,327	1,049	3,643	3,536	2,611	2,302
third	797	586	165	80	1,619	1,377	703	446
fourth	147	87	14	21	545	380	67	59
fifth	37	48			100	89	17	12
sixth	28	10			45	29		
seventh	5	5			11	12		
eighth	10	5			13	16		
ninth	1	5			5	13		
highest decile	3	1			3	1		

26 poor families w/ 1988 hshld income > 1988 national median & 47 poor families w/ 1985 hshld income > 1988 national median

71 poor families w/ 1988 hshld income > 1988 national median & 77 poor families w/ 1985 hshld income > 1985 national median

Sources: March 1986 and March 1989 Current Population Surveys (microdata files).
[1]Household income distribution
[2]Family income distribution

regarded as pooled rather than nonpooled and if persons living as nonrelatives in a family household were regarded as family members.

Table 3.4 also shows that for both 1985 and 1988 when income distribution is specified in terms of household income only a very small number of poor families are in the upper half of the distribution, whether poverty is defined at the 100 percent level or the 125 percent level. When family income is used to specify income distribution, there are no poor families in the upper half of the distribution.

In interpreting the data on poor families by family income as opposed to household income, one should be aware that some family households consist of more than one family and for a small number of those families the combined income of the families that form one household is sufficient to place them in the upper half of the income distribution.

Tables 3.2 and 3.3 provide information as to the sensitivity of the 100 percent standard as compared to Criterion 1.1, the standard that is closest in definition to the official poverty standard. Between 1985 and 1988, there was a decline of 1.7 million in the number of persons in families and 1.1 million in the number of persons in households who were officially classified as poor (see table 3.2). The same data indicated that over the same period the same number of persons, whether in families or in households, were classified as needy. Virtually all of the net decrease in the numbers of poor persons as measured by the 100 percent poverty standard occurred among those who according to Criterion 1.1 were classified as marginally needy. The same general findings apply to poor families whether Criterion 1.1 is applied to the household income distribution or the family income distribution. All of the net improvement took place among families classified as marginally needy.

Conclusions and Recommendations

A proper criterion of poverty or unmet physical need should be direct, comprehensive, consistent, convenient, and, most especially, accepted. By direct I mean that the criterion measures unmet physical need directly rather than estimating it indirectly.

A criterion or threshold is comprehensive if it encompasses every relevant aspect of unmet need; it is selective if it leaves out some aspect of need or resources.

By consistent I mean that the criterion assigns everyone who is found in the same circumstances with regard to unmet physical need into the same need classification. A criterion of physical need ideally is convenient, that is, it is relatively simple to apply to the data and to generate estimates of poverty or unmet need. The 125 percent standard is a very good example of a criterion that is convenient.

A standard of physical need is similar to legal tender: it must pass the test of public acceptance. The importance of public acceptance derives from the fact that need is a normative concept and acceptance of a given standard indicates that there is wide agreement to the effect that the standard conforms to value systems of large numbers of persons.

The official 100 percent standard outperforms all others in this regard because it has been used widely and effectively for twenty-five years. For that reason, it is futile to attempt to replace it unless one can prove (1) that it is seriously flawed and (2) that a replacement standard does not create insurmountable problems, such as a much greater cost to develop the required information for its application and use.

These five characteristics are instructive as to the performance of the three proposed criteria of need versus the 100 percent standard and the 125 percent standard.

By including both the minimal-living and the income-distribution dimensions of physical need, Criterion 1.1, Criterion 1.2, and Criterion 1.3 are more comprehensive than both the 100 percent standard and the 125 percent standard. As to directness, the three suggested criteria of unmet need match the performance of the official standard because all four use the same basic income information to specify the critical values or thresholds. By comparison with the 125 percent standard, however, Criterion 1.1, Criterion 1.2, and Criterion 1.3 are superior because no attempt is made to demonstrate that inflating the poverty thresholds by 25 percent actually relates to unmet physical need and draws in only those persons with unmet need. Indeed, the empirical evidence indicates that the 125 percent standard counts as poor large numbers of persons and families who are not needy.

When income distribution is specified in terms of household income, all three criteria of unmet need are more consistent than the two official poverty levels with regard to persons in need because the two poverty standards count among the poor in both 1985 and 1989, 0.9 million to 1.3 million persons in households where income exceeds the national median. Finally, since the Census Bureau already generates the data required under Criterion 1.1, Criterion 1.2, and Criterion 1.3, these three criteria of unmet need are as convenient to use as the two official poverty standards. See figure 3.4 for a summary comparison of the two official poverty standards and the three criteria of unmet physical need.

In 1965 Orshansky described the 100 percent poverty standard as "still relatively crude" and the food-income relationship as an "interim guide" to poverty thresholds (3, 12). Some twenty-three years later, Sawhill confirmed that even though the poverty concept turns importantly on the absolute vs. relative issue it is difficult to say which of the two is the superior (1077). Even today the Census Bureau, which collects the data and publishes the official poverty estimates, acknowledges the need for an alternate level because the official poverty standard does not meet certain analytical requirements (Series P–60, No. 163, p. 156).

Criterion 1.1, which produces estimates of persons and families in need that fall between the 100 percent figures and the 125 percent figures, outperforms the 125 percent standard in terms of being more direct, more comprehensive, and more consistent. Since both derive from the same data base, Criterion 1.1 is as convenient to use as the 125 percent standard. In addition, Criterion 1.1 is more sensitive than the 100 percent standard as to net changes occurring over time among these poor persons and poor families who are neediest of all.

The evidence from the Current Population Survey argues for a two-dimensional criterion of need, similar to Criterion 1.1, that classifies as poor or needy all persons and families (1) below the official poverty threshold and (2) in the lowest decile of the income distribution. A criterion such as that is a better comple-

Performance Characteristics	Official Poverty Standard		Criterion of Unmet Physical Need		
	100 percent	125 percent	1.1	1.2	1.3
Comprehensive — encompasses all aspects of unmet physical need	**both inferior:** both exclude income-distribution aspect of unmet physical need		**all three superior:** all three include income-distribution aspect of unmet physical need		
Direct — measures unmet physical need directly rather than estimating it indirectly	**equivalent:** uses same income information to define thresholds as three criteria of unmet physical need	**inferior:** no attempt to show how 125 percent standard relates to unmet physical need; counts as poor many persons and families who are not needy	**equivalent to 100 percent standard superior to 125 percent standard:** uses same income information as 100 percent standard to define thresholds and shows how all three criteria relate to unmet physical need		
Consistent — assigns everyone with same unmet physical need to same need classification	**both inferior:** both include many persons and some families with household income above national median		**all three superior:** none defined as needy with income above the second decile; none defined as marginally needy with income above the second decline unless at same time person or family is below minimal-living standard		
Convenient — simple to apply to data and generate estimates of unmet physical need	**equivalent:** both poverty standards and all three criteria of unmet physical need use data from the same Census Bureau source				
Accepted — conforms to values of the majority	**both superior:** particularly 100 percent standard which the majority has been used widely and effectively for more than 25 years		**all three inferior:** even so, 100 percent standard has been criticized for excluding income-distribution aspect of unmet physical need		

Figure 3.4. Comparison of two official standards of poverty and three criteria of unmet physical need

ment to the 100 percent standard than is the 125 percent standard because it probes more deeply into the question, What does it mean to be poor?

Notes

1. See Burns (275–89) for more on the three major attitudes toward the unemployed: potential contributors to economic output, threats to the income of others, and human beings in need.

2. Becker's 1961 monograph on benefit adequacy in unemployment insurance is very instructive on the meaning of physical need and the role of the state in provisioning unmet physical need.

3. In terms of income distribution, among families with some *earned* income, inequality of earned income declined slightly between 1949 and 1984 (Levy, 164–65). Even though the official poverty rate in 1984, based on information from the Current Population Survey, was 14.4 percent, only 5.9 percent of all persons were classified as poor in all twelve months of that year, according to information from the Survey of Income and Program Participation (Ruggles and Williams, 7). The so-called always-poor poverty rate for 1984 is all the more significant for our purposes given the relatively high annual rate of unemployment—7.5 percent—for that year (see Statistical Abstract, 377). See note 12 for further comments on the CPS and the SIPP.

4. The principle of subsidiarity states that a larger and more powerful unit of society, such as the state, should not undertake to perform functions that can be handled as well by smaller and less powerful units, such as individuals and their families, but rather should offer help where necessary to enable smaller units to function at full capacity (Becker, 4).

5. Treatment for an addiction, this writer agrees, is a need. Whether it is a social question depends on the treatment success achieved through private means and the personal and social destructiveness of the untreated addict.

6. Methadone treatment, it seems, operates in this manner.

7. Reducing this risk is a worthy objective and a program that helps the needy and *as a consequence* curtails criminal behavior clearly is better than an aid program that does not have this secondary effect.

8. Sociologist Mayer is severely critical of defining and measuring physical need in terms of income. She recommends, instead, a "hardship scale" based on food, housing, and medical-care needs (Mayer, 40–68).

9. The official use of the term "near-poor" has emerged recently and

refers to persons whose income is between the official poverty threshold and 125 percent of poverty (see Series P–70, No. 15-RD–1, p. 40).

10. The income-distribution data are constructed in a way that disregards size of family and size of household. Thus, a person with a small annual income who lives alone is counted in one of the lower deciles of the income distribution. The same person with the same personal income but living in a multiple-worker family very likely would be placed in a higher decile.

11. A criterion of need constructed on the basis of a regional income distribution, it can be argued, reflects more accurately the comparisons that people make when they match what they have against what others have than does a criterion that uses a national income distribution. Demonstrating how such a criterion actually operates is not within the scope of the work undertaken herein.

12. During the 1980s a new survey known as the Survey of Income and Program Participation (SIPP) was launched by the Census Bureau and has begun to supply income data that are more detailed than the CPS data as to sources, are collected every four months, and are reported every month. The SIPP data may be used to construct additional measures of unmet physical need. (See Williams for a brief description of the differences in measuring poverty by means of the CPS data and the SIPP data. See Series P–70, No. 13, for a SIPP report based on the financial support networks that supplement the income of persons living in different households.)

13. See Series P–60, No. 155, for a report on noncash benefits from the CPS. See Series P–70, No. 14, for a report on the attachment of persons to the welfare system based on SIPP data. See Series P–60, No. 164-RD–1, for an experimental report on the effect of benefits and taxes on income and poverty based on data from several sources including the CPS but not SIPP.

14. Family income is the combined annual income of all persons who are related to one another by birth, marriage, or adoption who at the time of enumeration are living together. Household income is the annual income of all persons living together at the time of enumeration whether those persons form a family or not. Persons living alone or with others to whom they are not related are included in the count of persons in households but not in the count of persons in families. All persons who are not members of households are regarded as living in group quarters (Series P–60, No. 163, pp. 154–58).

15. An alternate poverty level developed by the Census Bureau some years after the official poverty standard in order to meet the "needs of the analysts of the data" (Series P–60, No. 163, p. 156).

16. Included among the ten in 1985 are the three thousand persons in households who are nonpoor according to the 125 percent standard but are classified as needy under Criterion 1.3.

References

Becker, Joseph M., S.J. *The Adequacy of the Benefit Amount in Unemployment Insurance.* Kalamazoo: The W. E. Upjohn Institute for Employment Research, 1961.

———. *Shared Government in Employment Security: A Study of Advisory Councils.* New York: Columbia University Press, 1959.

———, William Haber, and Sar A. Levitan. "Policy Recommendations." In *In Aid of the Unemployed,* edited by Joseph M. Becker. Baltimore: The Johns Hopkins Press, 1965.

Braybrooke, David. *Meeting Needs.* Princeton: Princeton University Press, 1987.

Burns, Eveline M. "The Determinants of Policy." In *In Aid of the Unemployed,* edited by Joseph M. Becker. Baltimore: The Johns Hopkins Press, 1965.

Congressional Budget Office. "Measuring Poverty." Appendix A in *Reducing Poverty Among Children.* Washington, 1985.

Etzioni, Amitai. *The Moral Dimension: Toward a New Economics.* New York: The Free Press, 1988.

"Final Report on Family Budgets: Cost Increases Slowed, Autumn 1981." *Monthly Labor Review* 105, no. 7 (1982): 44–46.

Griffin, James. *Well-Being: Its Meaning, Measurement, and Importance.* Oxford: Clarendon Press, 1986.

Halladay, Allan. "The Significance of Poverty Definition to Australians." *Australian Journal of Social Issues* 10, no. 1 (1975): 46–50.

Howard, Michael. "Poverty Lines in the 1980s: Rejection or Redevelopment?" *Social Security Journal* (December 1982): 1–12.

Korpi, Walter. "Approaches to the Study of Poverty in the United States: Critical Notes from a European Perspective." In *Poverty and Public Policy: An Evaluation of Social Science Research,* edited by Vincent T. Covello. Cambridge: Schenkman Publishing Co., 1980.

Le Troquer, René, P.S.S. *What Is Man?* Translated by Eric Earnshaw Smith. New York: Hawthorn Books, 1961.

Levy, Frank. *Dollars and Dreams: The Changing American Income Distribution.* New York: The Russell Sage Foundation, 1987.

Lutz, Mark A., and Kenneth Lux. *Humanistic Economics: The New Challenge.* New York: The Bootstrap Press, 1988.

80 / Edward J. O'Boyle

Mack, Joanna, and Stewart Lansley. *Poor Britain*. London: George Allen and Unwin, 1985.

Marshall, Alfred. *Principles of Economics*. 8th ed. New York: The MacMillan Company, 1948.

Mayer, Susan E. *Who Is Poor: An Assessment of Income and Other Determinants of Material Well-Being*. Ann Arbor: University Microfilms International, 1986.

Orshansky, Mollie. "Counting the Poor: Another Look at the Poverty Profile." *Social Security Bulletin* 28, no. 1 (1965): 3–29.

Ruggles, Patricia. *Drawing the Line: Alternative Poverty Measures and Their Implications for Public Policy*. Washington: The Urban Institute Press, 1990.

Ruggles, Patricia, and Roberton Williams. "Transitions In and Out of Poverty: New Data from the Survey of Income and Program Participation." U.S. Bureau of the Census, SIPP working paper, December 1987.

Sawhill, Isabel V. "Poverty in the U.S.: Why Is It So Persistent?" *Journal of Economic Literature* 26, no. 3 (1988): 1073–1119.

Smith, Adam. *An Inquiry into the Nature and Causes of the Wealth of Nations*. New York: Random House, The Modern Library, 1937.

Townsend, Peter. "Poverty as Relative Deprivation: Resources and Style of Living." In *Poverty, Inequality, and Class Structure*, edited by Dorothy Wedderburn. London: Cambridge University Press, 1974.

———. *Poverty in the United Kingdom: A Survey of Household Resources and Standards of Living*. Berkeley: University of California Press, 1979.

U.S. Bureau of the Census. Current Population Reports, Series P–60, No. 155, *Noncash Benefits: 1985*. Washington, 1987.

———. Current Population Reports, Series P–60, No. 163, *Poverty in the United States: 1987*. Washington, 1989.

———. Current Population Reports, Series P–60, No. 164-RD–1, *Measuring the Effect of Benefits and Taxes on Income and Poverty: 1986*. Washington, 1988.

———. Current Population Reports, Series P–60, No. 166, *Money Income and Poverty Status in the United States: 1988 (Advance Data from the March 1989 Current Population Survey)*. Washington, 1989.

———. Current Population Reports, Series P–70, No. 13, *Who's Helping Out? Support Networks Among American Families*. Washington, 1988.

———. Current Population Reports, Series P–70, No. 14, *Characteristics of Persons Receiving Benefits from Major Assistance Programs*. Washington, 1989.

———. Current Population Reports, Series P–70, No. 15-RD–1, *Transitions in Income and Poverty Status: 1984–85*. Washington, 1989.

———. Current Population Survey. March 1986 and March 1989 (microdata files).

———. *Statistical Abstract of the United States: 1989*. Washington, 1989.

Williams, Roberton. "Measuring Poverty with SIPP and the CPS." U.S. Bureau of the Census, SIPP working paper, December 1987.

Zimbalist, Sidney E. "Recent British and American Poverty Trends: Conceptual and Policy Contrasts." *Social Service Review* 51, no. 3 (1977): 419–33.

4

Government Participation to Address Human Material Need

Anthony E. Scaperlanda

The title of this essay implies at least three questions. First, should government participate in society's attempts to address the material needs of its members? If the answer to this question is at all positive, which I assume it is, then two other questions follow: What participation should this be? And how much of it? In this essay I will identify some general guidelines within which to situate the last two of these questions. To constrain the essay's scope, I have limited my examples to contemporary experience in the United States.

It is far from radical to hold that government should participate in meeting human material need; both proclaimed principle and actual practice suggest that there is little controversy on this matter. On the matter of principle, for example, even such a chary advocate of government participation as Alfred Marshall nonetheless recognized government participation as a fact, and in cases of "underclass poverty" thought government intervention to be necessary (714–15). From a somewhat different ideological perspective, Wallace Peterson has recently decried the "long and lingering neglect of power by economists" and noted that "the exercise of power is strongly tempered by the state of the economy" (388–89). His point, like Marshall's, is that power should be used by the people through government for the protection and well-being of those persons who are either disadvantaged or potentially so. And until contemporary conditions favorable to a more generalized exercise of economic power develop, initiatives encouraging government to intervene on behalf of those with unsatisfied material needs will have to emanate from corporate America if Peterson is correct that "the modern corporation stands almost alone in the power it exercises in the market economy" (381). Harry Trebing suggests several points of departure if the future requires the restoration and revitalization of purposeful government activity on behalf of the general public. On the matter of praxis, virtually no one argues against public schools and universities, police and fire departments, some public housing, and some level of other government activities such as public health and disaster relief that meet human material need. Table 4.1 profiles the major government social assistance programs currently in place and table 4.2 summarizes parallel social insurance programs. The messages conveyed by "assistance" and "insurance" indicate why most of the controversy revolves around what kind and how much government participation is optimal. Because it is more controversial, government participation in providing social assistance is the focus of this essay.

This controversy has often involved the rhetorical use of "government intervention" to describe government participation. In the *American Heritage Dictionary of the English Language*, the definition of "intervene" ranges from "to enter or occur extraneously" through "to come in or between so as to hinder or modify" to "to interfere, usually through force or threat of force." Thus the phrase "government intervention" rhetorically embeds negative connotations and thereby substantially predetermines the conclusion of any discussion of the role of government in society. The negative connotations of intervention can be (and have been) exacerbated by policy makers intent on getting government "off the backs of the people" (one reading—reduce the taxes of our supporters). And, in turn, the rhetoric can lead to mean-spirited policy changes of the sort that David Hamilton identifies vis-à-vis AFDC (Aid to Families with Dependent Children) during the Reagan administration. Thus, to eliminate the rhetorical bias embedded in the word "intervention," my emphasis is on government participation, of which cooperation, facilitation, interven-

Table 4.1
Cash and Noncash Benefits for Persons
with Limited Income, 1987
(millions of dollars)

	Total	Federal	Federal Percent of Total
Social Assistance (Total)	158,735	114,912	72
Cash Assistance	42,542	27,925	64
AFDC[1]	18,440	9,987	54
Supplemental Security Income[2]	13,743	10,832	79
Pensions for needy veterans	3,793	3,793	100
In-Kind Assistance	116,193	86,987	75
Food & Nutrition	21,004	19,837	94
Food stamps	12,479	12,479	100
School lunch program	3,281	3,281	100
Women, Infants and Children	1,664	1,664	100
Housing	13,191	13,191	100
Lower income assistance	8,125	8,125	100
Low-rent public housing	2,161	2,161	100
Medical Care	60,692	34,956	58
Medicaid	50,010	27,960	56
Veterans	5,035	5,035	100
General assistance	3,370	0	0
Energy Assistance	2,104	1,892	90
Education (higher)	10,223	9,722	95
Jobs and Training	3,853	3,782	98
Services[3]	5,126	3,607	70

Source: U.S. *Statistical Abstract, 1990*, Tables 580 and 608.
[1]Aid to Families with Dependent Children
[2]Allocated 24 percent to persons aged, 2 percent to persons blind, and 74 percent to persons disabled
[3]82 percent for social services provided under Title 20 of the Social Security Act

tion, and protection are several possible forms.[1] Within this perspective, it is recognized that in some instances the electorate may select some form of government intervention to redress a particularly difficult societal problem.

Material Need Defined

As Edward O'Boyle says in chapter 3, neoclassical economics conventionally subsumed material need within the concept

Table 4.2

Social Insurance, 1987

(millions of dollars)

	Total	Federal	Federal Percent of Total
Total	415,023	345,082	83.0
Old age, survivors, disability, health	288,498	288,498	100.0
Public and railroad employee retirement	78,683	50,623	64.0
Unemployment insurance and employment services	18,055	2,956	16.0
Workers' compensation	27,053	2,816	10.0

Source: U.S. *Statistical Abstract, 1990*, Table 576.

of "wants." O'Boyle himself takes a conventional stance by focusing on marginal material needs when, for example, he says that "the social economics of human material need is really the social economics of *unmet* human material need." If an economic system should function to meet at least the minimum material needs of the persons living within it, and if unmet material need exists, then the private together with the public participants in economic activity are by definition either inefficient or their aggregate participation is inadequate. In my eclectic analysis of government participation, for purposes of analysis I assume that private activity to meet otherwise unmet needs is efficient. However, it may not be sufficient.

If one takes the percent of the adult population doing volunteer work as a general indication and notes that the percentage decreased from 52 percent in 1981 to 45 percent in 1987, the involvement of the private sector can be taken to be increasingly insufficient.[2] From a different perspective, in dollar terms private philanthropy has lagged in meeting demonstrated need. If private philanthropy had responded in the same proportion that public philanthropy did between 1970 and 1987, private philanthropy would have been 23 percent larger at the end of the period (*Statistical Abstract, 1990*, tables 577 and 620, pp. 352 and 372). Further, while recognizing that more rapid economic growth would substantially alleviate unmet material need, I nonetheless choose to deemphasize macroeconomic government policy that would stimulate growth in order to emphasize government participation that is targeted to directly respond to unmet needs.[3] Cognizant of Isabel Sawhill's observation that "what constitutes a minimum subsistence income is clearly socially defined and will therefore vary across cultures and historical periods" (1076), I recognize that a target level of needs fulfillment must be established as a condition for government participation in the meeting of those needs. As the United States approaches the twenty-first century, most citizens would identify not only food, clothing, and shelter as needs but also access to medical care sufficient to sustain life and to avoid or reverse damage to one's physical well-being. Access to an education that enables a person to be self-sustaining, together with adequate day care and residential facilities for children and elderly adults, both to provide for them and to free others to work on a regular basis, are reasonably included as needs. Adequate transportation also is essential to get to and from work, the doctor, the grocery store, and so on. The list of needs that are essential to a minimal standard of living could be expanded, of course.[4]

In fact, as Samuels says in chapter 1, the "specific content of 'needs' is and must be worked out in the total socioeconomic process." However, society has, arguably, already "worked out" some consensus on needs. For example, in 1991 most people would define shelter as more than a roof overhead. The rhetoric of "shelters for the homeless"—the proverbial roof—implies that shelter has come to be equated with "home," witness the work of organizations like Habitat for Humanity. Whether it be a room, an apartment, or a house, whether rented or owned, in a colloquial sense this might be a place of shelter that a person "could call my own": a place that provides stability not just for psychological reasons, but for practical reasons as well—for receiving mail from potential employers as well as from relatives; for providing a center from which to receive medical care, education, and other social services; and for providing a stable environment for children. Shelter, that is, is a comprehensive and complex concept in the United States in the 1990s. The same is true about clothing and food. "Adequate" clothing is not just a body covering but includes notions of cleanliness and style that encourage or at least allow a certain degree of self-esteem. In addition to allaying brute hunger, food is expected to provide nutrients that contribute to health and well-being.

Basically, society has "worked out" effective definitions of the minimal level of need fulfillment that it expects, even though they are complex and subject to ongoing debate at their margins. In the U.S., the poverty index—originally developed at the Social Security Administration in 1964 using the Department of Agriculture's 1961 economy food plan—is a statement of the money income that is needed to satisfy the minimal needs of families of various sizes. Another way to measure society's expectation is to ask the personnel directors or the managers of a McDonald's, a landscaping firm, and the loading dock at a Marshall Fields store what sort of health (including strength and stamina), dress, education, and work habits, among other criteria, would be expected of an average employee at work and at the company picnic. The responses to such a question would explicitly identify the characteristics that employers would like relatively unskilled workers to possess and implicitly would identify the minimum level of material need fulfillment that is required if the characteristics are to be present.[5]

Why is the satisfaction of material needs so important? Basically the assumption is that until material needs are met, a person has little chance of effectively participating as a productive and politically aware member of society. Marshall, for example, has said:

> And in addition to the Residuum, there are vast numbers of people both in town and country who are brought up with insufficient food, clothing, and house-room; whose education is broken off early in order that they may go to work for wages; who thenceforth are engaged during long hours in exhausting toil with imperfectly nourished bodies, and have therefore no chance of developing their higher mental faculties . . . Even when they are well, their weariness often amounts to pain, while their pleasures are few; and when sickness comes, the suffering caused by poverty increases tenfold . . . And though a contented spirit may go far towards reconciling them to these evils, there are others to which it ought not to reconcile them. Overworked and undertaught, weary and careworn, without quiet and without leisure, they have no chance of making the best of their mental faculties. (2–3)[6]

This statement not only implicitly defines Marshall's sense of the minimal material needs of the 1890s but explicitly declares that a person in poverty has little chance of developing the mental skills that enable him or her to be a more complete participant in society in general and in the workforce in particular. Considering the level of skills that work of the 1990s will require, Marshall's observations are even more crucial today then they were to the 1890s. Until minimal material needs are met, the average person does not have the "foundation" from which to engage in activities that result in a full development of an individual's human potential. Society, properly, has an interest in citizens who fully develop their potential both because they are more informed and interesting and because as participants in the labor force they are more productive. Therefore, through government as well as through private channels, society addresses that interest by investing in programs that insure that minimal human needs are met.

Guidelines for Government Participation in Meeting Minimal Human Material Needs

At one extreme, libertarians and many pure neoclassical economists favor an analytical model that minimizes government participation in meeting human material needs. They favor enough government presence to permit private participants in economic activity to pursue their self-interest. If self-interest is pursued without resistance, the invisible hand with its "trickledown" fingers would take care of human need. At the other extreme, proponents of a centrally planned economy would have a few "wise people" at the top of the economic-political hierarchy identify the minimum human needs of the populace and put in place regulations to ensure that these needs are met.

Theoretically, either model might work well in a particular circumstance. For example, the neoclassical model could work if all producers were of relative similar size, if they were similarly endowed, if there were an abundance of them, and if other institutions in the society were geared to insuring a sufficient distribution of output to every person. In wartime or other disaster circumstances, urgency might dictate the centralized model. However, regardless of the theory, practice so far has proven that neither of these extreme models is sufficiently universal or flexible to effectively and efficiently meet the minimal material needs of all of the people most of the time. Therefore, I propose an eclectic model that draws the good from both as the model on which to found policy.

My eclectic approach recognizes that U.S. society, to say nothing of societies in other countries or the international relationships among these societies, is extremely complex, and there is no expectation that it will become less complex. In the light of society's complexity, policy should be designed to elicit the maximum number of solutions to problems from the workings of the private economy. Thus, the government policies that influence production and distribution by private citizens should be continuously reviewed and modified in order to better insure that private activities, including those that may introduce or promote economic insecurity, do not reduce the well-being of any citizen below the minimal level. A variant of this is that policies always should be designed to meet the minimum human needs of each member of society.

Further, my position is that because the U.S. and other societies are pluralistic, it is impossible for anyone or any small group to identify the minimal human material needs of everybody and/or policies to meet those needs. Such efforts are likely to be misguided, at least some of the time. Therefore, if meeting the minimal needs of all people requires some aggressive, central government participation, the eclectic model must incorporate at least two political constraints. First, centrally made definitions of need must be determined through a democratic process and must stand on hard information about unmet material need rather than ideology if they are expected to closely reflect the preferences of the people in need. Second, policies to address minimal needs should be drawn in consultation with the persons to be affected by them, the persons best able to identify these needs.[7]

Samuels asserts in chapter 1 that the definition of human needs must be arrived at by trial and error, or "worked out" as he put it. Just as needs must be worked out, so must the policies designed to address them. The working out of needs involves an evolutionary process from which emerges either social conventions or social institutions to meet the needs. In this connection, Robert Sugden recently has made the point that "conventions are not chosen; they evolve" (93). For example, as attitudes favoring equal opportunity and affirmative action have been codified and implemented, the need for child care has become a more apparent need; a need for which social conventions are still evolving. The conventions that exist at any moment in the evolutionary process provide "order in human affairs" and are "self-perpetuating" (97). Similar to Clarence Ayres's definition of institutions, conventions bind their beneficiaries to the past because individuals or groups either comfortable with or favored by a convention, of course, wish to retain it (42–50). Even though some individuals or groups may be harmed by the convention, its existence manifests the prominence or leverage of the favored during its evolutionary development.[8]

Because conventions tend to be static and not subject to periodic, systematic evaluation, it is quite possible at any point in time that the conventional solution to a perceived need no longer relates to that problem. The forces working within the society's fabric have altered the weave and/or texture of the fabric, but the techniques for caring for the fabric remain fixed. For example, referring back to the child care need, there continues to be a desire in some quarters for an "extended family type" child care in the midst of a U.S. society where increasingly that is becoming impractical.[9] From the basis of what might be called convention analysis, corrections, modifications, and adaptations of conventional solutions could be derived. One form of government participation in resolving problems of human need could be insuring that the task of evaluating existing conventions is continually undertaken and completed.

What forces work within society to affect its weave and texture? Population growth, resource availability, and technological change are three.[10] Although other forces exist, I think few analysts would dismiss any of these three as being other than central during a normal period of time. The interactions among and between these forces and societal conventions are far too complex to explore exhaustively in this essay. However, in order to illustrate the nature of the role of each in a more complex analysis of the workings of conventions, I will take up each of these three briefly.

First, population growth and resource availability interact in various ways in shaping society's conventions. (The age distribution of the population is also important but is not incorporated into this example.) For example, in a country with a small and slowly growing population, the conventions by which claims are made on nonhuman resources are drastically different from those in a country with a large and/or rapidly growing population. In the former case, the rules are likely to be geared toward easy and sweeping resource transfers, often resembling giveaways, aimed at encouraging resource development. In the latter, the conventions will more likely reflect the need to minimize conflict as members of society clamor for sufficient resources to sustain life. Or in another scenario, conventions that encourage spreading work around are predictable when population is great relative to other resources, while conventions that encourage intense work are predictable when population is more scarce than other resources.

There also occurs a dual interaction between resources and technology. Technology can be defined for the purposes of this essay as society's accumulation of tools and implements together with the knowledge needed to use them. Technology, in fact, defines what society labels as resources. Petroleum, for example, became an important resource only when developments such as the internal combustion engine, petrochemicals, and plastics were technologically feasible. The rich prairie soils of America's heartland were of little use to farmers until the development of a plow capable of breaking the prairie sod. Such examples constitute one type of interaction. Another type involves excessive technological pressure on resources. New technology that converts a product of nature into a resource often then proceeds to consume the newly defined resource as if it is unlimited. Only later are the resource limitations recognized. Whether it is a lake's capacity to regenerate or the atmosphere's limited capacity to absorb sulfur dioxide that is recognized, it is increasingly clear as we approach the twenty-first century that even such basic and presumably "free" resources as water and air, whose abundance was previously unquestioned, are limited. It is clear that technological developments and natural products interact to define what society labels resources and ultimately to identify the limits of these resources. In response to these interactions, social conventions evolve. Among the abundant examples that could be cited, the evolution of society's attitudes toward and efforts to control automobile emissions are widely known.

Population and technology likewise interact. The contemporary complexity of technology dictates more and modified demand for education of the social body. The upward shift in the education market's equilibrium is exacerbated by the diminished numbers of working-age members of U.S. society. These pressures have facilitated society's acceptance of spouses employed outside the home and in some cases have made such work a necessity. In turn, modifications of work practices have necessitated modifications in child care conventions and in shopping and leisure practices, among others.

The force for change emanating from the forward thrust of the technological process is pervasive in these interactions. Although its specific characteristics are evolving, over the centuries the effects of technical change have been sufficiently positive to generate the label "technological progress." This technological change, of course, inevitably has required change in a society's conventions or institutions. Whether it be the changes included in the "enclosure movement" that took place in England between the fourteenth and eighteenth centuries or those surrounding child care in the U.S. in the latter part of the twentieth century, social institutions always must be modified to accommodate technological change. Otherwise social dislocations will occur. Within this framework, and in any era, human resources (working-age population) and natural resources are relatively established over a fifteen- to twenty-year period. Thus, within that time horizon, the crucial variables to be analyzed are the existing static social conventions and the often disruptive forward-pushing forces of technology. In a dynamic setting, the tendency of each is constantly being challenged by the other, and policy and participation must be adjusted to accord with the degree to which the center, under this interactive pressure, has shifted.

It is important to observe the parallels between the operations of technology and those of social conventions. The technological process involves the use of tools and implements to produce something. In the use of tools and implements, a modification may occur that produces a technological breakthrough that may then either be publicized or set aside to be rediscovered only when an on-the-job problem arises. Conventions such as patent laws and collusive practices will, of course, influence the rate at which knowledge about new discoveries is disseminated. However, regardless of impediments to dissemination, it is fair to say that discoveries that build on previous knowledge are being implemented continuously and that the effect on society is dynamic; society's institutions must adapt to the new technological environment if an optimal use of the new technology is to be attained.[11]

U.S. citizens in the 1990s are accustomed to rapid technical change. Beginning almost a century ago with the advent of the motor car, as the automobile was originally called, the average citizen has been exposed to rapid technical change in all areas of life, from transportation and communication to the home and workplace. And whether in response to computerization of the production line in an automobile production plant, to the computerization of the office environment, to the microwave in the kitchen, or to the answering machine on the telephone, work rules and habits must change if people are to function in the environment created by new technology.

Policy making is a pragmatic enterprise. And Clarence Ayres's theory of economic progress, which postulates the interactions between technology and society's institutions, illustrated above, can serve as a guide to pragmatic policy making and can incorporate the best from the neoclassical and central planning models into the policy making process. I propose using Ayres's model to discuss the participation of government in the collective endeavor of meeting human material needs over a twenty year time horizon. (Since Ayres built on the work of Thorstein Veblen, this model is often referred to in the literature as the Veblen-Ayres model.) I propose this horizon because, in the absence of drastic changes in immigration laws, twenty-year population projections are rather certain, the twenty-year natural resource base is also rather well defined, and in the absence of unforeseen, dramatic new technology, the path of technological progress is relatively predictable. Within this time period one can expect that technology will continue to change both vertically and horizontally; vertical referring to improved technology and horizontal to its dissemination to areas not now possessing it. We know that, because social conventions or institutions are slow to adapt to technical change, social dislocations and their consequent human hardship will occur during this process. As a partner in the process, government can work to minimize hardship by developing and implementing policy using Ayres's model as a guide in the development and implementation of policy to meet the material needs of those disadvantaged as the economy and society adjust to new technology.

Examples of the Analytical Framework Applied

The application of this analytical framework foregrounds two broad categories of government participation. First, government should conduct its normal, nonhuman-need activities in such a way as to minimize negative externalities. Technology, as it modifies human material needs and other social conventions, inescapably calls for the modification of government policies as well. Government activities must be constantly monitored in an attempt to exclude from them the institutionalization of counter-productive policies and practices. Second, because technology continuously modifies the fabric of society, in a democratic society citizens must be ready to identify unmet human needs and their representatives in government must be receptive and re-sponsive to the needs identified. Regarding government partici-pation that is specifically addressed to meet human needs, I have argued elsewhere, in a different context, that instead of maximizing the power of a technocratic, bureaucratic public agency, we should optimally and publicly encourage existing semipublic institutions, or foster new ones, that provide objec-tive information to those with unmet needs, enabling people in need to make more informed choices as they seek to satisfy their needs. Ideally, both private and government agencies, as well as semipublic (government sponsored but not controlled) agencies would compete in providing information to insure, insofar as possible, that all information is cross-checked (Scaperlanda,

136). Such competition would insure bureaucratic efficiency as well, exposing and then pressuring out of existence any agency whose ratio of good information to bad proved too costly. John Smithin has pointed out that John M. Keynes thought that semi-public bodies ("semi-autonomous bodies" he called them) would operate "solely for the public good as they understood it" and with all "motives of private advantage" excluded from their deliberations. Keynes further observed that the English experience was that successful "bodies" of this nature came to be both an accepted and then integral part of the social fabric (Smithin, 213).

General Government Policy and Human Material Need

I turn first to government participation in economic life that is not targeted toward unmet human need. Stavins and Jaffe recently demonstrated "that the depletion of forested wetlands in the Mississippi Valley . . . has been and is currently exacerbated by federal water-project investments, despite explicit federal-policy to protect wetlands" (337). Their statistical analysis leads to the conclusion that private landowners, responding to the unintended economic incentives resulting from federal flood control and drainage projects, since 1934 have converted 1.15 million more acres from wetlands to other uses than would have been converted in the absence of the government participation (349). Obviously, government participation can and does distort the use of resources in unanticipated ways. Ayres's pragmatic, eclectic model would allow the government to better foresee such and avoid them, especially if there is an adverse impact on members of the society with unmet material needs.[12]

The plight of the homeless, which has become so acute in recent years, provides an example of potential distortion allowed by the income tax interest deduction for home mortgages. Currently the federal income tax code permits the deduction of interest on a home mortgage of one million dollars, no questions asked. Consequently, those who can qualify often apply for large loans and build very large houses whether they are really needed or not. I hypothesize that a lower cap on the amount of interest that can be deducted would produce fewer large loans and greater numbers of smaller houses. If this occurred, the reduced demand for loans and building materials would lower the prices of both, thereby making housing more affordable for people who are less well-off.

Government policy bears differentially on the needy in other ways as well.For example, poorer persons are more likely to live near toxic waste dumps or other hazardous places than are the more affluent. Government policy often permits the continuation of such pollution, rationalizing that to impose environmental standards would be harmful to the international competitive position of the firm or industry in question. Yet, in other instances, such as automobile pollution controls, questions of competition are set aside and the U.S. standard is applied to all producers of whatever nationality. (Localized toxic waste dumps affect only the people, often the poor, who live near them; pollution from automobiles affects both the poor and the rich.) There is no reason such a pattern could not be applied universally. Let me propose a method. First, the U.S. government would apply the desired standards to American firms and calculate from this experience the cost of implementing the standards. Then a tariff equal to that cost would be levied on imports unless and until the foreign firm exporting to the U.S. could demonstrate that it too meets the U.S. standards. This tariff would not discriminate against foreign producers. Rather they would be treated identically with U.S. firms. At least two benefits would accrue from this approach. First, it would assure to some U.S. citizens a healthier living environment.[13] Second, it would stand to benefit the citizens of other nations as well if foreign firms that opted to meet the U.S. standards, in the interests of simplicity and efficiency, also applied the U.S. standards in their own countries.

State government participation in meeting the material needs of the poor also must be considered. For example, modification of legal practices concerned with divorce and child support could benefit a number of persons with unmet needs. As Sawhill and others have pointed out, female-headed households are more poverty-prone than others. The cost of obtaining a divorce and often the continuing cost of obtaining or maintaining the awards of the divorce decree compound rather than alleviate the poverty of these households.[14] This problem should be addressed. State government might provide legal aid for anyone with a poverty-level income who wants it; or the offending spouse might be required to pay all legal fees whenever there is an abridgement of the original decree. Or the law might require that child support payments be made through a government office, with the proviso that if payments are not made, the state immediately garnishees the wages or attaches the property of the delinquent spouse. The person receiving child support should be guaranteed regular payment and should be protected from the legal fees incurred to either enforce the law or to be protected from harassment. Such divorce laws would materially assist a number of female-headed households to meet more of their material needs.[15]

Targeted Government Policy and Human Need

Next, I turn to targeted government participation in meeting material needs. Although Sawhill, in her survey "Poverty in the U.S.: Why Is It So Persistent?" says that "from a more scientific perspective, we still understand very little about the basic causes of poverty," she does report that some understanding exists (1113).[16] First, she finds that "the existing 'official' measures of poverty in the United States have proved useful" (1112) in reaching conclusions such as: "the greatest success story is the decline in poverty among the elderly" and "the failure to conquer poverty cannot be attributed to the failure of antipoverty programs . . . they reduced poverty but it is hard to say by how much" (1113).

The official measures, by focusing on components of the poverty process, also identify causes of poverty that lie beyond the reach of antipoverty programs, narrowly defined. For example, general economic stagnation and recession together with demographic trends are declared to be the probable reasons for the "rather modest progress in the face of a large increase in real spending for income transfers and for human capital programs targeted on the poor" (1113). Moreover, "some basic needs— medical care in particular—are met more adequately now than in the past, and this does not show up in most measures of poverty" (1113).[17]

Most important is the fact that the definitions of poverty have been the foundations for studies that have contributed substantially to our general understanding of the great diversity among those who are poor (Sawhill, 1112–13). Therefore, as we approach the twenty-first century, policies can be tailored and targeted more precisely to such diverse populations as the temporarily poor and the unskilled and uneducated who comprise the so-called underclass, each of whom faces different problems that require imaginatively different solutions. Other cases of poverty between these extremes can be addressed with still other policies.

In this spectrum, underclass poverty is the most difficult for which to formulate policy, temporary poverty the easiest. Beginning with the most difficult, who belongs to the underclass? According to Mincy, Sawhill, and Wolf, an individual could be said to belong to the underclass if past or current activities have "severely constrained their life chances" so that the probability of their prospects of rising from the most impoverished level of society "are unacceptably low." Citing several other studies, they go on to say: "A related approach would define the underclass as all adults who are chronically dependent on socially unacceptable forms of income such as money from crime, from public assistance, or private charity" (451). For greater precision in policy formation and greater efficiency in policy implementation, it may be useful to distinguish what Mincy and others identify as the behavioral underclass—those persons "whose upward mobility is constrained by their own behavior"—from the structural underclass—those for whom upward mobility "is constrained by background factors over which they have no control" (451).[18] The former may require behavior modification or rehabilitation in addition to the training and other "cultural literacy" opportunities necessary to eliminate the entire structural underclass.

How large is the total underclass in the United States? Recognizing that every neighborhood, the average size of which is four thousand people, has some diversity, scholars use statistical profiles of neighborhoods to answer this question on the assumption "that the underclass tends to live in low-income or bad neighborhoods and to congregate in ghettos that are economically, socially, and racially segregated."[19] Based on these profiles Mincy and others estimate that in 1980 there were about five million people equally distributed between "poor" neighborhoods, where 40 percent or more of the people live in poverty, and "bad" neighborhoods, where, in addition to "straightforward poverty," there is a high incidence of adolescent high school dropouts, of single parenthood, of welfare dependency, and of male joblessness (451).[20] In 1980, there were 880 bad neighborhoods disproportionately concentrated in large Northeastern cities of the United States, with an education profile of high school dropouts at 63 percent of persons over age twenty-five, and with a racial profile of disproportionately large concentrations of blacks (59 percent) and Hispanics (10 percent) compared to "non-bad" neighborhoods (451).

What is alarming is that between 1970 and 1980 "the number of poor neighborhoods rose by 75 percent, and the number of bad neighborhoods by 331 percent." And while cautioning that care must be taken in interpreting these findings, Mincy and others conclude as follows:

> What we know unambiguously is that the number of people living in neighborhoods where the incidence of low income and dysfunctional behavior is high increased substantially between 1970 and 1980 and at a much more rapid rate than the number of poor or badly behaved people in the nation as a whole. These neighborhoods, which we call underclass areas, are the site of much of the crime, welfare dependency, school dropouts, poverty, and other social problems that not only affect the life chances of the children residing in such areas but also impose costs on the rest of society. (452)

What should be the role of government in dealing with such an underclass? The findings of Mincy and others show that in the absence of action, society pays a cost. Thus, expenditures on attempts to eliminate the underclass through processes that result in the meeting of its material needs are not, and therefore should not be viewed as, a gross increase in cost. Because society bears a cost in the absence of government participation, the net increase in cost of a program should be less than the actual outlay, and if the government participation is very successful, the people rescued from the underclass will make a positive financial contribution to society. That is, the taxes paid by former members of the underclass could exceed the additional cost involved in enabling them to escape from the socioeconomic conditions that are associated with being a member of the underclass. To answer the question of the role of government and to make intelligent use of the experience of other societies with these problems, one can refer to Alfred Marshall's solution for eliminating the Residuum—clearly the English underclass of a century ago.

Since Marshall's prescription for dealing with the underclass is poignantly stated, I will quote him.

> A beginning might be made with a broader, more educative and more generous administration of public aid to the helpless. The difficulty of discrimination would need to be faced: and in facing it local and central authorities would obtain much of the information needed for guiding, and in extreme cases for controlling, those who are weak and especially those whose weakness is a source of grave danger to the coming generation. . . . The most urgent among the first steps toward causing the Residuum to cease from the land, is to insist on regular school attendance in decent clothing, and with bodies clean and fairly well fed. In case of failure the parents should be warned and advised: as a last resource the homes might be closed or regulated with some limitation of the freedom of the parents. The expense would be great: but there is no other so urgent need for bold expenditure. It would remove the great canker that infects the whole body of the nation: and when the work was done the resources that had been absorbed by it would be free for some more pleasant but less pressing social duty. (714–15)

It is clear that Marshall advocated a long-range, active, and firm policy stance toward the underclass, focused on the next generation. Adequate food, clothing, shelter, and other basics should be provided by government so that the next generation has at least the minimally acceptable home environment. If the current older generation among the Residuum cannot productively use what government provides, Marshall advocates government intervention as the mode of participation. Implicitly he would initially advocate in-home training in such matters as housekeeping, personal finance, and personal hygiene. If the underclass did not cooperate, a warning would be issued. If the warning were not heeded, Marshall would take the children and place them in foster homes as a last resort.[21] Thus, Marshall's government participation would begin as government intervention and, if necessary, progress to government intrusion. He deemed such drastic shock tactics reasonable given the great barriers to be overcome and the huge societal benefits emanating from success.

The point of referring to Marshall's solution is not to advocate foster homes. Rather, it is to illustrate that even a revered neoclassical economist would support government intrusion to achieve what is perceived as an ultimate good. Further, in the contemporary world, if the only solution society can identify is to remove a child from its home environment, extreme care must be taken to insure that the replacement environment is a nurturing one. In addition, this could be one situation in which a semipublic agency would be the most humane approach to handling the problem.

In the face of the human needs of the behavioral underclass in the contemporary United States, Alfred Marshall's ideas are quite instructive. While some of Marshall's policies may strike us as extreme, nonetheless a very activist role by all levels of government, especially in the decayed and decaying neighborhoods, may be necessary to help create an environment that will enable the next generation to escape the underclass. Because, if undertaken, the various forms of intervention will challenge many definitions of freedom, care must be taken to insure that interventions are reasonable and just. And as Marshall indicates, the lifting of the underclass requires large infusions of resources; the process of human rescue and rehabilitation is labor intensive and expensive. A number of specific programs are currently in place in the U.S., but they need better funding and/or reform.[22] Experience with semipublic organizations monitoring and, if necessary, helping to manage individual family units is limited and dispersed. If the U.S. is going to get serious about eliminating "the great canker that infects the whole body of the nation" (Marshall, 715), the experiences that do exist in these areas should be compiled. In turn, general guidelines should be extracted from existing data and tested in carefully monitored pilot programs so that subsequently they could be implemented at large.

Contemporary research has refined our understanding of the modern Residuum. Some persons in the behavioral underclass may spontaneously respond to opportunities to escape the underclass and thereby modify or eliminate detrimental behavior without government intrusion into their personal lives. And escape from the structural underclass should be possible in the presence of the right opportunities and with targeted remedial work to provide missing background factors.[23] William Wilson after surveying the poverty literature has concluded that, in addition to secondary means-tested and race-specific policies to overcome background deficiencies, what is really needed is a universal program. He has summarized the program by saying:

> that the problems of the ghetto underclass can be most meaningfully addressed by a comprehensive program that combines employment policies with social welfare policies and that features universal as opposed to race- or group-specific strategies. On the one hand, this program highlights macroeconomic policy to generate a tight labor market and economic growth; fiscal and monetary policy not only to stimulate noninflationary growth, but also to increase the competitiveness of American goods on both the domestic and international markets; and a national labor-market strategy to make the labor force more adaptable to changing economic opportunities. On the other hand this program highlights a child support assurance program, a family allowance program, and a child care strategy. (163)

The problem is not that Wilson's vision is misguided. Rather, it is that current political activity at the national level seems incapable of reconciling revenues with expenditures at all, much less in a nondeflationary way. Until taxes and spending are sufficiently reconciled so that there is a general impression that equilibrium has been achieved, fiscal policy as an effective policy instrument will be unavailable and the resulting burden placed on monetary policy will continue to bias its application. Thus, the outlook is not good for implementing, in the near future, the macroeconomic policy for which Wilson calls.

It seems to me that in the near future even job creation will have to be targeted for poor and bad neighborhoods. Otherwise, targeted programs to overcome background deficiencies will only further frustrate the participants from the underclass if they become prepared for new work and no work exists. Recognizing Wilson's arguments that targeted programs have been less successful sustaining political support than nontargeted ones (119–20), if success in eliminating the underclass is to be achieved in the contemporary world, courageous and effective political leadership will be required. Therefore, assuming that with the assistance of governments, members of the underclass and other poor people have available enough food, clothing, shelter, and other amenities, education becomes an important key, perhaps *the* key, to upward economic and social mobility. We know this. Further, we know that we need educational reform and funding.[24] Progress is slow, however, because of the lack of political commitment to sufficient funding and because "institutionalized nay-sayers" fear the personal implications of educational reform and therefore impede change. Of funding for education that would make at least all members of the next generation functional literates, Marshall asserts: "To this end public money must flow freely" (718).

Unlike underclass poverty, short-term poverty is relatively easy for government to deal with. Presumably, persons who are temporarily impoverished are already equipped with the will, the experience, and the skills to rebound from adversity, and they may be particularly reluctant to accept assistance. To spare the pride of those in short-term poverty, emergency allocations such as food stamps should be available quickly and automatically for at least several weeks, or until paperwork can be processed if the need for longer-term assistance is anticipated. (This is the equivalent to a monetized food pantry. And the administrative structure might make use of existing food pantries to distribute this sort of assistance.) Also, clothing stamps might be developed to provide children's clothes and clothes that an adult would need to interview for a new job if unemployment or underemployment is the cause of the temporary poverty.[25] Moreover, society will be less disrupted if people in short-term poverty are not evicted from their housing. Quick loans for two or three months' rent or mortgage payments should be made available at low interest through local banks or credit unions or through a specialized agency, after which repayment could be made over the course of a year or two. If poverty is not overcome within the allotted time period, the loan can be forgiven (covered by public assistance) on the same schedule as payments were anticipated. The aim is to prevent a deterioration in standard of living that increases the vulnerability of the short-term poor to sickness, disease, and homelessness and thereby pushes them toward the underclass. If this can be accomplished, the diminishment of human dignity will be minimized even as the public cash outlay will probably be smaller.

In addition to food, clothing, and shelter, those in short-term poverty may benefit from counseling of various sorts (i.e., financial, job search). Government should participate with the private sector to provide these services. For all short-term assistance, the expectation is that efficiency will be increased and the diminishment of the recipients' dignity minimized the closer the locus of control is to the recipient of the assistance. Thus, government cooperation with and through private agencies active in the communities where the needy live should minimize mistakes and promote optimal efficiency (an efficient operation that is sensitive and responsive to individual need).

For poverty of an intermediate term (longer than six months but not so long as to draw those involved into an underclass environment), the food, clothing, and shelter provisions would have to approach the character of a program. Much of the U.S.'s public social assistance that is summarized in table 4.1 is geared in this direction now. However, the components of contemporary public assistance could be more effectively deployed if a single administration handled both food stamps and housing assistance, for example. Even when both are available, the potential recipient usually has to make application for assistance at two places. Consolidation of the application processes would not only facilitate the extension of assistance but, in addition, would reduce the administrative cost thereby reducing the "burden" on the taxpayers.

The word burden is placed in quotes because a popular attitude toward social assistance programs is that they are a burden on the society. The major social insurance programs that are identified in table 4.2 also are due individuals as a right. However, the right to social insurance is viewed by the general public in a more positive light than the light in which the right to social assistance is viewed. The reasons for this difference in perception are complex and deep-seated. However, one of the manifestations of this different perception is a mistrust of the recipients of public assistance. This mistrust results in society's application of means tests to insure that no recipient obtains assistance in excess. In turn, the person in need may feel that personal dignity is threatened and self-respect diminished by having to repeatedly respond to means tests. Since means tests will probably continue to be used in response to taxpayers' demands, the consolidation of the application process that I advocate will minimize the number of means tests required and thereby minimize the diminishment of the dignity of the applicant. Further, experience with less complicated and less intrusive procedures and tests eventually may lead to general attitudes that encourage the use of social assistance programs. If such a change in attitude transpires, assistance programs will be viewed more like insurance programs and may experience a more generous attitude toward funding.

Gary Burtless has documented the decline in real funding of social assistance over the last decade or so. He has also observed that the hypothesized increase in the labor market participation by single mothers that rationalized the decrease in AFDC assistance during this period has not materialized in fact (70–71). Given the negative findings of the experiment with decreased assistance, U.S. society may wish to test the hypothesis that "success encourages further success" or "improvements in circumstances beget desires for further improvements." Such an experiment would require not only an attitude that access to social assistance is a right of anyone who needs it, but substantial funding increases would also be needed, at least initially.[26]

The programs that are in place are generally underfunded

relative to contemporary need.[27] For example, cutbacks during the 1980s greatly reduced the stock of affordable housing, the availability of food stamps, nutrition for young mothers, infants, and children, and the administrative infrastructure of all programs. Administrative cutbacks and the resulting heavier case loads for social workers have reduced access to knowledge of programs and procedures and thereby have made the programs less accessible to the poor. Reduced time to obtain information about benefits from a social worker penalizes not only the impoverished but society at large, for society incurs the costs of work time missed because of the time required to straighten out the consequences. Thus, some restoration of recent funding reductions may be a positive investment for the U.S. In addition, experiments with more generous assistance as a means of encouraging its recipients to be more active in the marketplace seem worthwhile. In this instance, "throwing some money" at the problem is equivalent to saving it rather than throwing it away.[28]

Yet money alone is not the complete answer. Institutional reforms are needed to simplify the process of obtaining assistance. A lighter case load for social workers could and should translate to more "quality" time with each client.[29] If the case worker had the time and was empowered to effectively operate as a broker for all manner of assistance, the client could obtain in one place a package of support to meet his or her human needs, a step that also would be a mark of respect for the client in an age when the comfortable equate time with money and money with the worth of a human being.[30] (Conceptually this is not unlike the development of a financial package that private colleges provide for prospective students. Only the sources of the support differ.) If funding is available and if there were the equivalent of a financial adviser with comprehensive knowledge of financial assistance available and that being received, a greater probability of meeting the human needs of those in extended poverty should result.

The financial adviser/social worker would also be able to assess the probabilities and possibilities of a person escaping the impoverished state. With this information, a plan targeted to the individual's specific situation could be devised for achieving that escape. Training and education will be essential in many cases. Career planning, liaison with training and education institutions, support during the process (including child care and other support services), and a placement service at the end of the road all effectively complement the ongoing process of welfare assistance.[31] When the opportunity for employment arises, relocation expenses should be made available, as needed. This might take the form of a grant to include reasonable and necessary moving expenses as well as the required deposit on an apartment.[32] All of these institutional reform measures coupled with more adequate funding would add up to a genuine welfare "program," in contrast with the scattershot, disconnected potpourri of services currently in place and difficult to access, especially for those most in need.

Conclusions

I return to the question: What should be the kind and extent of the participation of government in meeting the human material needs of residents of the United States of America? First, governments should continually review all policies to insure that they do not unintentionally distort the distribution of income to the disadvantage of the poor. Second, various levels of government should work in concert to insure that meaningful employment is available for everyone able and willing to work. Third, for those who cannot work, various government programs should be coordinated to insure that every person has, by right, access to adequate food, clothing, shelter, and other amenities in order to attain a level of living at least above the poverty line. All services for a given individual should be coordinated by one social worker. And the procedures and their administration should be designed so that a person's human dignity is not diminished in the process of exercising their right to the assistance. Fourth, emergency assistance should be increased and made more easily accessible to the temporarily impoverished.

Fifth, society must attack the problem of underclass poverty. Attack is a carefully chosen word because meeting the needs of the people in this type of poverty requires an effort tantamount to an attack. Some dimensions of underclass poverty may call for seemingly harsh measures if they are to be addressed at all effectively. Other aspects will require firm direction and training as well as maintenance assistance during the process. In general, if underclass poverty is to be overcome, the attack on it must be multifaceted and administered by a "government" that has the authority to cut through bureaucratic ensnarements much the way a military government in a conquered country is able to after a war. Such an all-out attack will be most effective if it builds on democratically constituted community organizations and if it explicitly establishes a process to further the development of community government institutions so that democratic control of required reforms can be phased in on an established timetable.

Sixth, and the most important if there is to be a serious effort to meet the material needs of everyone, government participation should create a positive, broadly shared discourse about society's responsibility toward the well-being of all. I began by arguing that, rhetorically, "government participation" is preferable to "government intervention" because in recent decades the public discourse has been poisoned by negative attitudes toward the poor that have been encouraged and shaped by a political ideology that results in bestowing advantages and benefits on those who are economically privileged. Political leadership that focuses the nation on poverty as an eradicable condition could substantially reduce resistance to policy initiatives and increase the public's recognition of the problem. Basically, I am optimistic that if the human material needs of the poor are more clearly and publicly recognized, the body politic will support the programs necessary to meet them. A century ago, Marshall commented that "devotion to public well-being on the part of the rich may do much, as enlightenment spreads, to help the tax-gatherer in turning the resources of the rich to high account in the service of the poor, and may remove the worst evils of poverty from the land" (719).

As social economists have long argued, meeting the basic human material needs of the people in the U.S. is possible. The resources are available, but the rhetoric of many prominent political leaders has worked to destroy the political will to mobilize those resources to meet the apparent needs. If government can come to participate by providing more positive leadership, the past and current experience the country has had with programs to meet the needs of the poor together with the theoretical and analytical infrastructure economists have provided will serve well as a foundation for the new generation of programs that are required.

Notes

1. Warren Samuels recently explored some aspects of the economic role of government. Noting that government's involvement in economic matters is both complex and fundamental, he says, "law-government is not exogenous to the economic system and the economic system cannot exist independent of law and government" (432).

2. This trend is not likely to be reversed because the participation of women in the workforce is not likely to be reversed. And when anyone is formally employed less time is available for volunteer activities. (The participation of women as volunteers decreased from 56 percent to 47 percent of the population of women between 1981 and 1987.) (*Statistical Abstract, 1990*, Table 617, p. 371.)

3. If national government deficit financing is correlated with stimulative macroeconomic policy, the experience of the 1980s should have been extremely stimulating. Yet the 1990 *Economic Report of the President* (328) reports that poverty in the U.S. was a bigger problem in the 1980s than it was in the 1970s. Does this mean that without the Reagan budget-deficit stimulation the U.S. economy would be in a deep recession/depression with many more unmet needs than are currently apparent? Or does it mean that the stimulation distorted economic activity so that those whose needs already were abundantly fulfilled received most of the benefit? If the second alternative is the more accurate, the fact that over one million additional families fell below the poverty line between the late 1970s and the late 1980s is evidence that the benefits of stimulation have not trickled down to the poor as rapidly as supply side policy makers expected. The implications of these changes for the productivity growth required as a basis for an improving standard of living have been explored by Litan, Lawrence, and Schultz. Not unexpectedly they recognize that "the Nation's well-being is dependent on the skills of its people," and that "in the end poor families need more income if they are to provide an environment in which their children can learn" the skills needed by the society (30–31). Nord and Sheets have concluded that job training programs may

not be successful in the long run because of a "lack of jobs that pay sufficiently well to maintain long-term labor force attachment" (196). They based their conclusion on an empirical study of 226,023 single mothers living in a metropolitan setting that analyzed the effects of AFDC payments and other factors on the labor force participation and underemployment of single mothers.

4. An extensive discussion emphasizing the evolution of the concept "human needs" can be found in Braybrooke.

5. The phrasing of the question is important in this "employer-in-the-workplace" approach. For example, Thomas Monaghan, founder of Domino's Pizza and owner of the Detroit Tigers, was recently quoted in the *National Catholic Reporter* as saying that a family of four "could have an adequate, balanced diet on an annual food budget of $150–$300" (Bellant, 5). The question is not what he thinks people can survive on. Rather, it is would a person in such straits possess the personal characteristics (i.e., dress, hygiene, skills, and stamina) to work for him. One might speculate that a Tiger pitcher on such a budget would have little time to practice and insufficient stamina to complete many innings.

6. By Residuum Marshall meant "persons who are physically, mentally, or morally incapable of doing a good day's work with which to earn a good day's wage and perhaps some others" (714).

7. This concept is often referred to as the "Principle of Subsidiarity." For an example of this, see the U.S. Roman Catholic bishops' recent pastoral letter on the U.S. economy entitled *Economic Justice for All*.

8. John Elster recently explored the subject "Social Norms and Economic Theory." He distinguishes social norms from "the convention equilibria described in Robert Sugden's accompanying article" by noting that Sugden explains that "the evolution of a convention equilibrium is guided by whether the conventions lead to a substantively better outcome" whereas he argues that "many social norms do not benefit anyone" (100). It seems to me that an argument based on the assumption that a norm or a convention will prevail if it benefits no one and possibly is detrimental to some is seriously flawed. Even if society is not composed of individuals with perfect knowledge and ideal rationality as Sugden asserts that game theorists posit, it is not unreasonable to assume that members of society will shed norms that somehow became institutionalized but that have no constituency and that cause harm to members of society. Thus for purposes of this chapter, I ignore Elster's distinction between social norms and social conventions and use either convention or institution.

9. During the September–November 1986 period, only 41 percent of

the children under five years of age of working mothers were cared for by the father (14.2 percent), a grandparent (18.2 percent), or another relative (8.7 percent). One can speculate that as the current generation of working mothers moves into retirement they will be less inclined to be engaged in child care than is the current generation of family members providing child care.

10. Readers familiar with the work of Clarence Ayres will recognize that this is basically an Ayresian model. Reference can be made to Ayres, 1952, chapters 2 and 3, for example, or Wendell Gordon, 1980, chapter 2, for a full and systematic presentation of the model.

11. Wendell Gordon explores these characteristics on pages 10–16.

12. Kevin Deno's conclusion that "public capital appears to play an important role in manufacturing firms' output supply and input demand decisions" provides another example of why the ramifications of government policy must be understood (409). If the U.S. government wanted to explicitly or implicitly impose "fiscal federalism" on the states, the national policy makers should have recognized that the private sector would be injured if states did not instantly have both the legal and the financial ability to offset decreased national financing of public capital.

13. George Ladd has recently modified a neoclassical utility function by adding a scalar measure representing the quality of the consumer's environment and found that if price reductions or income increases adversely affect environmental quality their effects can be negative on consumer welfare (56).

14. As of the spring of 1986, only 53 percent of the 1.1 million women with incomes below the poverty line received child support payments that were due. This compares with 74 percent for all women due child support (*Statistical Abstract*, Table 611, p. 369).

15. The assumption is that most divorce proceedings are more financially disadvantageous to the female when children continue to live at home. It is also assumed that after the divorce children usually live with their mother. Incorporating Patrick Raines's interpretation of Frank Knight that the family is "the appropriate place to begin remedying social ills, including and especially the misuse of power, injustice, and poverty," the aim of public policy should be to minimize the potential for disruption of positive intrafamily relations (283).

16. As to whom should be targeted, Sawhill notes that although shifts in the composition of households that have occurred in the last four decades have been significant, for practical purposes the family living at one address is the most feasible entity toward which to direct assistance to meet human needs (1080).

17. Robert Aponte, in his review of the literature on urban poverty, concludes that "on balance, it appears that the extent of poverty is not exaggerated by the official poverty formula" and that the formula is quite useful on a number of counts (171).

18. Using different terminology, the structural underclass can be said to be a function of "social isolation" and the behavioral underclass a function of that plus a "culture of poverty." For a discussion of these concepts, see Wilson, p. 61 or chapter 6.

19. Neighborhood, as the concept is used in scholarly studies, is defined by the U.S. Bureau of the Census. Although size requirements and other constraints are imposed so that the data collected for each neighborhood are reliable for analytical purposes, the unit defined as "neighborhood" is not necessarily devoid of human meaning. Since the Census Bureau attempts to draw neighborhood boundaries so that the socioeconomic group within each neighborhood is relatively homogenous, the area so defined as neighborhood also reflects a human-social as well as a statistical dimension.

20. Evidence of the importance of these background traits has recently been presented by Corcoran, Gordon, Laren, and Solon (362–66).

21. Frank Knight's warnings about transferring functions from the "private family" to the "political state" (Raines, 282) should be kept in mind when developing policy. Relying on the principle of subsidiarity, perhaps an optimal solution is to have the policy developed and implemented by a semipublic local or neighborhood entity that reflects, as much as possible, the values embodied in the concept "private family."

22. For example, nominal federal outlays on food assistance remained almost constant between 1985 and 1987. And expenditures on housing benefits declined in these years even in current dollar terms. In real terms both of these classifications of noncash assistance declined (*Statistical Abstract*, Table 580, p. 353).

23. Gueron (86) notes that the results of fifteen pilot projects, conducted between 1975 and 1980 "showed that structured, transitional, paid work experience could have positive long-term effects for very disadvantaged welfare recipients and could also be cost-effective for taxpayers." Thus, actual intrusion into neighborhoods may not have to be extensive; some will be required to "encourage" structure and some to "reign in" severe noneconomic, disruptive forces.

24. The process of designing and implementing reform, if community based, can strengthen neighborhood communities so that they are better able to take on other semipublic enterprises as opportunities arise.

25. Economic utility will be maximized if cash grants are used instead of stamps or vouchers. However, cash grants are usually not politically feasible. So, if assistance is to be provided, an alternative means such as stamps must be used.

26. Fundamentally, the question is one of distributing or rationing what is available for use. Churchill, focusing on the distribution of medical care, provides useful commentary on the interrelations of justice, needs, and rights.

27. In addition to a statistical profile of the major U.S. assistance programs for the last two decades, Burtless (57–78) discusses problems of the current programs and the potential for reforming them. Reforms that would emphasize seeking employment or preparing for employment have been reviewed by Gueron (78–98).

28. Tienda (376) recently reported that the longer women in Chicago are dependent on welfare the less likely are they to enter the work force, and "that policy initiatives designed to reduce the length of welfare spells should focus both on individuals and environments that sustain dependent behavior." Thus, substantial expenditures early in the dependency process have a better chance of being effective than lesser annual expenditures over a protracted period of time.

29. I am assuming that people who enter the social work profession do so because they care about the well-being of everyone in society. Further, I assume that if they are not overworked and are adequately mentored and supervised they will develop into caring, effective professionals.

30. Burtless (60) recently said that "within a given state, eligibility criteria in different programs are not always coordinated and methods for measuring income are inconsistent." A first step in the right direction would be a harmonization of definitions and criteria.

31. Klerman and Leibowitz (287) recently published results that "suggest that the more generous tax treatment of child care expenses" along with other factors "have tended to promote earlier return to work among new mothers during the 1980s."

32. Deposits on apartments vary by location. A common practice might be the first and last month's rent plus a security or damage deposit. Such an amount is often impossible for a person trying to overcome an impoverished state. Consequently it is not unusual to find working people having to live in shelters for the homeless while they accumulate the base amount needed to acquire a home of their own. The process of overcoming poverty probably can be accelerated if a few obstacles such as the ability to make the required deposits can be overcome. If the process can be accelerated, taxpayers will benefit.

References

Aponte, Robert. "Urban Poverty: A State-of-the-Art Review of the Literature." Appendix in *The Truly Disadvantaged* by William J. Wilson. Chicago: University of Chicago Press, 1987.

Ayres, C. E. *The Industrial Economy*. New York: Houghton Mifflin Company, 1952.

Bellant, Russ. "Millionaire Says Poverty Is Exciting." *National Catholic Reporter* 26, no. 19 (1990): 5.

Bishops, U.S. Roman Catholic. *Economic Justice for All: Pastoral Letter on Catholic Social Teaching and the U.S. Economy*. Washington, D.C.: National Conference of Catholic Bishops, 1986.

Braybrooke, David. *Meeting Needs*. Princeton: Princeton University Press, 1987.

Burtless, Gary. "The Economist's Lament: Public Assistance in America." *Journal of Economic Perspectives* 4, no. 1 (1990): 57–78.

Churchill, Larry R. *Rationing Health Care in America: Perceptions and Principles of Justice*. Notre Dame: University of Notre Dame Press, 1987.

Corcoran, Mary, Rodger Gordon, Deborah Laren, and Gary Solon. "Effects of Family and Community Background on Economic Status." *American Economic Review* 80, no. 2 (1990): 362–66.

Council of Economic Advisers. *Economic Report of the President*. Washington, 1990.

Deno, Kevin T. "The Effect of Public Capital on U.S. Manufacturing Activity: 1970–1978." *Southern Economic Journal* 55, no. 2 (1988): 400–23.

Elster, Jon. "Social Norms and Economic Theory." *Journal of Economic Perspectives* 3, no. 4 (1989): 99–117.

Gordon, Wendell C. *Institutional Economics: The Changing System*. Austin: University of Texas Press, 1980.

Gueron, Judith M. "Work and Welfare: Lessons on Employment Programs," *Journal of Economic Perspectives* 4, no. 1 (1990): 79–98.

Hamilton, David. "Welfare Reform in the Reagan Years: An Institutionalist's Perspective." *Journal of Economic Issues* 24, no. 1 (1990): 49–56.

Klerman, Jacob Alex, and Arleen Leibowitz. "Child Care and Women's Return to Work After Childbirth." *American Economic Review* 80, no. 2 (1990): 284–88.

Ladd, George W. "Welfare Paradoxes of Endogenous Externalities." *Review of Social Economy* 48, no. 1 (1990): 41–56.

Litan, Robert E., Robert Z. Lawrence, and Charles L. Schultze. "Improving American Living Standards." *The Brookings Review* 7, no. 1 (1988/89): 23–31.

Marshall, Alfred. *Principles of Economics.* 9th ed. London: Macmillan and Co., Limited, 1961.

Mincy, Ronald B., Isabel V. Sawhill, and Douglas A. Wolf. "The Underclass: Definition and Measurement." *Science* 248 (1990): 450–53.

Morris, William, ed. *The American Heritage Dictionary of the English Language.* New York: American Heritage Publishing Co., Inc., and Houghton Mifflin Company, 1969.

Nord, Stephen, and Robert G. Sheets. "The Relationships of AFDC Payments and Employment Structure on the Labour Force Participation and Unemployment Rates of Single Mothers." *Applied Economics* 22, no. 2 (1990): 187–99.

Peterson, Wallace C. "Market Power: The Missing Element in Keynesian Economics." *Journal of Economic Issues* 23, no. 2 (1989): 379–91.

Raines, J. Patrick. "Frank H. Knight's Contributions to Social Economics." *Review of Social Economy* 47, no. 3 (1989): 280–92.

Samuels, Warren J. "Some Fundamentals of the Economic Role of Government." *Journal of Economic Issues* 23, no. 2 (1989): 427–33.

Sawhill, Isabel V. "Poverty in the U.S.: Why Is It So Persistent?" *Journal of Economic Literature* 26, no. 3 (1988): 1073–1119.

Scaperlanda, Anthony. "Human Capital and Economic Progress in Eastern Europe: A Veblen-Ayres Perspective." In *Institutional Economics: Contributions to the Development of Holistic Economics,* edited by John Adams. Boston: Martinus Nijhoff Publishing, 1980.

Smithin, John N. "The Composition of Government Expenditures and the Effectiveness of Fiscal Policy." In *New Directions in Post-Keynesian Economics,* edited by John Pheby. Brookfield, Vt.: Gower Publishing Company, 1989.

Stavins, Robert N., and Adam B. Jaffe. "Unintended Impacts of Public Investments on Private Decisions: The Depletion of Forested Wetlands." *American Economic Review* 80, no.3 (1990): 337–52.

Sugden, Robert. "Spontaneous Order." *Journal of Economic Perspectives* 3, no. 4 (1989): 85–97.

Tienda, Marta. "Welfare and Work in Chicago's Inner City." *American Economic Review* 80, no. 2 (1990): 372–76.

Trebing, Harry M. "Restoring Purposeful Government: The Galbraithian Contribution." *Journal of Economic Issues* 23, no. 2 (1989): 393–411.

U.S. Bureau of the Census. *Statistical Abstract of the United States: 1990.* 110th ed. Washington, 1990.

Wilson, William J. *The Truly Disadvantaged: The Inner City, the Underclass, and Public Policy.* Chicago: University of Chicago Press, 1987.

5

The Need for Work as Such

Self-Expression and Belonging

Edward J. O'Boyle

> Due to [participation], the self and the commu-
> nity are, in a way, contiguous and are neither
> strange nor opposite to each other.
> —Wojtyla, 42

> [A]t the root of all human alienation through
> structured relations transmitted by objects, we
> must posit alienation as stemming from man
> himself.
> —Wojtyla, 55–56

The need for work as such along with physical need are the two fundamental needs that flow directly from the materiality of human nature. For that reason, these two needs, taken together, are referred to as human material need.

This essay proceeds from three main premises. First, a human being in the workplace is an instrument of work but more fundamentally is a person and for that reason matters much. In chapter 3, this person is called *Homo socioeconomicus*. Second, work is organized and performed through two main modes or channels conforming to the duality of human nature. Those modes or channels are referred to herein as individual contribution and teamwork. Third, work provides two main opportunities that also conform to the duality of human nature. In these pages, those opportunities are called self-expression and belonging.

In the section immediately following, individual contribution and self-expression—the one mode and the one opportunity that reflect the individual side of the person—are addressed at some length. Later this writer discusses teamwork and belonging—the one mode and one opportunity reflecting the social side of the person. In both sections, the need for work as such is demonstrated as being twofold corresponding once again to the duality of human nature.

In what follows, person and work are presented in the context of the secular world. No attempt is made to introduce the sacred as is done, for instance, by John Paul II in his encyclical *On Human Work* where work is affirmed as sharing in the activity of the Creator (57–59). In other words, the need for work as such which is addressed in these pages is purely secular.

The Significance of the Need for Work as Such

Work may be defined as any activity that produces a good or service of some utility, beauty, or both, whether the work is paid or unpaid and whether it is done for hire or not. Included under this broad definition are paid employment, unpaid employment in a family business, voluntarism, and leisure activities (including home production). Work, according to Jaques (and this writer concurs), is any human behavior that is goal-directed and that "requires the continuous play of thought, imagination, judgment, and decision making" (viii). Jaques's definition of work is much wider than the definition employed in conventional economics. Indeed, because Jaques includes parenting in his definition (viii), work has a meaning herein that is wider than is commonplace even in contemporary society.

The common good of workplace communities has two aspects—objective and subjective. Producing a specific good or service through the common action of individuals is the objective aspect. Liberating participation from within the various individuals who work together—Schumacher refers to this as liberating "ourselves from our inborn egocentricity" (4)—is the subjective aspect of the good of such communities. Of the two, primary consideration is to be given to the subjective aspect (Wojtyla, 45). For that reason, providing opportunities for self-expression and for belonging and thereby meeting the need for work as such is the primary goal of workplace communities.

Human beings are more than mere instruments of work. Humans beings are ends in themselves and therefore meeting their needs including the need for work as such is more important than the things that they produce[1] or their efficient utilization as instruments in the production of goods and services.

When it comes to production theory, conventional economists focus on instrumentality, and either set aside the problem of human dignity or presume that human material need is satisfied entirely through money. Social economists, in contrast, insist that instrumentality is subordinate to dignity and that because of the duality of human material need human beings are not satisfied by money alone. Human beings *need* work itself.

Self-Expression: Meeting the Need of the Individual Being for Work as Such Through Individual Contribution

The duality of human nature means that human nature has two sides: the individual and the social. As an individual being, *Homo socioeconomicus* is unique, solitary, autonomous, self-centered, and self-made.

Individual Contribution

Work affords persons as individuals an opportunity to produce something of utility or beauty by contributing skills and talents that are uniquely theirs. The process of hiring, for example, is an activity that by definition is performed individual-by-individual on the basis of each one's suitability for the work to be done and the labor contract, whether formal or not, represents a commitment made by a person as an individual to contribute in some unique way to the production of some good(s) or service(s).

Production is organized to incorporate the contributions of workers as individuals not primarily for the benefit of the individual workers but mainly due to the fact that every human being has a special endowment of skills and talents and typically a wide variety of individual skills and talents are required in the process of production. Skills and talents differentiate one person from another and for that reason reinforce one's individuality. Quite apart from the technical skills required in producing a given good or service, Varney identifies twelve task responsibilities and seven maintenance responsibilities that are necessary "for the team to sustain a concentrated effort in the direction of a specific task" (Varney, 55–57).[2]

The act of hiring is an individual act in which a person is evaluated and judged to be capable of making a contribution as an individual. Notice, in this regard, every job has its own (though not unique) title and work space. It is not just a figure of speech to call it "my desk," "my bench," or "my machine." Notice too that compensation is tied to individual contribution and is paid to persons as individuals.

The act of terminating too is an individual act even though it sometimes is done in groups, such as through a reduction in force. It is the terminated individuals who bear any burdens that are associated with the action. The group, on the other hand, has no material needs apart from those of its individual members. Individuals have material needs because they truly *are*; groups do not because strictly speaking they are a figure of speech.

A major task for the person who holds a supervisory position is to draw from the individual workers all that they are able to contribute to the process of production. In this regard, the orchestra director is a particularly instructive model. Human beings are unique economic resources in that human beings alone among resources have the free will to withhold some of their productive energies. Bennis, according to Albrecht, estimates that over 60 percent of workers think that neither they nor their co-workers give their best efforts on the job (33).

Hamermesh was the first to estimate how on-the-job leisure affects production. Using detailed time diaries from two household surveys to determine whether on-the-job leisure represents unproductive shirking or productive socializing, Hamermesh concludes that "additional time spent in on-the-job leisure at least partly represents unproductive shirking rather than productive schmoozing" (132).

Especially instructive for our purposes here is how Hamermesh represents the problem of unproductive shirking for the typical employer. Rather than construing it in terms of searching for ways to encourage employees to willingly contribute more of their productive energies and rewarding them accordingly, Hamermesh represents unproductive shirking in terms of tightening the supervision of employee break time (132–33). For Hamermesh, who affirms conventional, neoclassical economics, it is reasonable to allocate more resources to monitoring the way in which workers allocate time on the job because shirking reduces the revenues of the firm but not its costs. For those of us who affirm social economics instead, it is more sensible to restructure the work itself to make it more attractive and to reward the employees for the additional work effort on grounds that a more attractive workplace makes for a *permanent* increase in work effort and revenues more so than does tighter supervision of break time.

A private and personal decision to withhold some of the energy that one might contribute to the process of production is further evidence as to the individuality of the person.[3] Jaques asserts that creativity emerges when individuals find or are given an opportunity to work at their full capacity and in that sense "*all* work is creative in principle" (vii; emphasis added).

Crosby provides a definition of creativity that expresses the concept appropriately for this writer's purposes in what follows. Workplace decision making may be classified as either programmed or nonprogrammed. Programmed decision making refers to tasks where formal, rational procedures, such as a formula or computer program, have been put in place for passively producing answers in given situations. Nonprogrammed decisions require conscious control because standard guidelines are not readily available. Nonprogrammed decisions demand an active involvement of certain mental faculties, the functioning of which is called creativity (Crosby, 15). The effect of applying creative ability in an industrial setting is Crosby's way of defining innovation (43). Nothing is more damaging to creative performance than a false sophistication that serves as a shield that masks insecurity (Crosby, 89).

Typically, improvements in the contributions made by individuals that bear on the process of production as opposed to the product itself come in small increments because changes in the origins of any such improvements—the will and the intellect—commonly are gradual rather than radical. The Japanese workplace practice of *kaizen* pursues continuous rather than intermittent improvement in quality and efficiency. Revolutionary breakthroughs in Japan are regarded as belonging to an older paradigm (Gross, 22). Albrecht suggests why this is so.

> [C]reative and innovative activity is not necessarily separate and distinct from the day-to-day "efficiency" activity. It isn't as if a working person does something routine all day and then takes a break every now and then to do something creative. And it isn't as if the creative activity has nothing to do with the work. The routine work is the logical starting place for new ideas. The innovative activity is quite properly interwoven with the efficiency activity and serves to improve it in time. (Albrecht, 47–48)

In several site visits to manufacturing establishments in Louisiana during the mid and late 1980s, I observed this practice, which is described as "1000 small improvements." In the U.S., year-after-year improvements that make the product better, more reliable, and cheaper helped advance the semiconductor and computer industries from memory chips with one bit of data storage to four million bits. In autos, small improvements led to automatic transmissions as a replacement for manual transmissions, to power steering, and to power brakes (Port, 16).

From time to time, improvements take place that are better characterized as entrepreneurial as opposed to gradual. Just-in-time manufacturing, the personal computer, aluminum building studs, diapers, and liquid diet supplements for some of the elderly, and the network model of business organization are examples of several different types of entrepreneurial activity. Schumpeter argues that the central quality necessary for success-

ful entrepreneurship is persistence—the will to continue in the
face of heavy resistance and opposition (132). Entrepreneurship
underscores the role of the human will as one of the origins of
improvement.

The U.S. economy tends to affirm entrepreneurship. The
Japanese economy underscores the significance of gradual improvement. This contrast in experience and emphasis suggests
erroneously that the two are fundamentally different, that entrepreneurship is creative activity and gradual improvement is not.
Both, indeed, are creative because both are products of self-
expression. Both, therefore, are legitimate ways for workers to
meet the need for work as such that derives from their individuality.

Of late, however, this difference between the Japanese
economy and the U.S. economy has been narrowing in part
through the wider adoption and application of total quality management (TQM) in the U.S. TQM utilizes certain quality management practices developed in Japan after World War II. TQM,
which first caught the attention of U.S. companies in the late
1970s and early 1980s, is an approach to managing business
operations and workplace activities that encourages employees
to continuously improve both as individuals and as team members. A 1991 U.S. General Accounting Office (GAO) report identified an open corporate culture as one of six common features
contributing to improved performance at TQM companies and
a spirit of innovation as one of four attributes of a corporate
culture that is flexible and responsive (GAO, 8–10, 29–35). In
other words, under TQM entrepreneurship in established U.S.
firms increasingly is fostered through an emphasis on gradual
improvement.

The need for work is individual in part because the only
way for persons to engage in work is by contributing skills and
talents that are uniquely their own. In some cases the good or
service produced actually bears the visible imprint or signature
of the individual. In manufacturing, for example, it is common
for the person who has inspected and packed the goods for
shipment to insert a personal slip of paper in the package as a
way of identifying the responsible party. In nonmanufacturing,
it is commonplace for employees to wear identification tags, to

introduce themselves to their customers, or both. In other cases, the contribution of any one individual may be completely submerged in the contributions of many other individuals and may never be visible to the user or consumer. Nevertheless, the contribution of the individual is no less real for being hidden.

Just as the performance of an orchestra depends on the separate contributions of the various individual members, so too every good or service produced reflects the contributions made by each one of the individuals involved. Thus contribution means that in the process of production the whole of the good or service produced is comprised of its individual parts.[4] By affirming individual contribution as one of the two main channels for organizing and performing work, we insist that individuals make a difference even when that difference is not readily observable.

Self-Expression

Human beings have a need for work that is individualized because if work effort is entirely socialized or homogenized (i.e., work is organized as if everyone who works is perfectly interchangeable) the individual so subordinated may become in effect more object than person. Thus, personhood and the dignity that attaches to personhood rest on the contribution of the individual to work (broadly defined).

We are not saying that the human being who works, ipso facto, is more of a person than the one who does not. Personhood is not a continuum. Our argument is, instead, if a person works the work must be individualized because otherwise that person may be reduced to a mere instrument in the workplace and thereby would be deprived of personhood. Further, whether deprived of the opportunity to work or deprived of work that utilizes one's endowment, the person foregoes some self-expression and becomes less than all that he or she can be. The need for work as such derives in part from the need of the person as a unique, solitary, autonomous, self-centered, and self-made being to contribute something special and lasting and reflects an interest in one's individual being (self-interest) that is necessary to that person's survival.

The very endowments of skills and talents that differ from one individual to another and that make possible the production of a wide variety of goods and services mean that the need for work that is to be fulfilled through individual contribution is not the same from one person to the next. Given continuous change in a market economy (demand) and much individual freedom in preparing for work and in choosing where and for whom to work (supply), the individual need for work as such must be addressed through methods that are continuously changing and that may fall short of fully accommodating that aspect of the need for work.

In an imperfect world, the task of meeting the individual need for work as such therefore is ever challenging and stressful. In general, the longer this need remains unmet—as with the unemployed, for instance—the more difficult it becomes to address it successfully because with the passage of time idle skills and talents tend to deteriorate through *nonuse*.

There is, however, a positive side to all of this. Human beings are unique resources in that, even though they can withhold some of their productive energies, the very *use* of their skills and talents as instruments of work can lead to an *enhancement* of those skills and talents. For all other resources, *use* signifies *depletion*.[5]

Thus, the relationship between work and self-expression is not linear with work as cause and self-expression as effect. Rather, the two are so intertwined that each one at once is both cause and effect. Further, it is self-interest—a proper concern for one's own well-being—that prompts the individual contribution. In a market economy where individual income depends importantly on the economic significance of one's contribution, self-interest is essential to survival.

It is not uncommon for improvements in the workplace to have the same essential characteristics as creativity in the studio or on the stage. Artistic creativity is the development of an entire work that is not only unique but also complete. The artistic creation stands by itself and invites comparison with creations of the past. In essence, entrepreneurship is no different. The same can be said for craftsmanship. Indeed, sometimes it is quite difficult to differentiate art from craft. Further, both art and craft appropriately are called "work."

For sure, many improvements in the workplace are not entrepreneurial. Neither do they proceed from craftsmanship. Nevertheless, even what appear to be the most mundane kind of improvements in the workplace can be important forms of self-expression and make for significant improvements in self-respect. Two examples come to mind from a recent site visit I made to a jewelry manufacturer in Lafayette, Louisiana.

Stuller Settings produces gold jewelry from pure gold. In the company's foundry department, where the gold bars are melted and rendered into pellets for casting and into rolled sheets, the foreman called the visitors' attention to one workman who was pleased to demonstrate a method he had devised that reduces the amount of scrap in manufacturing flat-shape jewelry from rolled sheets.[6] In several other departments, where assembly operations take place, the workers are assigned carrel-like work stations that are illuminated in part by means of individual fluorescent lamps. Individual improvements in performance are recognized by affixing gold stars (the type that teachers have used for years to reinforce achievement among elementary-school students) directly to the lamp.

Neither of these two examples point to improvements that require artistic or entrepreneurial talent. They do, however, reinforce the significance of opportunities for self-expression which include opportunities to demonstrate one's improvement and to symbolically display one's improvement record. The lesson is that even ordinary workplace improvements that proceed from the contribution of a given individual can produce noteworthy improvements in self-respect and may have a far greater impact on self-expression and self-esteem than on unit cost, price, profits, or quality.

The role of the supervisor, therefore, encompasses not only evoking the full contribution that each individual is capable of but also recognizing and rewarding the various steps taken in the direction of achieving an individual's full potential. To some extent, self-expression, as with virtue, is its own reward. Even so, recognition and reward are required because human imperfection makes each one of us unreliable judges of the significance of our individual contributions. Self-deception, in other words, is an inevitable risk that attends self-expression.

Only a shortsighted supervisor would begrudge individual workers opportunities for self-expression on grounds that such opportunities conflict with the principal objectives of the company. Workers whose need for self-expression is unmet are dissatisfied workers and that dissatisfaction, in turn, encourages them to withhold some of their productive energies, to become less efficient, and to be less concerned about quality. Thus, any unresolved conflict between labor and management, whatever its origin, results in an increase in the cost of production, a deterioration in quality, and either a decrease in profits, an increase in price, or both.

Belonging: Meeting the Need of the Social Being for Work as Such Through Teamwork

Sociality, no less than individuality, is at the very core of personhood. Sociality means that in the workplace a human being by nature needs to be united with others in a common task not just to accomplish that task more successfully but also to develop more fully as a person. Teamwork, in other words, helps transform economic resources into goods and services and at the same time and even more importantly leads to a further unfolding of human beings as persons. Belonging, no less than self-expression, is critical to personhood.

Teamwork

Work affords persons an opportunity to produce something of utility or beauty not only by contributing skills and talents that are uniquely theirs but also by participating and interacting with others on a common task. Two persons working alongside one another is not teamwork unless there is some reason for the two to communicate as to how the work is to be done. Proximity is not closeness and membership is not participation.

Lindeman calls teamwork "acting jointly" (112) and Wojtyla insists on "acting jointly with others" (31). Given global competition and the economic advantages that attach to the division of labor, teamwork is a *requirement* of the modern workplace.

Teamwork is the intertwined individual contributions of two or more persons toward the production of a good or service such that it is difficult to clearly and completely differentiate one contribution from another and to divide all of the responsibility for the final results among the various individuals involved. Thus, teamwork introduces another duality: responsibility that is both individual and collective.

Teamwork is organized by enlarging human motivation from individual goals pursued competitively to include common goals pursued cooperatively. To be successful, teamwork requires a blending of self-interest and a genuine concern for others.[7] This blending is achieved (if at all) with some difficulty.

Cooperation helps organize the workplace by socializing the individual so that others at work on the same task are viewed as partners. Competition organizes the workplace by paying the largest rewards to the workers with the best performance records. Others, therefore, are viewed as rivals. The blending is difficult precisely because every member of the team must strike a personal balance in the perception of others on the team as partners and as rivals such that the whole may become greater than it otherwise would be through a team-inspired enrichment of the contributions made by the various individual team members. To illustrate, the dynamics of an orchestra in concert may inspire or drive an individual member to a performance level beyond what might be achieved by that individual performing alone. Any failure in this regard means that the whole may become less than that through a team-induced impoverishment of individual contributions.[8]

Teamwork, for sure, enhances self-expression by enhancing one's endowment (mainly through one-on-one and group on-the-job training). It cannot be otherwise because in the first instance teamwork depends on individuals contributing their individual skills and talents and, as stated previously, the very utilization of the endowment makes it self-reproducing.

Teams may be small and simple or large and complex. Two tradesmen carrying a length of pipe on a construction project and two truckers driving their 18-wheelers in tandem are examples of the first type. A large group of senior managers and technical specialists working on a start-up project such as a new manufacturing facility and a surgical team undertaking a heart-lung transplant are examples of the second type.

Whether large or small, complex or simple, all teams have one thing in common: necessity or efficiency. That is, a team may be necessary in the sense that there is no other way to accomplish the task at hand or a team may outperform autonomous individuals on the same task. Additionally, teams may be permanent or ad hoc, entrepreneurial or managerial; completely contained within a single operating unit or encompass several units in line or in parallel; single-skilled or multiskilled; self-managed or hierarchically run. Formally, they may be called natural work groups, field service teams, problem-solving or employee-involvement groups, cross-functional support teams, start-up teams, human resources teams, task forces, and the like (see O'Dell, 38ff).

The centrality of both individual effort and teamwork in the workplace argues for a dual system of rewards to separately recognize each. In a real sense, such a system reflects and reinforces the duality in human nature: one part individual being, the other part social being. For purposes of organizing and administering the workplace, the dual-rewards system presents the same delicate assignment of balancing between the perception of others in the workplace as rivals and the perception of them as partners, that is, a weighing of competition and cooperation as foundational organizing principles. O'Dell, a consultant to the American Productivity and Quality Center, has found that reward systems have not kept pace with the reorganization of the workplace to emphasize the importance of teamwork. Her first recommendation in modifying reward systems relates directly to minimizing employee competition and to reinforcing cooperation (38, 45).

There are numerous options available to the company that seeks to reward its workers on the basis of collective effort as well as individual contribution. Gain-sharing is one method that has won some favor in the U.S. although it would be an exaggeration to describe its utilization as widespread. At General Electric's transformer plant in Shreveport, Louisiana, hourly workers receive their regular weekly pay on Friday. In addition, every Wednesday these workers receive their gain-sharing pay, which is based importantly on plantwide savings in labor time on defect-free units of production.[9]

For many firms with gain-sharing plans, the financial reward is relatively small alongside the worker's regular earnings. For a few, such as Lincoln Electric, which is a Cleveland manufacturer of small electric motors and welding equipment, gainsharing actually doubles the base pay of the typical worker (Baldwin).

Cash bonuses tied to achieving predetermined goals or milestones is another way or recognizing collective effort. In-kind bonuses is a third. Stone Container Corporation, for example, in 1988 gave a color television set to each one of its twenty-two thousand employees for "helping make Stone an industry leader" (*Bayou Kraftsman*, 10). One year later, Stone gave each employee a VCR. At Stone's paper mill located in Hodge, Louisiana, the motto is "At Hodge, the difference is teamwork." A site-visit by this writer in 1988 confirmed that the motto is more than mere public relations puffery.

In-kind bonuses may be linked to specific performance goals. At Atlas Refining in Shreveport the program provides a variety of items that individual workers may select as a bonus for achieving certain predetermined safety goals. An unusual feature of the program at Atlas is that the goals are defined in terms of the team, not the individual. The program was established to reinforce the importance of team members carefully observing the actions of others on the team, particularly in situations that are hazardous. The payoff to an oil refinery from a successful safety program is self-evident.[10]

A collective "pat-on-the-back" is another form of reward for team performance. This method is used by Martin Marietta in New Orleans where problem-solving work groups are called system refinement teams (SRTs). This facility produces the external fuel tank for the space shuttle and SRTs were established to help promote zero-defect production. Every month one SRT is identified and honored for its performance. At the end of the year, the best SRT is selected and sent as a team at company expense to witness a shuttle launch.[11]

On occasion, the reward for teamwork is rudimentary: the employees get to keep their jobs. That is, sometimes reorganizing the workplace around teamwork is a last-ditch effort by the senior management to protect the financial viability of the enterprise. In 1988, I visited an AT&T manufacturing facility in Shreveport that was physically and administratively reorganized into large teams called "focused factories" in order to protect several thousand jobs from the stiff competition that followed divestiture at AT&T in the early 1980s. Some might be inclined to dismiss this reward with a certain cynicism about the company's true motives. My strong impression is that the reorganization actually saved about three thousand jobs that otherwise probably would have been lost and that the employees there had a strong perception of one another as partners in the workplace.[12]

Belonging

Just as self-expression is the fruit of individual contribution, belonging proceeds out of teamwork. Belonging is the sense that one is an important member of the team in terms of its ability to accomplish its mission. Dempsey expresses belonging in the language of the typical worker: "[A]ny day I'm missing they scramble around to get my spot covered" (254).

Work has two central actions: thinking and doing. When a person works completely alone and isolated from all other human beings, these two actions by definition are joined. When a person works in the company of others, these two actions may become separated. Indeed, it is not at all unusual in a modern industrial society to assign the thinking to one set of persons (management) and the doing to another (labor) and, furthermore, to identify thinking as a prerogative of management.

People cannot be joined into a team if the two central actions of work divide them. Given that thought precedes action and determines it, the doers inevitably will be regarded as less important than and therefore subordinate to the thinkers. Teamwork becomes much more difficult in a work environment where the parties involved are divided into two unequal groups.

Teamwork depends on management's valuing workers sufficiently as human beings to actively involve them in the decisions as to how the work is to be done. Belonging is the fruit
of such valuing. This involvement, which affirms the workers
as more than mere instruments of work, provides them with
additional means for effectively caring for one another on a
regular basis. Thus, workmates are more likely to be caring
toward one another when management is caring toward labor.[13]

In brief, belonging proceeds from teamwork and teamwork
proceeds from caring. Individuals belong when others care
enough to involve them not just in doing the work itself but
also in thinking about how the work is to be done.[14] Further,
caring is possible only when human beings are seen mainly as
persons with material needs and not as objects or even as human
resources.

Tischner explains the connection between teamwork (which
he calls "solidarity") and caring as follows:

> Conscience is the foundation of solidarity, and the stimulus
> for its development is the cry for help from someone wounded
> by another human being. Solidarity establishes specific, inter-
> personal bonds; one person joins with another to tend to one
> who needs care. I am with you, you are with me, we are
> together—for him. We—for him. We, not to look at each other,
> but for him. Which comes first here? Is "we" first, or is "for
> him" first? The communion of solidarity differs from many
> other communions in that "for him" is first and "we" comes
> later. First is the wounded one and the cry of pain. Later,
> conscience speaks, since it is able to hear and understand this
> cry. This is all it takes for communion to spring up. (9)

Caring presupposes not just a willingness to do what is
morally right but also a willingness to discern what is right.
Calling it "moral perceptivity," Dyck defines the disposition to
discern what is right as

> the ability to vividly imagine, that is, both to feel and perceive,
> what other persons feel and need, and how they are, or would
> be, affected by our attitudes and actions. This ability, when
> operative, informs our decisions as to whether there are moral

claims upon us in a given situation, and if there are, which and how stringent. Thus, as one of the ways in which what is obligatory is revealed to us, this ability or sensitivity is an essential part of what we mean by our sense of obligation. Having a sense of obligation requires or entails having this virtue. (111)

Dyck insists that moral perceptivity is essential to caring or love of neighbor and that love of neighbor, in turn, is requisite for human community (110–13). Since community cannot exist without moral perceptivity and since the members have a duty to maintain and support their community in order to protect the good that they derive from it, moral perceptivity is an obligation under contributive justice.

Belonging is significant because there really is strength in numbers. Belonging means being more secure than one would be if one were entirely alone. Families certainly provide security, but given the centrality of labor income and that families do not control the workplace as they did prior to the industrial revolution, families cannot provide adequate security in the modern age. Teams may become workplace families that provide some assurance that the individual members are not alone in meeting their own physical needs and the needs of their dependents in a market economy. Notice in this regard that some business establishments even call themselves "family." Notice, too, that the root of "company"—a common word for a business establishment—refers to persons who break bread together (*Company*, back cover).

Our argument reduces to the following. Human beings form teams in the workplace not only to produce a good or service more efficiently but also to develop more fully as persons. Belonging is no less essential to personhood than is self-expression and physical need.

Belonging proceeds from teamwork and enhances it and teamwork, in turn, proceeds from caring, that is, from a genuine concern for the needs of the other persons who are members of the team. Caring, in turn, requires a willingness not only to do what is morally right with regard to other persons but also to discern what is right.

At rock bottom, the need of every human being to belong, which if met enhances personhood, is grounded in a special aspect of contributive justice that is called moral perceptivity. This means that belonging is not so much something that others confer. Rather, it is acquired by each individual through the willingness to feel and perceive what others feel and need and to be especially sympathetic with regard to their unmet need. Individuals are more likely to be caring toward one another when they see one another not so much as instruments of work but as ends in themselves.[15]

Self-Expression and Belonging: Special Risks and Problems

Special risks and problems attend the need for self-expression and the need for belonging and the steps taken to meet those needs. More specifically, there are special risks to *Homo socioeconomicus* from self-expression and belonging. In the following, the two aspects of the need for work as such are discussed in turn.

Self-Expression and Destruction

Whether they originate on the shop floor, in the boardroom, in the research institute, or the backyard workshop, methods of self-expression that are creative in an entrepreneurial sense are, as Schumpeter pointed out years ago, destructive in precisely the same ways. First, entrepreneurial creativity may destroy an old product or service entirely. Second, creativity by the entrepreneur may dismantle an old process of production. Third, innovation may idle certain resources previously used to produce a given good or service or render them useless. Fourth, an established producer may lose a market to an entrepreneur or have it closed off. Fifth, and last, creativity may produce considerable organizational change and even chaos.

"Creative destruction" is the term attributed to Schumpeter which describes the various risks to *Homo socioeconomicus* from self-expression that is creative in an entrepreneurial sense. The greater the emphasis placed on individual self-expression in the workplace, the greater the destructive potential, that is, the greater the threat to the economic security of workers, their families, and their companies.

Thus, success in meeting the need for self-expression in the workplace (but not in the home) makes the task of provisioning physical need through work more difficult. Institutional arrangements are required whereby the conflicting demands of each may be balanced. This conflict alone guarantees a significant role for government unless human beings are unwilling to accept any responsibility for the ways in which meeting their own need for self-expression or their own physical need may be harmful to other human beings.

Belonging, Conformism, Avoidance, and Discrimination

Participation is a turning in the direction of another self on the basis of personal transcendence, toward the fullness of truth of this other self. Participation confirms the self and permits the individual to unfold, to attain self-realization in interpersonal ("I-Thou") relationships and social ("We") relationships.[16] Alienation is the antithesis of participation. It means that the aggregation of all individuals, each one a unique "I," is unable to develop into a genuine "We." Alienation annihilates all values by which one human being knows another as a second "I." Community is disfigured, and in place of "neighbor" there is only "other," "stranger," or in the extreme "enemy."

Solidarity is a readiness on the part of the individual to complete by one's act that which others complete jointly. Solidarity is the basic expression of participation whereby a human being finds fulfillment by adding to the fulfillment of others.[17] Opposition, an attitude that is related to solidarity, is a legitimate form of participation because opposition means that the individual is searching for a definition of the common good that permits the individual to participate in the community more fully and more effectively.

Conformism replaces real participation with the illusion of participation. Conformism replaces unity, which derives from authentic participation, with uniformity. In that sense, conformism is an affect by which the individual acquiesces to the demands of the community in order to avoid any unpleasant consequences. In conformism the human self agrees that the community takes the self away from one and, at the same time, takes oneself away from the community. The "lackey" is the prototypical specialist in conformism. Just as conformism avoids opposition, avoidance skirts conformism. Avoidance is a retreat in that it seeks no engagement. It is an absence of participation and therefore an absence of community. Avoidance is a way of not giving expression to solidarity or opposition. Avoidance may be justified when participation in the community is impossible, that is, when the community lacks a common good. Under those circumstances, avoidance is an exit from the community. The "loner" is the prototypical specialist in avoidance.

Wojtyla explains how conformism and avoidance deplete human vitality.

> In conformism and avoidance, the human being is convinced *that the community is taking away his self, and that is why he attempts to take his self away from the community.* In the case of conformity, he does it by maintaining the appearances; in the attitude of avoidance, he seems not to care about appearances. In both instances, something very vital is taken out of the human being. It is that dynamic quality of the self that enables it to perform acts and authentically fulfills the self through these acts in the community of being and acting "jointly with others." (52; emphasis in the original)

Conformism is sociality in acquiescence. Avoidance is individuality in retreat. By depleting the vitality of the worker, both are ways by which *Homo socioeconomicus* may fall short of achieving full potential as a person.

Belonging inevitably raises the issue of discrimination, that is, the exclusion of a specific person or persons from a given group on the basis of such characteristics as gender, national origin, race, age, or religion. Exclusion and the possibility of discrimination are inevitable because in order to act the group must establish boundaries (see note 17).

In a market economy, the boundaries are determined importantly by the nature of competition. Persons are hired (included) or released (excluded) because the very survival of the firm requires it to utilize only those resources that can be employed profitably.

A central requirement for dealing successfully with discrimination is the elimination of arbitrariness in the process of inclusion/exclusion. To root out any arbitrariness, persons with superior responsibilities in a business enterprise are duty-bound to share the benefits and the burdens of the group in approximately equal fashion.

Thus superiors have a duty to treat women no differently than men and blacks as they would whites, unless there is compelling justification for preferential treatment as with, for example, the handicapped as regards to parking spaces and access to a building. Belonging leads to discrimination when men and women in positions of responsibility in the workplace do not meet their obligations under distributive justice.

Concluding Comments

Figure 5.1 summarizes our comments on individual contribution and self-expression, on teamwork and belonging. This summary representation of the arguments presented in this essay may lead one to the unfortunate conclusion that analytically differentiating between individual being and social being means that person is two rather than one.

In addition, the two may be seen as inevitably engaged in a lifelong zero-sum struggle. That is, by nature a person develops more fully along one dimension of the dual nature only at the expense of the other dimension. If that were so, human beings invariably would be schizophrenic.

Person is one, not two, because the individual being and the social being that are the constituent parts are so intertwined that it is virtually impossible to separate them. The employer does not hire the social being or the individual being but the whole person who is at once one-of-a-kind and alike, independent and dependent, self-determining and conditioned by the environment, perfectible and subject to imperfection. The person who is whole is fully individual and fully social. Further, the whole person is a material being with two principal needs: physical need and the need for work as such.

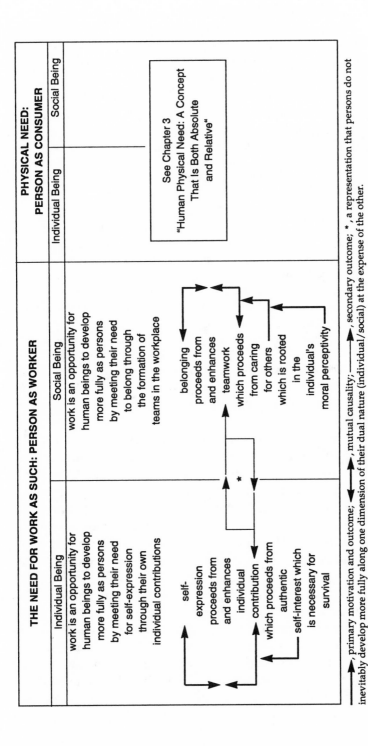

THE NEED FOR WORK AS SUCH: PERSON AS WORKER		PHYSICAL NEED: PERSON AS CONSUMER	
Individual Being	Social Being	Individual Being	Social Being
work is an opportunity for human beings to develop more fully as persons by meeting their need for self-expression through their own individual contributions	work is an opportunity for human beings to develop more fully as persons by meeting their need to belong through the formation of teams in the workplace	See Chapter 3 "Human Physical Need: A Concept That Is Both Absolute and Relative"	
self-expression proceeds from and enhances individual contribution which proceeds from authentic self-interest which is necessary for survival	belonging proceeds from and enhances teamwork which proceeds from caring for others which is rooted in the individual's moral perceptivity		

➤, primary motivation and outcome; ◀▶, mutual causality; ➤, secondary outcome; *, a representation that persons do not inevitably develop more fully along one dimension of their dual nature (individual/social) at the expense of the other.

Figure 5.1. Person and human material need

If families and workplace teams are at all comparable, Bradshaw suggests why human beings are not inevitably engaged in a zero-sum drama.

> One of the paradoxical aspects of functional and healthy families is that as individuation increases, togetherness grows. As people separate and move toward wholeness, real intimacy becomes possible. The poet says "The mountain to the climber is clearer from the plain." We need separation in order to have togetherness.
>
> Needy and incomplete people seek others to make them complete. They say "I love you because I need you." Individuated persons who have faced aloneness and separation knows [sic] they can make it alone. They seek a partner because they want to love, not because they need to be completed. They say, "I need you because I love you." They offer love out of generosity, rather than need. They are no longer fantasy bonded. (55)
>
> The mature relationship I like best is two people making music together. Each plays his *own* instrument and uses *his own unique skills*, but they play the same song. Each is a whole and complete. Each is independent and committed. (47; emphasis in the original)

For the employer and the workplace this means that it is virtually impossible to foresee precisely what the human being will become as the personhood of that human being unfolds in part through work. The real challenge in the workplace is to provide opportunities that will allow individuals to become all that they can be because maximizing those productive energies—which also are uniquely expansive—is at the very center of productivity and productivity is critical to meeting physical need.

For the economist and economics this means that our work begins and ends with the person. The personalist foundation means that economics most fundamentally is the study of the person from two special perspectives: *worker* and *consumer*. It is as worker that the need for work as such is represented and met and it is as consumer that physical need is articulated and fulfilled. And it is the centrality of human material need to economics that leads to an insistence that, properly understood, our discipline more accurately is called "social economics" and at the same time makes it a moral science.

Notes

1. I mean the things themselves and not the physical needs they may satisfy.

2. The twelve task responsibilities are: initiator-contributor, opinion seeker, opinion giver, coordinator, evaluator-critic, energizer, information seeker, information giver, elaborator, orienter, procedural technician, and recorder. According to Varney, these are the seven maintenance responsibilities: encourager, compromiser, follower, standard setter/ego ideal, harmonizer, gatekeeper/expediter, and group observer/commentator.

3. Withholding energy through group action in a social conflict such as a strike is evidence of the sociality of the person.

4. In the section on sociality and the need for work I argue that the amount of the good or service produced and its quality depends on teamwork as well as on individual contribution.

5. As with all economic resources that are living things, human beings are reproductive and, as with resources that are animals, human beings are subject to fatigue and are reinvigorated by means of regular periods of rest. However, human beings alone among economic resources are able to learn new skills and acquire new talents.

6. In manufacturing gold jewelry, scrap is very valuable. Stuller Settings has installed special filters in its ventilation system to capture and retrieve the tiny gold filings that are produced in its grinding, buffing, and polishing operations.

7. Three years ago I visited Bollinger Machine Shop and Shipyard, a family-owned and operated shipyard in south Louisiana that employs about 250 workers. Before the decline in oil prices and U.S. oil production in the early 1980s Bollinger produced one-of-a-kind customized "boat trucks" for use in servicing offshore oil rigs. To survive after the decline in the U.S. oil industry, Bollinger bid on and won a U.S. Coast Guard contract to manufacture several identical, high-speed boats for use in interdicting illegal drug shipments.

The work was organized around two identical, side-by-side production lines that competed with each other to see which one could deliver a finished vessel first. Each boat was built in 550 steps that were grouped into sets of related tasks and assigned to various teams in the production line. To instill cooperation up and down the line, any team that was idle because the team immediately up the line had not finished its assignment on time was sent home without pay. This harsh financial incentive for cooperation worked because of the large labor surpluses in "the oil patch."

8. This type of enrichment commonly is known as synergy and impoverishment of this sort typically is called entropy. *Synergy* and *entropy*, it appears, are words that derive from physics (Albrecht, 24–25) and are not appropriate to the personalism advocated in these pages. Enrichment and impoverishment, in contrast, are much better suited.

9. From information supplied by General Electric senior management at the Shreveport facility during a site visit in 1984.

10. From information provided by Atlas Refining officials during a site visit in 1986.

11. From information provided by officials at the Martin Marietta facility in New Orleans during a site visit in 1985.

12. This reorganization also included the adoption of just-in-time manufacturing principles, the installation of line-stop switches at every workstation, and the introduction of statistical process control.

13. Clearly, workers may be caring toward one another when labor and management are pitted against one another as adversaries. That kind of caring, however, is likely to be short-lived because to some extent everyone's capacity and willingness to be caring is depleted by the hostile labor-management relationship.

In the same way, workers initially may be caring toward one another during a protracted work stoppage or a large and long-lasting workforce reduction. Under those circumstances, however, emotional and financial stress depletes the personal resources that make caring possible and effective.

14. In a 1984 site visit to the General Electric plant in Shreveport, I asked a security guard in the reception area what it was like to work there. The guard explained that she did not work there because she was employed by a security service under contract to G.E. but that she wished that she worked for G.E. because "they care about their workers." This plant was the first recipient of the U.S. Senate Productivity Award, State of Louisiana, for its gain-sharing program.

15. For many, a belief in the common origin of all human beings is a powerful reason for caring for others. Further discussion along these lines, however, leads out of the secular domain and into the sacred, which previously was excluded from the scope of this chapter.

16. Wojtyla's "The Individual and the Common Good: Toward a Theory of Participation," in *Toward a Philosophy of Praxis* is very instructive on participation, conformism, avoidance, and discrimination.

17. Smith and Berg identify this phenomenon—the paradox of individuality—as one of the four paradoxes of belonging. In their own words, "the paradox is that the group gains solidarity as individuality is legitimated, and individuality is established when the primacy of the group is affirmed." They refer to the other three paradoxes as identity, involvement, and boundaries. The paradox of identity conceives of the individual as deriving meaning from belonging to the group which at the same time derives meaning from its individual members. The paradox of involvement is that in order to develop the detachment needed for self-reflection an involvement is demanded that makes detachment seem impossible. The paradox of boundaries is that boundaries make it possible for a group to act and at the same time limit what the group can do (89–108).

References

Albrecht, Karl, with Steven Albrecht. *The Creative Corporation.* Homewood: Dow Jones–Irwin, 1987.

Baldwin, William. "This Is the Answer." *Forbes* 130, no. 1 (1982): 50–52.

Bradshaw, John. *Bradshaw on the Family.* Deerfield Beach: Health Communications, 1988.

Company: A Magazine of the American Jesuits (September 1983).

Crosby, Andrew. *Creativity and Performance in Industrial Organization.* London: Tavistock Publications, 1972.

Dempsey, Bernard W., S.J. *The Functional Economy: The Bases of Economic Organization.* Englewood Cliffs: Prentice-Hall, 1958.

Dyck, Arthur J. *On Human Care: An Introduction to Ethics.* Nashville: Abingdon, 1977.

Gross, Neil. "A Wave of Ideas, Drop by Drop." *Business Week,* special 1989 bonus issue on innovation in America (no date): 22–30.

Hamermesh, Daniel S. "Shirking or Productive Schmoozing: Wages and the Allocation of Time at Work." *Industrial and Labor Relations Review* 43, no. 3, special issue (February 1990): 121–S—133–S.

Jaques, Elliott. *Creativity and Work.* Madison: International Universities Press, 1990.

John Paul II. *On Human Work.* Boston: St. Paul Editions, no date (see Wojtyla below for a work originally published prior to his election as Pope John Paul II).

Lindeman, Eduard C. *Social Discovery: An Approach to the Study of Functional Groups.* New York: Republic Publishing Company, 1924.

142 / Edward J. O'Boyle

O'Dell, Carla. "Team Play, Team Pay—New Ways of Keeping Score."
    Across The Board 26, no. 11 (1989): 38–45.
Port, Otis. "Back to Basics." *Business Week*, special 1989 bonus issue
    on innovation in America (no date): 14–18.
Schumacher, E. F. *Good Work*. New York: Harper and Row, Publishers,
    1979.
Schumpeter, Joseph A. *Capitalism, Socialism, and Democracy*. New York:
    Harper and Brothers Publishers, 1950.
Smith, Kenwyn K., and David N. Berg. *Paradoxes of Group Life: Under-
    standing Conflict, Paralysis, and Movement in Group Dynamics*. San
    Francisco: Jossey-Bass Publishers, 1987.
Stone Container Corporation. *Bayou Kraftsman* (2d qtr. 1988).
Tischner, Jozef. *The Spirit of Solidarity*. Translated by Marek B. Zaleski
    and Benjamin Fiore, S. J. San Francisco: Harper & Row, Publishers,
    1984.
United States General Accounting Office. *Management Practices: U.S.
    Companies Improve Performance Through Quality Efforts*. Washington,
    1991.
Varney, Glenn H. *Building Productive Teams: An Action Guide and Re-
    source Book*. San Francisco: Jossey-Bass Publishers, 1989.
Wojtyla, Karol. "The Individual and the Common Good: Toward a
    Theory of Participation." In *Toward a Philosophy of Praxis*, edited
    by Alfred Bloch and George T. Czuczka, 24–52. New York: The
    Crossroad Publishing Company, 1981.

6

Social Management
and the Self-Managed Firm

Severyn T. Bruyn

The concept of social management refers to a corporate administration oriented to people as well as to profits. Technically speaking, a corporation must always be oriented to people in order to
survive, but over time we have seen American business paying
increasing attention to employees as part of corporate policy.
This social orientation has thus become a management goal
along with the economic goal of the corporation.

The long-range trend in the organization of corporations
has been from systems of command governance to systems of
mutual governance that optimize each worker's capacity for
self-management. In this historic sense, social management has
come to mean a system of work which aims to increase the
satisfaction and well being of employees, develop their personal
resources, and cultivate self-management skills, while at the
same time increasing productivity and profits. It means that
management has found it important to integrate social and economic goals in order to become more competitive in the marketplace.

Most recently, social management has come to signify a
trend toward increasing employee participation in managing
work teams and overseeing work systems. The process of increasing employee participation began as far back as the 1920s,

when employers found it profitable to put suggestion boxes on the factory floor so that workers could contribute ideas on improving production. It continued with the establishment of labor-management committees that jointly determined rules on production and safety in the use of machines and advanced further with Scanlon Plans and other profit-sharing plans instituted by management with labor participation. Today it includes quality circles, quality of worklife projects, autonomous work groups, labor-management committees, and so on. Social management has been a process of experimenting with increasing degrees of worker participation in running the operations in the firm, including recent experiments with labor representatives on boards of directors.

A theory of self-development is implied in social management, based on the premise that the self is an entity constructed in a social context, an idea that began with the philosopher Georg Wilhelm Friedrich Hegel in the nineteenth century and was later developed by the sociologist George Herbert Mead and others in the twentieth century. The self of each person requires participation with others in order to grow and expand as a part of the reduction of alienation. Each person develops himself or herself through role-taking, by participating with wider and wider sets of groups, and thus understanding others more as a "generalized other," as a part of his or her own self. American management has been finding that when people participate with others in higher levels of authority, they often increase not only their own personal resources but the effectiveness of the firm through their understanding of the larger organizational system of which they are a part.

European and Scandinavian nations have taken big steps in this direction of social (self) management and found the practice quite resourceful. In West German corporations, for example, labor is not only involved in worker councils at middle levels of management, but also has coequal participation (called codetermination) with management on the board of directors. The German model has been so successful that the European Economic Community has been discussing a plan recommending it as a model for development by all member nations.

Each European nation, however, has special problems in the

implementation of labor participation and none can realistically serve as a simple model to be replicated by other nations. According to critics, one of the macro problems they all exhibit is state "corporatism," which means that big organizations—labor, capital, and government—rule the nation. Both big unions and big business are now seen as too powerful, collaborating at the top, and the government is seen as too much involved in mandating the changes. For many scholars of self-management, there is still much to be done beyond the European scene to decentralize and de-statify economic life.[1]

By contrast, American corporations have been emphasizing experiments in the workplace and in middle management in ways that are conducive to greater degrees of employee control over work. The last two decades have been marked by a concern for the quality of worklife, including job rotation, job enrichment, and job enlargement, and today a variety of innovations are occurring around the concept of work time (Sirianni, 23).[2]

Another basic trend in labor development in the United States is the recent growth in employee-owned corporations, a development which has been promoted through Employee Stock Ownership Plan (ESOP)[3] legislation. As we shall see, worker ownership in this case does not necessarily mean that a majority of workers own their firms. Yet like the trend to worker participation, the trend toward employee ownership shows strong signs of continuing.[4]

This double trend toward increased levels of worker participation and ownership is so important to the future of the American economy that we will now take time to examine the empirical data concerned with how well those trends have been developing in the last few decades. The promotion of self management may offer a way for the business society to evolve a new economy that is both decentralized and humanized.

Growth of Self-Managed Firms

Over ten thousand firms with more than eleven million workers have employee-ownership plans today, a trend simulated largely by federal Employee Stock Ownership Plan (ESOP) legislation. Most of these workers are employed by companies with less than 15 percent worker ownership, but about 1 million are employed by companies that are 15 to 50 percent worker-owned, while about one thousand firms, with a total of about a half-million employees, have 51 to 100 percent ownership.

Employee ownership characterizes companies like Science Applications (six thousand employees) and W. L. Gore Associates (three thousand employees) and significant portions of employees in such key industries as airlines and trucking. Employees are majority owners in many large companies, such as Davey Tree (two thousand six hundred employees), Life-touch Studies (four thousand), and Parsons Engineering (seven thousand). Employees also own 100 percent of the stock in many large companies, such as Avondale Industries (ten thousand employees), Weirton Steel (seven thousand), Pamida (five thousand), and OTASCO (three thousand) (Blasi & others, viii, 1). But the trend toward employee ownership is only half the corporate self-management story.

The trend toward employee participation in management has increased in tandem with that toward employee ownership. In 1982, in one of the first studies of U.S. corporate experiments with human resource programs, the U.S. Stock Exchange estimated that about 14 percent of the forty-nine thousand companies studied had such programs as job enlargement and rotation, employee participation in management training, labor-management committees, autonomous groups, and quality circles, while 70 percent of the companies with over five hundred employees were seeking to involve workers in new forms of decision making. Significantly, only 3 percent of the managers interviewed believed that participative management was only a passing fashion.[5]

The two trends are taking place because they are productive and profitable, and public opinion research suggests that they will continue in the future. A U.S. Chamber of Commerce poll revealed that 84 percent of the workforce wants greater participation in management decisions, and a Peter Hart Associates poll showed that 66 percent of the workforce would prefer to work in an employee-owned firm.

It seems likely that employee ownership and management will merge and become an integral part of corporate life in the next few decades, but the process is not without pitfalls. While many observers suggest that the two trends of worker participation in management and worker ownership of the firm have positive long-term advantages—for example, they contribute to a more productive economy, augur a significant advance in the capacity of corporations to become fully self-managed, increase the level of enterprise autonomy, and foster the economy's becoming a self-regulating system—other observers see these two trends as mere fads of the time, which actually complicate the problems of free enterprise. How can we evaluate these trends? Is there need for facilitative legislation in their regard? What do studies suggest about the future?

Let us now examine studies on the performance of firms which are heading in the direction of becoming fully self-managed. Some scholars describe such firms, which are approaching a majority of employees involved in management and ownership, as "relatively self-managed."[6]

Performance of Self-Managed Firms

Although relatively self-managed firms seem on the whole to contribute to both social and economic development, they still have problems to solve in becoming the most effective enterprises for the future. They contribute toward social development insofar as they cultivate greater human resources and add to the quality of life in the firm and to the well being of local communities, and they contribute to economic development by their ability to increase the level of efficiency and lower the costs of enterprise management. But the manner in which they develop is critical to their success. They require a favorable legal environment and management consultation in order to avoid the pitfalls that some have faced in the last decade.

We now look at ten potential benefits deriving from the unique nature of self-managed firms. In each case we present the problems that may arise and possible methods for solving these problems.

Preventing Plant Closings

There are many possible reasons for shutdowns. Top executives may want to move a firm to where labor is not organized or move overseas to save labor costs. They may close a plant because a subsidiary—purchased as part of a conglomerate deal—is found to be incompatible with the parent organization, or they may decide that it is more profitable to cease operations as a tax write-off. A firm can shut its doors at the choice of its owner. But especially when earnings do not match the expectations of top executives, shutdowns become a way to increase profits. In other words, even in highly profitable firms major layoffs are deemed necessary simply to increase the level of profits.

Such was the case with the Library Bureau, a furniture factory in Herkimer, New York. Taken over by Sperry Rand in 1955, in the succeeding two decades it yielded a profit in every year but one. In 1976 Sperry Rand nevertheless decided to close the Library Bureau down, declare a tax loss, and sell its valuable machinery, because although the plant was making money at the time it was not up to the standard of 22 percent on invested capital that was expected by Sperry Rand executives. Furthermore, it had no organic connection to the main lines of Sperry Rand's activity in electronics and machines. The executives looked upon it as a liability which only complicated smooth management operations, and it was more trouble than it was worth to the parent corporation. A shutdown was averted by alert employees who, initially against the wishes of management, collected money among themselves and with the help of the community purchased the firm at the last minute.

A firm's shutdown for whatever reason is always harmful in some measure and can sometimes devastate a community. The Library Bureau case (and others like it) is significant because it kept itself and a network of local institutions and small businesses from going under or from being detrimentally affected, and it prevented a drain on the public coffers for welfare and unemployment compensation (Whyte, 20ff).

Whatever the reason for a business shutdown—cheaper labor elsewhere or to take a tax write-off—executives know that the government will assume responsibility for welfare payments to the newly unemployed. The costs of such unnecessary shutdowns have been significant when measured not only by government welfare payments but also in the struggle required by local communities to find additional resources to cope with the deterioration and problems that inevitably crop up when there are not enough jobs to go around.

Although it is difficult to measure the extent of plant closings and relocations, they commonly are recognized to be destructive of community life. Detroit used to determine the number of plant shutdowns by asking Detroit Edison how many factory electricity cutoffs had occurred in a given year! A study by Wayne State University reported 278 plant shutdowns in Detroit between 1970 and 1976; the city staggered under the subsequent problems of family instability, crime, and drugs. The Ohio Bureau of Economic and Community Development measures plant closures by equating them with the number of companies that stop filing franchise tax forms. An acceleration of shutdowns so measured in 1981–82 appeared to push state job-loss figures close to seventy thousand.

Buyouts by employees are therefore an important method for saving jobs. According to a Senate Select Committee on Small Business in 1979, no employee buyout had failed during the 1970s, and the total number of jobs preserved in the decade through such buyouts was estimated to be between fifty thousand and one hundred thousand, a considerable plus in terms of job preservation.

Because of the positive experiences with employee buyouts some analysts have suggested that government could provide a better environment for them; buyouts could be facilitated as a protection against plant closures, especially those that threaten vulnerable localities. It has also been suggested that firms whose employees have a greater say in management decisions, for example, ESOPs with pass-through voting rights, have special value in helping to stabilize the local economy. Encouraging the development of self-managed firms, therefore, should reduce the likelihood of shutdowns that carry so dear a social price.

Some recent worker buyouts have failed, seemingly for two reasons: (1) lack of careful feasibility studies to determine the capacity of a firm to compete; and (2) lack of knowledge among employees about how to organize a self-managed company so that it cannot be bought by outsiders after it becomes successful. An example of the first reason for failure was the case of

Rath Meatpacking in Waterloo, Iowa. Rath, which had not mod-
ernized its equipment under its conventional management, sus-
tained a loss of $14.6 million in 1972 and was consistently in
the red from 1975 through 1978. In 1979 the workers decided
to provide the equity capital to keep it afloat and were able to
buy the plant in June 1980. Although the union and workers
cooperated energetically to bring the organization around, the
effort failed; the meat packing market is extremely competitive,
and Rath required not only top management skills but modern
technology to survive. The lesson: industry overcapacity and
turbulent market conditions can overcome even a highly motivated and skillful attempt to save a company (Meek &
Woodworth).

An example of the second reason for failure was the case
of the Vermont Asbestos Group. Its original owner, General
Aniline and Film (GAF), announced it would close the Vermont
mine because it was worried about the remaining reserves and
the need to install antipollution equipment required by the Environmental Protection Agency—a $1.25 million outlay. Within
ten days, the president of Local 388 of the Cement, Lime and
Gypsum Workers Union called a meeting to discuss a buyout.
The final financial package included a mix of state and federal
guarantees, a GAF mortgage, and two thousand shares priced
at $50 per share, and in 1975 the workers took possession. They
experienced quick financial success but were soon quarreling
over the right of board representation and access to information
from the board. The new firm had been organized as a conventional business with shareholder power based on the amount
of money that managers and workers had invested at the time
of purchase rather than on the principle of one person, one
vote; since these amounts differed for each individual, voting
rights were also unequally distributed. A wealthy local contrac-
tor subsequently bought out the company because some disaf-
fected employees were willing to sell him their shares. In this
case, the initial employee buyout could be described as an economic success but a social failure, since the employees succeeded
in averting a shutdown but did not have adequate instruction
on how to organize and operate a self-managed firm, and consequently ended up back where they started from.

These problems can be resolved through providing employees with professional consultant assistance in making feasibility studies and in organizing a self-managed company that can operate in both their short-and long-range interests.

Maintaining Local Stability

Some absentee corporations tend to exploit the financial resources of the community and to draw capital away from it. Self-managed firms, however, can stop this outflow and become a more positive force for community development.

Serious capital outflow problems are created through plant closings because each plant closure has a ripple effect. A study in Youngstown, Ohio, showed that the loss of five thousand jobs with the shutdown of the local steel and tube company actually meant the loss of an additional 11,199 jobs connected to the steel business. Furthermore, the whole process began with a parent company that did not update its technology and took the loss of its subsidiary as a tax write-off (Stillman, 140).

But the problem of capital outflow goes beyond shutdowns. Absentee-owned companies draw income excessively away from a community and then distribute it elsewhere, causing a loss of circulating capital at the local level. Floyd Agostinelli has demonstrated how the export of profits from local chain enterprises in poor city neighborhoods (e.g., McDonald's) results in a major loss of investment capital to the locality; he argues that the pattern is unfair, and that localities with a high incidence of absentee ownership thereby tend to deteriorate. The diminishment of financial autonomy undermines cohesion, which permits social ills to proliferate (Agostinelli, Rice).

The presence of a significant number of relatively self-managed companies means that the local government has dependable tax revenues and that other enterprises can gain from the intralocal free flow of capital. Also, as we have suggested above, companies with high degrees of employee ownership and participation in management are less likely to shut down arbitrarily (or run away to another country or terminate a subsidiary for a tax write-off) and are more likely to maintain a continuing presence in the community, to keep capital circulating there.

In sum, there is reason to believe that higher levels of local employee ownership and control preserve the stability of community life. Policies supporting the growth of self-managed firms could have enormously favorable cost-benefit ratios for the state, not the least element of which is the possibility of reducing taxes.

Although absentee ownership has amply manifested its negative aspects, an overemphasis on employee ownership and participation in management also has its drawbacks; an overemphasis on local control could be regressive and lead to provincialism. The task is to find the right balance between outside and inside controls over the local economy. Many factors are important to consider in developing self-managed firms so that they are able to maintain a healthy commerce with the outside world, for example, recognizing that self-managed companies can be large (nationwide) and yet decentralized in a manner that yields autonomous local controls; making contacts through trade associations; utilizing government resources for overseas marketing and production opportunities; and developing arrangements (e.g., community land trusts) that permit multinational corporations to operate locally in such a way as to protect local interests.[7]

Enhancing Productivity

Scientific data show high levels of efficiency and productivity among companies with increased employee participation in management or increased employee ownership. Studies on these two trends are extensive but here we reference only a few done by well-known researchers.

Increasing levels of worker participation in management have greatly profited hundreds and probably thousands of companies in the United States. For example, job-enrichment and participatory-management experiments at Harwood Manufacturing Company, involving one thousand employees, raised productivity by 25 percent. At the Monsanto Corporation, 150 machine operators and maintenance personnel began a participatory experiment that led to a 75 percent increase in productivity. A study of nine companies representing Scanlon Plans averaged 23.1 percent higher productivity than theretofore. There is no question about the overall value of such ventures for companies, even though some have failed and others are controversial. The fact is that companies that have been sincerely interested in collaborating with workers and unions to take these steps on an experimental basis have greatly benefited in social and economic terms.[8]

Studies also show a notable improvement in productivity of companies with high degrees of worker participation, compared with conventional companies. Research by Samuel Bowles and his colleagues demonstrates most persuasively at the national level that a causal relationship exists between the structure of labor and management and productivity: an adversarial structure is associated with low productivity, and worker participation at high levels of management correlates with greater productivity. Hence, they argue that a new social contract is needed to include labor in the governance of corporations (Bowles). Other scholars have also stressed the causal connection. Robert Reich (43), for one, asserts that increasing labor participation in corporate governance is an important route to higher productivity; this same issue has figured in many studies on Japanese management.[9]

Employee ownership also correlates with increasing productivity. One of the first studies to demonstrate a positive correlation was conducted by Michael Conte and Arnold Tannenbaum (3) of the Survey Research Center at the University of Michigan. Studying ninety-eight employee-owned companies heavily biased toward worker buyouts and non-ESOP firms, these economists found them 50 percent more profitable than the other companies in their industries. Further, *the more of the company the employees owned, the higher the ratio of productivity*.

A study by Thomas Marsh and Dale McAllister (612–16), using a list of fourteen hundred firms compiled by the U.S. Department of Labor, revealed that ESOP firms were more productive than non-ESOP firms. The ESOP managers overwhelmingly believed that the plan improved company performance. The most significant finding was that the ESOP companies had an average annual productivity growth rate of +.78 percent, compared to a rate of −.74 percent for comparable conventional firms.

The ESOP studies convinced Corey Rosen that employee ownership not only correlates with higher productivity, but also provides many more advantages for a company than worker participation alone. For example, he suggests that employee ownership can attract and keep high-quality, experienced employees in ways that short-term worker participation experiments cannot, an advantage of considerable importance to some industries. He points out that worker ownership—discussed as part of a company plan—can provide an essential synergy without which other factors would not work in leading to higher motivation and productivity. Worker ownership keeps motivating workers; worker participation motivates them for only the life span of the experiment. Moreover, a company's success may depend on its introducing new technologies (or a willingness to forego short-run earnings for long-run investment), which nonowning workers may fight against, but which employee owners can embrace because they see a longer term payoff for themselves.

Various other studies have demonstrated that both employee ownership and participation in management are associated on the whole with an increase in productivity.[10] In sum, the evidence is persuasive.

The problem with evaluating productivity rests in part on accuracy of measurement in research and in part on its singular value in corporate management. First, difficulties exist in measuring productivity in ESOP firms because the causal links between ownership and productivity are not made fully clear. Some studies suggest the link between ownership and the motivation of employees is enhanced by a sense of ownership but show only a statistical correlation with no real proof of a causal relationship. Also, measuring productivity in a technical sense is more problematical for firms engaged in service activities, such as restaurants, real estate, insurance, recreation, and education, although such firms are coming to constitute over 50 percent of the enterprise economy. Still, failure to show direct causation between ownership and productivity does not invalidate their correlation.

Second, productivity has a fascination for economists and business leaders because of its relation to the bottom line—that is, profits. This emphasis, as opposed to other values, such as free speech for employees, self-direction on the job, personal development, social justice, has been questioned extensively by liberal scholars, some of whom conclude that while the accent on productivity as the basis for judging the value of corporate life may be part of the advantages of a business system, it is also a part of the problem. The traditional focus on productivity should be assessed as only part of the larger value scheme of the corporation.

Reducing Absenteeism

In 1971 when General Motors headquarters announced its Tarrytown plant was about to be shut down, the plant manager approached union leaders to work with him to keep it open. Initial skepticism gave way to joint planning, resulting in a complete turnaround in operations: absenteeism dropped from over 7 percent to between 2 and 3 percent and by late 1978, there were only thirty-two outstanding grievances, down from two thousand. The key to the change was a plan that accented new values: decentralized responsibility, authority, decision making, and accountability (Simmons & Mares, 65).

Similar benefits of self-management are evident in the celebrated studies of Japanese firms, which continue to challenge American management today. One of the explanations offered for lower absenteeism and labor turnover and better product is that *higher levels of self-management within the Japanese workforce develop a sense of purpose, belonging, motivation, and meaningfulness in work.*[11]

The development of a harmonious workforce is sometimes resisted by union leaders who believe that the whole emphasis on "building a corporate family" and getting workers to "identify with the company" diminishes worker identity with the union. The effort to establish good "human relations" within a firm is seen by such leaders as a subtle method to maximize profits and destroy union power, and there have been instances when union solidarity has declined and unions have been destroyed (Parker).[12]

Business and labor leaders have suggested that this situation could be ameliorated with the establishment of improved resources for consultation (respecting both sides) on development of self-managed firms; establishment of an informational center to gather facts on how both labor and management can benefit in the long run under the right conditions; and creation on the part of business and labor leaders of a long-range plan of cooperative development in the construction of self-managed companies. In addition, the government might consider lending its agencies that are engaged in arbitration and conciliation to this process.

Curtailing Pilferage

Prior to a change to employee ownership at the Saratoga Knitting Mill, pilferage was a major problem serious enough to require a guard service. Following purchase of the plant by the employees the service was terminated, and the incidence of pilferage has remained at zero. Other cost savings were also observed, for example, the reduction of fabric loss. Under conglomerate ownership, apart from pilferage, fabric had been lost predictably through trimming and damage; 1 percent of the total manufacturing cost was regularly budgeted to cover the loss. During the first year of employee ownership, an amount equal to only .25 percent of net sales was attributed to loss of fabric.

Still other types of savings were documented. In the textile industry, an average of 20 percent of batches have to be re-dyed because the color is incorrect or inconsistent. Earlier Saratoga management allowed for this with a budget allocation of 3 percent of manufacturing costs; after the employee takeover, the re-dye costs for the first year amounted to only .25 percent of sales. In the words of one foreman, "Now that they own the plant, they take care of getting the colors closer" (Russell, chapter 4).

Business leaders in the United States have been seeking to stop pilferage through legislation that would give their top managers the right to investigate employees' lockers and to institute criminal charges against employees suspected of thievery. Pilferage is enormous, but the evidence suggests that there is a better alternative to taking away employees' privacy: providing incentives for the development of self-managed enterprises.

Although elimination of pilferage and stimulation of employee interest in quality control through employee ownership can be observed in individual cases of self-managed companies, no definitive conclusions can be drawn as to a linkage because there has not yet been a carefully conducted relevant survey. It is possible, of course, that pilferage could become a problem in a large worker-owned and -managed corporation in which workers do not identify with the firm, especially if employees did not know that they would personally be hurt thereby. For this reason, self-management consultants emphasize the importance of an employee plan for setting aside a portion of the profits for the workers themselves. When employees know collectively about the desirability of an efficient and honestly managed plant, corporate norms are established and internal surveillance is more easily accomplished.

It is well known that employees in newly formed self-managed firms have a flush of excitement about their new status, behaving for a period of time with extra care toward one another and with extraordinary motivation. In a later phase, they come face-to-face with everyday reality and the old habit patterns return. But based on observations spanning many decades (e.g., of the plywood cooperatives and the Mondragon system mentioned below), consultants suggest that positive values are maintained, concluding that even with the known fall from initial grace, employee concern for honesty and efficiency holds over time. In any event, more studies would allow us to estimate more accurately the long-range impact of ownership on inside pilferage and quality control.

It should be noted that conclusions about employee honesty and the special care given to the quality of products and services are drawn from observations of only fully self-managed firms. It is likely that big firms with small proportions of employee ownership or with short-term Quality of Working Life (QWL) projects could not manage these matters.

Contributing to Personal Growth

The experience of democratic participation in the workplace can positively alter people's attitudes and values as well as improve the quality of their work, and some researchers maintain that it can even make a positive change in self-identities. Although this is not universally true, there is a structural tendency for self-managed firms to cultivate a sense of personal autonomy and a broader set of human values that are frequently absent in other firms.

Raymond Russell noticed this tendency when he studied the worker-owned and -managed trash collection firms in San Francisco, reporting on the high level of teamwork among the workers. Interviews substantiated that the cooperation was based on a sense of mutuality in ownership and common responsibilities in management that were not present in workers in conventional firms. For example, partners in self-managed firms were more likely than other respondents to agree with the statement "In my company (or department), if each crew doesn't do their best, we all suffer." They were more likely to say they make an "extra effort" and to describe their relations with co-workers and customers as close and cooperative (chapter 4).

Other studies show that human values are cultivated in a self-managed workplace. In one such study Melinda Schlesinger and Pauline Bart looked at an employee-owned and -managed health company and found that the sense of autonomy and competence of employees increased along with their sense of social bonding (Schlesinger & Bart, 153).

Researchers suggest that the symbols of work often change in self-managed companies, leading to or reflecting changes in attitudes of managerial dominance. For example, at Consumers United Group, an employee-owned and -managed insurance company, the president put his desk in the middle of all the other desks; he said he had no need for special perquisites. The president of W. L. Gore Associates insists that there are no "employees," only "associates," and refuses to give out job titles. The new experiments with employee involvement seem to provide an environment in which such changes can emerge spontaneously; they add human dimensions to an enterprise.

The new experiments in worker ownership often add administrative structures that provide a greater degree of self-confidence and personal expression. At the employee-owned Frost Company, a Michigan manufacturer, every employee was put on salary, replacing the wage structure. At Quad/Graphics, management leaves the plant one day a year to let employees run it, symbolizing their responsibility as owners. The Herman Miller Company's annual report features pictures of all the employee owners. At American Trust of Hawaii, a special employee ownership day was established to celebrate the employee owners. Many companies symbolize worker ownership by abolishing special parking places, executive lunchrooms, and other pleasant but often unnecessary management perquisites (*Employee Ownership Report*, 2).

At fully self-managed firms these new structures go further to guarantee constitutional principles, usually attributed to a democratic government, such as free speech and free assembly, sometimes including tribunals in which all employees in the corporate work system are justly represented on a panel to hear cases of grievance. At the John Lewis Partnership in London, an employee-owned and -managed firm of twenty-four thousand, the company newspapers have policies whereby any employee can question management anonymously, and specific managers must promptly answer them. These John Lewis employees believe that they can be whistle-blowers without fear of reprisal; free speech and free assembly are considered part of the governing principles of the company.[13]

There is reason to believe that an employee's experience in a firm that encourages democratic participation in the workplace can lead to a greater degree of political efficacy and community responsibility. Carole Pateman (105), a well-known scholar of worker self-management, has argued that we "learn to participate by participating" and "feelings of political efficacy are more likely to be developed in a participatory environment." Max Elden offers empirical support for her position that participation increases a sense of political efficacy.

Although the change in corporate style seems to offer greater opportunities for personal development, it can also have its drawbacks. Some worker-owned companies offer mixed messages to employees and create a dissonance between the new structure and management conduct. For example, managers may tell employees they are owners and talk about common benefits, but established special perquisites stay in place, or only executives receive special bonuses. Mismatch between talk and reality can result in unhappy returns.

The dramatic change in style of work accomplished by top executives like those at Gibbons and Gore is not simply a natural outcome of an altered structure of work and ownership but also a function of personality and leadership style. A departure from traditional roles and relationships can sometimes have untoward results or be detrimental to human relations in a firm. The process of organizational development is actually very complex, with many varied leadership styles emerging, and the transition to a more fully self-managed firm usually requires careful joint planning and self-study among employees.

The critical point here is that a company in transition is living simultaneously in two competing worlds, and there can be varied negative outcomes. Employees can become overzealous in demanding rights or management can refuse to recognize the momentousness of the change. Managers must fashion new relationships to workers, who in some cases can remove them from office. The new relationships are best supported by an educational program in self-management.

In certain aspects, Edward Greenberg's study of the workers in the plywood cooperatives of the Pacific Northwest region of the United States showed very little differences in their attitudes from those of workers in conventional plywood plants. There was the common interest in job security and financial gain, and the common experience of stultifying work routines. "The rhythm of the machinery process imposes a kind of sameness to the actual work found in both kinds (self-managed and conventional) of plants." Yet Greenberg found a difference in the feeling of mutuality and caring, and in concern for the operation of the whole plant (184).

One final point: differences in attitudes and values among employees in firms becoming self-managed versus conventional firms are extremely resistant to measurement. This is so partly because of the difficulty in comparing positions and employee experience. But it is also true because the structure of a firm is only one among many major influences on the life of employees, others including early childhood, current family circumstances, religion, and politics.

Limiting Strikes

Although studies are lacking on the correlation between degrees of corporate self-management and strikes in the United States and Great Britain, there are studies from the longer-term experience of Scandinavian and European countries that show a significant reduction in the number of working days lost through strikes when firms include worker councils and labor representation on boards of directors. This difference first became evident several decades ago.

In the United States the number of working days lost per one thousand employees due to strikes for the period of 1964–73 averaged 1,247; in Britain, 633; and in France, 277. But in countries in which labor shared authority at top levels of the corporation, the hours lost were significantly lower. For example, in Sweden and West Germany the hours lost averaged 43 (Foreseback, 67). The evidence continues to suggest that when labor is trained and prepared to participate significantly at top levels of governance in corporations, labor unrest can be significantly reduced. This is one reason that the European Economic Community has considered the West German model of codetermination (fifty-fifty representation of labor and management on corporate boards) as a guideline for its members.[14]

The lack of systematic studies of this issue in the United States and some variability of experience in other countries lead to caution as to conclusions regarding positive connections between self-management and reduction of labor unrest. In former Yugoslavia, for example, the number of strikes in self-managed firms was larger than in other European countries and could be a case in counterpoint.

Former Yugoslavians asserted that the significance of the numerous strikes was lessened by the fact that they lasted only a few hours, during which time management responded to worker complaints. It is also believed by some that lower levels of education, political requirements for labor participation in management, and oppressive practices of the government are special reasons for these occurrences. The causes of the strikes are most often external to the life of the corporation.[15]

A study of the outbreak of strikes in Yugoslavia also suggests that they arose largely as a protest against political policies. Nevertheless, the existence of political factors (external to the corporation itself) as a cause for strikes may be suggestive of what the future could hold for the socialist states of the former Soviet Union that are seeking to take serious steps toward worker self-management.[16]

Strikes are absent in the system of producer cooperatives in Mondragon, Spain, but it took one short strike at the two-thousand-worker firm at Ulgor to awaken workers to the fact that they had to decentralize their pattern of administration. Leaders decided that large companies needed to develop a federal structure so that the private companies could maintain autonomy with their own boards of directors, and it was agreed that autonomous companies should remain at about the size of five hundred workers.

The evidence suggests that a reduction in strikes is likely among firms taking deliberate steps toward self-management in capitalist nations. But the continuation of stable labor-management relations may require employee training on how to work together under the new arrangements and may also require the formation of administrative committees (e.g., a grievance committee or labor tribunal).

The case of a strike in one worker-owned company in the United States should be noted here to illustrate problems in labor-management relations. In 1975, the Chicago-based Amsted Industries decided to shut down its lathe-making subsidiary in South Bend, Indiana, after five straight years of losses. It seemed inevitable that its five hundred workers would be laid off, but union and management worked with federal and local officials to raise ten million dollars for an ESOP buyout. In the first year, productivity rose by 25 percent, workers received bonuses, and the company won the largest contract in its history. A study conducted by the Economic Development Administration found that almost all employees felt that morale had improved, people were more conscientious about their jobs and had a greater sense of community, and there was less waste and absenteeism. Everything seemed to be operating perfectly. The union local even contemplated decertification from the United Steelworkers. Then problems arose.

The ESOP had been touted as a substitute for a pension plan, which was dropped in the buyout because of its costs to the company, but employees began to see that employee ownership could not be an adequate substitute. The union's international body filed suit in federal court to recover the conceded funds. Union members were already skeptical of the arrangement because it blurred the distinction between themselves and management, and the loss of the pension fund worsened their attitudes. Furthermore, the ESOP did not give workers the right to influence management policy by voting for the board of directors and despite worker's desires, management refused to permit pass-through voting. Workers were now dismayed by what they believed were half-truths given to them about the ESOP arrangement, and their union leaders began demanding an unlimited cost-of-living allowance, which the company said it could not afford. In 1980 the three hundred members of the Steelworkers local struck for nine weeks.

The lesson of this case is that the introduction of self-management into a company requires at minimum an educational program which tells workers the whole story and involves them in management training commensurate with both their interests and management's making the changes needed to accommodate the new plan.

Reducing Supervisory Personnel

In the traditional firm, the foreman is expected to be a coordinator and work scheduler as well as a police officer, assuring that people work properly. But many studies have shown that middle-level managers and supervisors become less needed in relatively self-managed companies. Bowles and his colleagues have studied the phenomenon at the national level and find the associated cost reduction through worker participation in management to be highly significant.

One of the first cases in which this reduction was noted

was with the employee buyout of Saratoga Knitting Mill. Under outside ownership, the plant employed three janitors. After the buyout, employees kept their own work areas clean and neat, so only one janitor was needed.

Christopher Gunn's study of worker cooperatives emphasizes that they "use significantly fewer supervisors than their conventional counterparts; the average in the co-ops is one or two per shift of sixty to seventy people as opposed to five to seven in conventional firms . . . Owner-members are willing to take direct action to solve production problems, and they also perform some of the policing function that supervisors and foremen perform in traditional mills. There is considerable peer pressure among owner-members to perform a job well" (Gunn, 111).

Greenberg estimates that conventional plywood firms usually have four times as many supervisors as firms of the same size structured as worker cooperatives. Studies suggest that elimination of middle managers in no way reduces productivity or product quality; a number of studies have shown that the plywood cooperatives are more productive and have higher quality products than conventional firms (1981, 31–33).

The introduction of self-management techniques threatens middle management and can be disruptive. Studies of Quality of Working Life experiments first revealed this problem, as John Simmons and William Mares (232) report regarding General Motors: "Democratization of the workplace threatens first-level supervisors and middle managers more than any other group. For years they have been taught to keep their noses clean and get the production out. Their rewards were promotions, money, prestige, and perhaps a chance to 'kick ass and take names' . . . Increased employee participation strikes at the heart of middle management's professional identity—indeed their very jobs."

The experimental organization of General Foods's new plant in Topeka, Kansas, proved to be one of the most participatory self-managed (flattened hierarchies) in U.S. business, and one of the most productive and profitable, but when General Foods sought to reproduce the experiment in some of its other plants, it found great resistance from middle management. It discovered that this type of change raises a question of identity:

Does the position of supervisor become equal to all other positions? If so, supervisors feel that they are moving from a higher status to a lower status. Some consultants have asked whether the supervisors should be "kicked upstairs" or the job eliminated entirely. General Foods was never able to replicate its successful experiment in its old plants, largely due to the resistance of middle management (Ketchum).

The lesson here is that success in self-management is achieved more easily in new plants and offices than in traditional settings. Although major experiments are possible in traditional settings, their success may take more time; the process requires a careful review of changes in status among longtime employees. The positive outcome of many experiments, however, points to a largely untried way to reduce some business costs. Consultants recommend that the new practices require more public attention and support in order to achieve maximum success.

Improving Survivability

This argument has not been studied extensively, but special cases have been observed with interest. For example, the Pacific Northwest Plywood cooperatives are noted for their capacity to live through difficult times while conventional firms in the same industry failed. Begun in the 1920s, the cooperatives survived the Great Depression because they made adjustments that traditional companies could not easily make, using methods such as collective decisions on pay cuts, time off, work rotation, and the like. Indeed, their survival helped them corner the plywood market and encouraged other plywood co-ops to develop following World War II. They still show higher productivity than conventional firms in the same industry, and their capacity to survive is stronger. Greenberg (184) is one among many observers of this phenomenon. [17]

> [Interviewer: Did you ever think of getting out during bad times?] No . . . instead of giving up, you fight all the harder. I mean, if things get tough, you know, why you don't all of a sudden go to work and somebody says . . . notice up there saying plant shutting down tomorrow because we're losing money. Here if we got to that point where it's shut down or

something, they call a stockholders' meeting. They'd say, now look if we take a 50 cent an hour cut in pay, we can keep going. Let's have a vote on it. So, we'd keep working. Everybody'd vote for it. We did that once before here a few years back when we had to.

Greenberg found the general mood of employees in conventional plants very different from the self-managed firms he studied. Rather than seeing themselves as a group acting to advance their collective interests and happiness, conventional workers perceived themselves as almost powerless, being used for the advancement of others, and subject to higher-ups' decisions. By contrast, he noted that among the plywood workers a "strong sense of mutuality, caring, and cooperation seems to come strongly to the fore during crisis times, a seemingly recurrent state of affairs for all of the plywood firms, given the instability of the industry in general."

As fully self-managed companies, the plywood cooperatives do not represent the same kinds of management style and mood of employees in partially worker-owned firms or even firms with high levels of worker participation in management. Reaching this stage of organization still represents a major process of change and development for conventional firms. Nevertheless, such a development would be worth public support, since among other benefits, it should be noted that when companies can solve their own problems during hard times, it reduces the need for restrictive legislation against shutdowns.

Eliminating Bureaucracy

The difficulties in managing overly large or conglomerate companies have been discussed widely. For example, Robert Reich has examined the unproductive character of financial manipulations which he characterizes as "paper entrepreneurialism," and many other observers have argued that such conglomerate configurations reduce the effectiveness of business. The slowly advancing trend toward worker ownership among U.S. firms, however, is a countervailing force for several reasons.

First, the fully self-managed company eliminates outside

stock purchases, insofar as employees in most cases can only sell their stock back to the firm. In other instances, the practice of purchasing companies and building conglomerate structures is slowed down considerably by the fact that all the employees must vote together on the sale of a firm. Even if the practice of one-person-one-vote were not in existence, high levels of employee ownership by means of ESOPs, in which pass-through voting rights are provided, go far toward stopping financial speculators' excesses.

Second, the organizational structure seems to be less bureaucratized in fully self-managed firms. Joyce Rothschild-Whitt (509–27) found that in the conventional firm, authority is resident in the office hierarchy with work administered through formal rules, direct supervision, a maximal division of labor, and specialization of jobs with maximal differentiation of income. In the fully self-managed firm the opposite occurs: authority is resident in the employees as a whole, with minimally stipulated rules, an accent on personal authority, limited reward differentials, minimal division of labor, generalization of labor, generalization of jobs, and demystification of expertise. As companies move toward becoming fully self-managed, it is reasonable to believe that they will shed levels of bureaucracy along with its red tape, impersonality, and other negative trappings.

The likelihood that big ESOP firms, with widespread ownership and pass-through voting rights, will move toward conglomeration is also unlikely. The case of the *Milwaukee Journal* can illustrate this point. As the company has grown by acquiring other companies and turning them into subsidiaries, employees in the newly purchased companies have complained that they were not included in the original ownership plan. The board of directors decided to admit them to ownership upon purchase of shares, which opened the door to their representation on the board as well. The extent to which the firm will continue to grow with a large command bureaucracy and with subsidiary employees on the board will be something to watch (Conrad and others).[18]

The experiences of many self-managed firms have suggested that employees of a firm self-impose a limit of about five hundred employees. When some relatively self-managed firms have grown sizable, the large organization was redesigned, for example, through new social inventions in corporate organization that provide accountability to the employee owners. Corporations of ten thousand to forty thousand employees exist in West Germany with fifty-fifty representation of workers on the board of directors, but they have also devised highly decentralized systems of divisional worker councils and shop-level ombudsmen.[19]

We have mentioned that the two thousand workers in the democratically managed corporations of Ulgor, in Mondragon, Spain, found its swollen bureaucracy to be intolerable and decided to decentralize into a confederation of smaller firms. The new corporation, Ularco, retained centralized functions in marketing and budgeting but key decisions involving work processes were made in the autonomous firms.

We also have mentioned social inventions at the John Lewis Partnership (twenty-four thousand employees) in London, where departmental newspapers allow for complaints to be printed anonymously from employees, to be answered directly by appropriate managers. Employee-managed and -owned firms seem to have a bent for creating alternatives to command bureaucracy.

While relatively self-managed companies show a tendency to reduce excessive bureaucracy, stratification, and differential rewards, and to promote a more egalitarian managerial system, the transition is not easily done. Three problems are critical to consider in the transition process: time, homogeneity, and emotional intensity.

Employees not well trained in self-management can take too much time making decisions in meetings; they can become too like-minded and/or can embroil themselves in differences in opinion that might not exist in conventional companies. Regular two-way communications may be good for morale in some cases but can also use up more of the workday than memos and one-way commands. Employees in relatively self-managed firms have found that they need to streamline meetings, reduce the number of meetings, and provide representational systems to handle grievances. Some consultants believe that self-managed companies attract like-minded members and hence there is need to cultivate diversity in ethnicity and political opinion while maintaining a sense of corporate community.

The more familiar face-to-face relations of smaller self-managed firms may be more humane than the impersonality of a bureaucracy but can also be more emotionally threatening. In a relevant parallel situation, a study of the New England town meetings found citizens reporting headaches and developing anxieties in anticipation of the meetings' conflictual character. To diminish their fears, townspeople utilized various devices, such as concealing critical thoughts, minimizing differences of opinion in seeking consensus, and other avoidance mechanisms (Lindenfeld & Rothschild-Whitt). One might assume that workers in self-managed firms may experience similar avoidance mechanisms.

Transition toward greater degrees of mutuality in decision making has its risks. While the learning process has begun in conventional firms experimenting with autonomous groups, QWL projects, and quality circles, the next steps can be still more taxing. Today employees in QWL programs are learning how to conduct meetings that can be sensitively led, but higher levels of comanagement require still more skill training.

The lesson for corporate and public policy is that steps toward greater self-management in business will likely require more training in managing intergroup relations to guarantee successful outcomes.

The Next Step

The two trends—worker participation in management and employee ownership—have each been cover stories for *Business Week* (May 15, 1989, p. 116; July 10, 1989, p. 56), with a positive outlook given to both. Employee involvement "is sinking in to the core of Corporate America." At the same time, employee ownership represents "a time of change that could take its place in history . . . Corporate America is rushing headlong into something that was, only a few years ago, almost universally unthinkable in executive suites: giving up billions of dollars' worth in equity—and crucial margins of power—to their work forces."

The eventual outcome of these two trends could be an entirely new democratic enterprise, called by some the "worker cooperative" and by others the "labor-managed firm." Experts do not all agree on an operational definition for this ideal type but it is clear that this type of firm is part of the logic of the future. Louis Putterman (1982, 140) has defined it as

> an enterprise in which ultimate discretion over all matters lying within its field of choice—e.g., what products to produce in which quantities (and at what prices) to produce and sell in a market economy; how to organize the production process; what contracts to enter into the suppliers, customers, lending institutions, etc.; how to allocate net revenues; and even what decision-making procedures to adopt—is in the hands of the firm's personnel, with each member having an equal vote regardless of what skills or managerial rank he or she may have. [20]

Many economists have challenged the capability of the producer cooperative (or the fully self-managed firm) to perform in an adequate manner because of its structure, arguing that cooperatives tend to degenerate over time into conventional firms. But the story is more complex and there is much evidence to the contrary, suggesting that cooperatives do in fact have a superior economic capability. If we add here that they also have a greater potential than conventional firms for reducing worker alienation and eliminating the necessity for state regulations, their evolution seems all the more probable.

It is important that we take a look at economists' arguments about what could limit the high performance of employee-managed firms in the market. We cannot go into technical details in this literature because it is so extensive and international in scope, but we can point to major issues and how they have been resolved.[21]

First, some economists argue that democratic firms over time tend to degenerate into conventional firms because they employ increasing numbers of hired labor—that is, workers who are not owners, thus leading them gradually back to a conventional firm (Ben-Ner, 247–60; Miyasaki, 909–31).[22] Although this is true in some cases many other types of democratic firms have placed restrictions on the use of hired labor, most notably the French, Italian, and Spanish (Mondragon) worker cooperatives. Indeed, the successful Mondragon system of producer cooperatives has been expanding for over thirty years, exceeding the productivity and profitability of the conventional firms in Spain without introducing any hired labor.[23]

Second, the way in which property rights are defined in a fully self-managed firm has important effects on its ability to maintain its unique democratic character, and some economists have argued that there have been problems in those areas. Furubotn and Pejovich base their criticism of property rights on a Yugoslavian concept of social property, which recognizes property rights as bundles of rights which can be separated and held by different parties. In this concept, society holds the final right to ownership of the firm's assets and rents these assets to the employees. In return for paying interest on the firm's capital and maintaining the book value of the assets in perpetuity, employees are permitted the right to use the assets and appropriate the income from their use without having the right to liquidate the firm. New investments must be taken through collectively owned reserves (Furobotn & Pejovich).

This model of collective ownership, which fits the legal system of Yugoslavia, does not fare well in the framework of U.S. laws due to pressures toward degeneration. Jaroslav Vanek has suggested two alternative models that might be more appropriate for the U.S. One is a shelter agency for the ultimate (basic) owners in a federation of self-managed firms. In this case, the ownership is divided between the federation as the basic owner (in place of Yugoslavia's reference to society), with the right of ultimate disposal of capital goods. Employees have the right to use the property and appropriate the surplus in perpetuity but the user-owner pays the basic owner the market rate of return on capital.

The other solution is to combine the basic and user rights to property in the same corporation while at the same time legally separating them. In this case, new incoming employees of the firm purchase a membership share and the money is used to set up an individual "savings account" in the firm. This account becomes a source of capital for investment by the firm and is returnable to the employee upon retirement. The membership share establishes the member's right to a share of the net book value of the firm's assets while voting rights and the right to a share of the surplus are then vested separately in the worker-members themselves as a function of their work in the firm.

This structure eliminates tendencies to degenerate in certain legal environments, for example, to underinvest and reduce membership, or to liquidate the firm when new members buy new individual accounts, and it has been supported by consultants and is operating most effectively in the United States. It does not mean that it is the only type that will be highly competitive with conventional firms, but its success has already been proven to be most effective in the context of U.S. business law (Vanek).[24]

Finally, some economists have claimed that democratic firms are not as efficient as conventional firms. But these arguments are based on the theoretical assertions of economic models—as in some of the earlier cases we have discussed—that do not meet the tests of reality. For example, Oliver Williamson claims that the cooperative firm is based on a set of internal transactions with the least cost. He offers the model of collective ownership in which member income is an average of group output, and strategic decisions are made in a general assembly of employees for strategic decisions. His model is also based on the assumption that the firm operates through an information network he describes as an "all-channel network." As the firm grows in size, the increasing number of members and quantity of information leads to more costs for information processing, communication, and decision making, which reduces the ability of the collective to respond to market changes and make quick decisions, thus contributing to a reduction in efficiency. Assuming therefore that a pyramidal structure permits a quicker response and reduces the cost in communications, he assumes that the cooperative firm will eventually degenerate and convert back to pyramidal form to compete in the marketplace. He also assumes that the democratic firm cannot fire its employees and has no management hierarchy (Williamson, 5–38).

However, the economic model of a collective is entirely removed from the reality of worker-managed firms which maintain a coordinating hierarchy. They are quite capable of firing their employees and meet annually in general assemblies to set basic operating principles as well as to elect officers to the board. Indeed, worker-managed firms continue to resemble ever more closely the decentralized firm which modern management is finding most effective in the current marketplace. This is another reason why they are likely to fit the needs of the future business market.[25]

Conclusion

There are signs from the union movement, state legislation, and trends toward social (self) management that the market is developing a solution to Marx's concern over labor alienation. One could also argue that worker self-management is a common frontier of change for both state socialism and capitalism, that changes taking place in socialist countries today appear to be moving in the same direction toward self management.[26]

The empirical evidence strongly suggests the benefits that would be derived from policies supporting relatively self-managed firms. Public support for worker participation and worker ownership will help to save jobs, maintain local flows of capital, and support community development. Firms moving toward higher levels of self-management have the potential to be more productive and efficient, to reduce absenteeism and labor turnover, to curb the extent of tardiness and sickness among employees, and to reduce pilferage. Further, they provide the best structure for employees to develop a sense of purpose and meaningfulness in their work, and have the potential to save money and increase efficiency by reducing the corporate costs of middle management and the multiple costs of bureaucracy. Finally, the evidence suggests that self-managed firms may lead to fewer social problems locally and a consequent lessening of the financial burden on government, since fewer tax dollars going out means that fewer tax dollars need come in. New public policies in support of the trends toward employee-owned and -managed companies should be helpful to corporations, their employees, and to the economy overall.

Notes

1. For an elaboration on the meaning of corporatism, see Schmitter (885–928) along with Salisbury.

2. Worker participation programs developed in the 1970s through experiments at General Motors, Ford, and Chrysler in cooperation with the United Auto Workers. But since they were found to add significantly to the productivity and profitability of the firm, they expanded rapidly to other corporations in the 1980s. These programs came to be called Quality of Work Life (QWL), Quality Circles, Labor Management Participation Teams, and Employee Involvement plans and now have become the rule in big companies like the Fortune 500.

3. An employee stock ownership plan is a type of deferred benefit plan. Many people have deferred benefit plans such as profit-sharing or pension plans that buy stocks and bonds and place them in a fund for the employees' use when they leave the company or retire. An ESOP does the same thing, only it buys stock in the company the employees work for. The shares belong to the employees, but they cannot sell them until they leave the company or retire. Until then a trustee holds the stock. For more information, see Rosen and Young.

4. For a detailed discussion of the data suggesting that the trends will continue in the future, see Rosen and others along with Bruyn and Nicolaou-Smokoviti.

5. The report concluded that one in seven companies with more than one hundred employees has some kind of human resource program, involving thirteen million workers overall (*People and Productivity*, 44). There also are several thousand labor-management committees operating today. See Talbott (7).

6. The fully self-managed company is owned by its workers, who vote on a per-person rather than per-share basis, and who are represented at significant levels of management, including the board of directors. Probably about a thousand such firms exist in the United States and serve as models for many thousands more that appear to be heading in the same direction. See Gunn (35) for a discussion of the ten requisites defining a fully self-managed company.

7. The way in which a balance of inside-outside control is maintained for local communities is discussed in Bruyn and Meehan.

8. Many of these experiments are described and summarized by Simmons and Mares.

9. On Japanese management, Cole estimated that one out of eight workers in Japan is participating in quality circles, which makes a difference in productivity. Vogel (15) points out how featherbedding

and labor's inflexible insistence on work rules contrast with Japanese styles of participatory management. He says that low productivity in the United States is due partly to workers' fear of losing their jobs, in contrast to Japanese workers, who eagerly seek technological change because they have a guarantee of permanent employment and a high level of participation in corporate governance.

10. Many of these studies are reported in Rosen, Klein, and Young (48).

11. Studies of Japanese firms have demonstrated the advantages of developing a more cohesive and participatory workforce. An early argument was made by Ouchi.

12. Workers often see management attempts to develop a harmonious company life as an insidious ploy to gain stronger control over labor. See Edwards along with Braverman.

13. These data are based on my personal interviews with members of the personnel department and employees at John Lewis Partnership in London.

14. For comparative studies on the effects of labor participation in higher management, see King and Van De Vall along with Jenkins. As self-managed companies develop, unions continue to play an important role in defending the rights of workers by assisting in pension funds, enabling firms to obtain loans, consulting with members on personnel problems, and so on. The assumption of these studies is that the overall economic costs of the adversarial system are thereby significantly reduced.

15. Obradovic and Dunn describe the political nature of the first strike in Yugoslavia in 1958. Reasons for the strike were low personal income, caused not by management but by the position of workers in the system of distribution. The relatively high costs of production and the relatively low prices of coal were at fault, and the miners protested to the government, which set the prices. Because they received no response from all the political bodies (the League of Communists and the trade union) and state organs at the commune and district levels as well as the republic of Slovenia and the federation, a strike became a more effective means for realizing their demands. Their protests were complicated by the fact that the media announced nothing about the strike because such reports were discouraged at the time. The character of strikes in socialist states thus can have a larger political significance than strikes in capitalist nations based on labor-management disputes.

16. These observations on the causes of recent strikes in Yugoslavia are based on reports of studies given during a conference on worker self-management ("Social Stratification: Comparative Perspectives")

that I attended at the Interuniversity Center in Dubrovnik in April 1986.

17. See also Berman along with Bernstein.

18. See also "Partners in Ownership" updated periodically by the Journal Company.

19. My visit to West Germany provided an opportunity to observe large-scale businesses that are organized with labor having 50 percent board representation and worker councils at the level of middle management, as well as interplant councils, government-labor-management tribunals, and ombudsmen. I also witnessed this same organization in U.S. subsidiaries in that country, such as Xerox and General Motors's Opel plant. There were problems in these structures, but the visit suggested to me that U.S. firms can adjust to major changes in administration and still remain highly productive, as is the case for West German companies.

In interviews with employees in smaller self-managed companies, such as Scott-Bader in Wallaston, England, they told me of the tendency for employees to number around five hundred. Expansion of a firm is not ruled out if hierarchy can be reorganized as a decentralized system of management. See Mead-Fox.

20. See also Putterman (1984, 171–87). The reader should note that such definitions are over-focused on the firm itself, in isolation from the rest of the system, as though firm members alone could have "ultimate discretion over all matters," such as "what products to produce in which quantities." Such an approach fails to recognize the power of the larger external market to influence such decisions. I deal with this faulty perception in Bruyn (1990, part 3) which recognizes the firm as part of a larger system of interaction that affects decisions made separately in each firm.

21. The technical arguments on these issues can be found in Egan.

22. Egan (15) criticizes the arguments of these economic models on the basis that they (1) fail to take account of noneconomic factors (they are not specified in the models), (2) fail to be supported by empirical tests, and (3) do not reflect the literature on labor-managed firms that disclaim taking on hired labor. Therefore, these economic models are inadequate. See also Russell (1984, 73–96).

23. For studies of the Mondragon model, see Oakeshott, Henk and Logan, Clamp.

24. The structure for combining basic and user owners in the same firm has been devised and implemented by a number of consulting agencies, including the Industrial Cooperative Association, 58 Day Street, Somerville, MA 02144. For a more technical discussion of this

structure, see Ellerman (62–78). We also should note that state laws in Connecticut, Maine, Massachusetts, New York, and Vermont have been altered to create a better legal structure for producer cooperatives.

25. The empirical research on self-managed firms referring to issues of income equity, internal structure, middle-management resistance, union resistance, organizational development, and community relations are discussed in Bruyn (1987, 82ff). See also Jackall and Levin.

26. The first Russian-style worker buyouts of state-owned firms have been arranged in a Moscow firm that manufactures food-processing equipment and in a building materials firm outside of Moscow. The buyouts were designed by Dr. Valery Rutgaizer, an economist who was also Deputy Director of the All-Union Center for Public Opinion Research. (The Center is headed by Tatiana Zaslavskaya, a leading Russian sociologist who was Gorbachev's pollster and an architect of perestroika.) Reports suggest that these transactions could set a precedent for the one thousand two hundred or so state-owned businesses in the Moscow region which have negotiated leasing agreements with the authorities during the previous year (*The Economist*).

References

Agostinelli, Floyd. *Community Development Credit Unions*. Washington: 1977.

Ben-Ner, Avner. "On the Stability of the Cooperative Type of Organization." *Journal of Comparative Economics* 8 (1984).

Berman, Katrina. *Worker-Owner Plywood Companies: An Economic Analysis*. Pullman: Washington State University Press, 1967.

Bernstein, Paul. *Workplace Democratization*. Kent: Kent State University Press, 1976.

Bowles, Samuel, David Gordon, and Thomas Weiskopf. *Beyond the Wasteland*. New York: Anchor Press, 1984.

Braverman, Harry. *Labor and Monopoly Capital*. New York: Monthly Review Press, 1974.

Bruyn, Severyn T. *The Field of Social Investment*. Cambridge: Cambridge University Press, 1987.

———. *A Future for the American Economy: The Social Market*. Stanford: Stanford University Press, 1991.

Bruyn, Severyn T., and James Meehan. *Beyond the Market and the State: Innovations in Community Development*. Philadelphia: Temple University Press, 1987.

Bruyn, Severyn T., and Litsa Nicolaou-Smokoviti. "Development To-

178 / Severyn T. Bruyn

ward Worker Self-Governance in the United States." In *The International Social Economy*. New York: Praeger, 1989.

Clamp, Chris. "The Mondragon Experiment." Ph.D. diss., Boston College, 1985.

Cole, Robert. *Work Mobility and Participation*. Berkeley: University of California Press, 1979.

Conrad, Will, Kathleen Wilson, and Dale Wilson. *The Milwaukee Journal*. Madison: University of Wisconsin Press, 1964.

Conte, Michael, and Arnold Tannenbaum, *Employee Ownership*. Ann Arbor: University of Michigan Survey Research Center, 1980.

Edwards, Richard. *Contested Terrain*. New York: Basic Books, 1979.

Egan, Daniel. "Organizational Degeneration in Self-Managed Firms: A Theoretical Survey." Working paper, Department of Sociology, Boston College, May 1988.

Elden, Maxwell J. "Democracy at Work for a More Participatory Politics: Worker Self-Management Leads to Political Efficacy and Participation." Ph.D. diss., University of California, Los Angeles, 1976.

Ellerman, David. "Horizon Problems and Property Rights in Labor Managed Firms." *Journal of Comparative Economics* 10 (March 1986): 62–78.

The Employee Ownership Report. Oakland: National Center for Employee Ownership, n.d.

"ESOPs: Are They Good for You?" *Business Week*, no. 3105 (May 15, 1989): 116–23.

Foreseback, L. *Industrial Relations and Employment in Sweden*. Stockholm: Swedish Institute, 1976.

Furubotn, Erik, and Svetozar Pejovich. "Property Rights and the Behavior of the Firm in a Socialist State: The Example of Yugoslavia." In *The Economics of Property Rights*, edited by Erik Furobotn and Svetozar Pejovich. Cambridge: Ballinger Publishing Co., 1974.

Greenberg, Edward S. "Industrial Self-Management and Political Attitudes." *American Political Science Review* 75, no. 1 (1981): 29–42.

———. "Producer Cooperatives and Democratic Theory: The Case of the Plywood Firms." In *Worker Cooperatives in America*, edited by Robert Jackall and Henry Levin. Berkeley: University of California Press, 1984.

Gunn, Christopher. *Workers' Self-Management in the United States*. Ithaca: Cornell University Press, 1984.

Henk, Thomas, and Chris Logan. *Mondragon: An Economic Analysis*. Boston: George Allen and Unwin, 1982.

Jackall, Robert, and Henry M. Levin, eds. *Worker Cooperatives in America*. Berkeley: University of California Press, 1984.

Jenkins, David. *Industrial Democracy in Europe*. Geneva: Business International, 1974.

Ketchum, Lyman D. "A Case Study of Diffusion." In *The Quality of Working Life*, vol. 2, edited by Albert Cherns and others. New York: Free Press, 1975.

King, Charles, and Mark Van De Vall. *Models of Industrial Democracy*. New York: Mouton, 1978.

Lindenfeld, Frank, and Joyce Rothschild-Whitt, eds. *Workplace Democracy and Social Change*. Boston: Porter Sargent, 1982.

Mansbridge, Jane. "Town Meeting Democracy." *Working Papers for a New Society* (May 15, 1973).

Marsh, Thomas, and Dale McAllister. "ESOPs Tables." *Journal of Corporation Law* 6 (Spring 1981): 551–623.

Mead-Fox, David. "Worker Self-Management in Ireland." Ph.D. diss., Boston College, 1990.

Meek, Christopher, and Warner Woodworth. "Worker-Community Collaboration and Ownership." In *Industrial Democracy: Strategies for Community Revitalization*. Edited by Warner Woodworth, Christopher Meek, and William Foote Whyte. London: Sage Publications, 1985.

Miyazaki, Hajime. "On Success and Dissolution of the Labor-Managed Firm in the Capitalist Economy." *Journal of Political Economy* 92, no. 5 (1984): 909–31.

New York Stock Exchange. *People and Productivity: A Challenge to Corporate America*. New York: Office of Economic Research, New York Stock Exchange, 1982.

"Nothing to Lease but Your Chains." *The Economist* (September 16, 1989).

Oakeshott, Robert. *The Case for Workers' Coops*. Boston: Routledge and Kegan Paul, 1978.

Obradovic, Josip, and William N. Dunn. *Workers' Self-Management and Organizational Power in Yugoslavia*. Pittsburgh: University of Pittsburgh Press, 1978.

Ouchi, William. *Theory Z: How American Business Can Meet the Japanese Challenge*. Reading: Addison-Wesley, 1981.

Parker, Mike. *Inside the Circle*. Boston: South End Press, 1986.

Pateman, Carole. *Participation and Democratic Theory*. Cambridge: Cambridge University Press, 1970.

"The Payoff from Teamwork." *Business Week*, no. 3114 (July 10, 1989): 56–62.

Putterman, Louis. "On Some Recent Explanations of Why Capital Hires Labor." *Economic Inquiry* 22, no. 2 (1984): 171–87.

———. "Some Behavioral Perspectives on the Dominance of Hierarchical over Democratic Forms of Enterprise." *Journal of Economic Behavior and Organization* 3, nos. 2–3 (June–September 1982): 139–60.

Quarry, Michael, Joseph Blasi, and Corey Rosen. *Taking Stock.* Cambridge: Ballinger, 1986.

Reich, Robert. "The Next American Frontier." *Atlantic Monthly* 251, no. 3 (March 1983): 43–58.

Rice, Graham. "Difficulties in Keeping Financial Capital in the Community." In *Financing Community Economic Development,* edited by Richard Schramm. Ithaca: Cornell University, 1981.

Rosen, Corey, Katherine Klein, and Karen Young. *Employee Ownership in America.* Lexington: D. C. Heath, Lexington Books, 1986.

Rosen, Corey, and Karen Young, eds. *Understanding Employee Ownership.* Ithaca: ILR Press, 1991.

Rothschild-Whitt, Joyce. "The Collectivist Organization: An Alternative to Rational-Bureaucratic Models." *American Sociological Review* 44, no. 4 (1979): 509–27.

Russell, Raymond. "The Role of Culture and Ethnicity in the Degeneration of Democratic Firms." *Economic and Industrial Democracy* 5, no. 1 (1984): 73–96.

———. *Sharing Ownership in the Workplace.* Albany: State University of New York Press, 1985.

Salisbury, Robert. "Why No Corporatism in America?" In *Trends Towards Corporatist Intermediation,* edited by Philippe Schmitter and Gerhard Lehmbruch. Beverly Hills and London: Sage Publications, 1979.

Schlesinger, Melinda, and Pauline Bart. "Collective Work and Self-Identity." In *Workplace Democracy and Social Change,* edited by Frank Lindenfeld and Joyce Rothschild-Whitt. Boston: Porter Sargent, 1982.

Schmitter, Philippe C. "Democratic Theory and Neocorporatist Practice." *Social Research* (Winter 1983).

Simmons, John, and William Mares. *Working Together.* New York: Knopf, 1983.

Sirianni, Carmen, ed. *Worker Participation and the Politics of Reform.* Philadelphia: Temple University Press, 1987.

Stillman, Don. "The Devastating Impact of Plant Relocations." In *The Big Business Reader,* edited by Mark Green. New York: Pilgrim Press, 1983.

Talbott, Vernon G. "A Brief History of Labor-Management Committees." *Workplace Democracy,* no. 56 (Spring 1987).

Vanek, Jaroslav. "The Basic Theory of Financing of Participatory Firms." In *Self-Management,* edited by Jaroslav Vanek. Baltimore: Penguin Books, 1975.

Vogel, Ezra. *Japan as Number One*. New York: Harper and Row, 1979.

Whyte, William Foote. "New Approaches to Industrial Development and Community Development." In *Industrial Democracy: Strategies for Community Revitalization*, edited by Warner Woodworth, Christopher Meek, William Foote Whyte. London: Sage Publications, 1985.

Williamson, Oliver E. "The Organization of Work: A Comparative Institutional Assessment." *Journal of Economic Behavior and Organization* 1, no. 1 (1980): 5–38.

7

Reconstruction of Mainstream Economics and the Market Economy

John B. Davis and Edward J. O'Boyle

As is clearly evident, the contributors to this volume generally believe that the reconstruction of market economics and the market economy involves adopting a more comprehensive, more holistic view of economy and society. For them, mainstream economics can be faulted for failing to explain real economic relationships and for its pursuit of an overly narrow, excessively scientific conception of the economy. The change in vision we believe necessary in economics is represented here by a general statement of the goals pursued by the alternative thinking in the essays in this volume and specific illustrations of what such an approach may uncover in the experience of everyday life. We thus first describe how we believe a rethinking of market economics involves a rethinking of human nature, and then go on to describe four recent examples in which innovative thinking about workplaces and neighborhoods permits people to address human need. From this we discern a number of lessons from a socioeconomic approach to the concept of need, which we believe should guide future research in economics. Respecting these lessons would do much to bring the practice of professional economists back into line with self-understanding of the people whom they study.

Social Economics: A Reconstruction of Mainstream Economics

Mainstream economics is widely recognized to have sacrificed a broad understanding of human nature for a restrictive model of rational behavior tailored to the requirements of a supply-and-demand explanation of the market process. Thus social scientists and humanists often bemoan the narrowness of contemporary mainstream economics, arguing that economists abstract from all that is interesting and difficult to explain in human behavior because it does not fit rational choice theory. Economists themselves are generally content to limit their interest in human nature to a narrow set of possible choice characteristics on the assumption that this does not prejudice their ability to predict economic behavior. The premise of the essays collected in *The Social Economics of Human Material Need* is that economic life cannot be adequately understood apart from a broad view of human nature. A rethinking of market economics consequently presupposes a rethinking of human nature, and both together are required for an adequate and informative account of human need.

Rethinking Human Nature

The chief fault in mainstream economics' characterization of human nature is its omission of the social dimension of human nature. Human nature is two-dimensional, both individual, as mainstream economics has always recognized, but also social, a fact ignored by most contemporary economists. Attention to the latter dimension, moreover, is essential to the analysis of individual needs, since understanding individual needs depends upon seeing individuals as members of a society with generally accepted standards of deservingness and personal well-being. Rethinking human nature, then, means first and foremost coming to an understanding of those social values that determine our conceptions of individual need and that explain the general standards society recognizes as defining human dignity and personality.

The omission of the social side of human nature is perhaps

most evident and most harmful in regard to mainstream economics' general stance toward public policy regarding markets. Perceiving economic agents as only individual in nature, mainstream economists abstract from social differences in wealth and advantage across individuals, and argue that because individuals only trade when they expect to make themselves better off, markets should be free from government intervention. Yet this recommendation gives tacit approval to a variety of undesirable market outcomes in the name of a defense of the social value of individual freedom. Moreover, when individuals' differences in well-being and consequent bargaining power are believed to be relevant to economists' analysis of markets, then defending the market process also requires attention to the terms and conditions on which individuals enter markets. This broader framework for economic policy, which typically entails concern for access to education, job training, equitable income distribution, fair tax burdens, safety in the workplace, discrimination, and so on, requires a greater vision of individual human beings in economic life than arises from the individualistic paradigm of mainstream economics.

Human beings taken in this larger perspective possess two fundamental material needs that derive from their nature as persons. First there is physical need. As living creatures, human beings clearly possess physical requirements for survival. There are many ways that this dimension of need can be expressed as dictated by differences across societies and individuals regarding the sorts of things that satisfy this basic level of need. Nonetheless, individuals' essential materiality makes the simple fact of physical need self-evident to us all. Second there is individuals' need for work. Because human beings are conscious, intentional creatures, they exercise their skills and capacities upon activities and objects of their work. An existence without activity is destructive of the individual, and thus individuals must be able to apply their talents with a conscious deliberation to insure their very survival as human beings. In mainstream economics, in which labor is treated as an input to production no different than any other input, this important dimension of life and need is altogether unrecognized.

What, then, are the social values that make possible this minimal conception of human need? As argued by Peter Danner above, freedom, equality, and community constitute the three principal social values that comprehend a broad conception of human nature as both individual and social. Freedom, of course, is well recognized in mainstream economics, since the expression of individual nature in market choices is central to the analysis of rational choice. Even equality as a social value receives significant attention from mainstream economists, since the standard efficiency critique of market power and monopoly presupposes that competition must be carried out on an even playing field. Yet as one would expect from the lack of attention in mainstream economics to the social side of human nature, mainstream economists rarely grasp the importance of community as a social value in economic life—this despite the fact that fraternity, free associativeness, and democratic participation are values deeply embedded in much of our life together in all its spheres.

A rethinking of human nature in economics, therefore, involves developing a better understanding of the human being's social side, particularly as explained by the social value of community, and then integrating this with an appropriately reformulated conception of the human being's individual side. In *The Social Economics of Human Material Need*, this has been taken to be tantamount to replacing the traditional view of the economic individual as *Homo economicus* with one termed *Homo socioeconomicus*. Practically speaking, this shift in focus entails the development of a research program in economics that devotes more attention to the variety and array of socioeconomic institutions that enable individuals to organize their interactions with one another in markets in a fashion suitable to their dual-dimensioned human nature. These institutions in the chapters above are broadly classified as those fostering competition, intervention, and cooperation—systems of organization that are respectively tied to the three social values of freedom, equality, and community. Within this broader framework for understanding human nature and economic behavior, the reality of material need can become the subject of economic policy making as theory in economics becomes more attuned to the genuine features of the world in which we live. It is to this task that this collection has been dedicated.

Rethinking Market Economics

What, however, are the specific deficiencies of mainstream economics with its one-sided view of human nature and the principles underlying economic organization in the modern economy? How precisely is it, that is, that the mainstream view of human nature and economic behavior produces oversights and misconceptions regarding the real world of economics in the theory that it advances? Recalling the circular flow of expenditure and income, we can identify two fundamental areas of concern, resource markets and product markets, from which further comment on the general view of the market system naturally follows.

In resource markets, where in mainstream theory firms purchase inputs for production, the highly individualist conception of economic agents enforces a conceptual separation between transactions and the individuals involved, the agents of firms, and members of households. Market economics as it is currently pursued only examines the immediate conditions of supply and demand of commodities without at the same time investigating the social and human aspects of market participants. But the individuals who offer goods and services as inputs to production possess a need for income and work that defines them as human beings. The individuals who bargain for the firm on the demand side possess similar needs in work and income. These further characteristics of individuals cannot be separated from our examination of the things—the resources—that they bargain over, since the true terms on which individuals interact in markets are those that follow from their overall human nature. A rethinking of market economics in the sphere of resource markets, then, requires an analysis that reunites transactions and a full understanding of market participants.

Integrating these aspects of the lives of individuals who transact with one another in resource markets, in fact, is something many of us do unconsciously. We are often aware of those with whom we deal and incorporate this awareness in our responses to others in markets. The problem with mainstream economics is that it formalizes market transactions on the narrowest of grounds, so that its conclusions typically discourage our better intuitions. In resource markets, it seems that it is only the characteristics of the inputs to production that determine the organization of production rather than the decisions of living individuals. Worse, when it comes to economic policy, we may be inclined to disvalue those sides of individuals that fail to receive ready statement in our supply-and-demand judgments about the functioning of markets. Should an individual, say, feel compelled to work at an undesirable wage and employment, mainstream economics is only able to say that for an individual happening to possess such-and-such a laboring capacity and other resources this choice must have been preferred to another not pursued (even more unfortunate!) or it would not have been taken. Mainstream economics, then, cannot begin to investigate felt compulsion and the extent to which it is located in individual need, because it lacks a means of examining the broader aspects of human nature that enter into market decisions.

There are similar difficulties with mainstream economics' analysis of product markets. Because the traditional approach concentrates its attention on the goods and services that pass from firms to consumers, allowing the individuals involved to enter into the explanation in only the narrow choice theoretic sense, the full range of rationales behind production and consumption in a society are obscured. Thus, should consumers, say, convince producers that they believe certain goods and services are harmful to the natural environment, this expression of opinion regarding the need for a healthy environment only gets registered in mainstream economic thinking as an unexplained change in preferences. Of course it may well be fair to say that such choices reflect a kind of reasoning that can be characterized as rational and utility-maximizing. But this takes us very little distance toward understanding actual product markets, since our understanding of the deeper rationales and intentions behind individuals' decisions is central to our judgments about the differences between the markets in which individuals interact. Thus, it is only when we incorporate our fullest view of human nature and its attendant behavior in both its individual and social aspects that we are likely to gain insight into the operation of markets.

In the market economy, then, supply-and-demand analysis represents only a first step in explaining individuals' economic interaction. Employers and employees and buyers and sellers all complete their transactions with one another in exchanges that have foundations in more than simple responses to relative scarcities. While we observe the allocation and reallocation of resources across alternative uses in conjunction with the operation of the price mechanism, there is more that needs to be said to explain how the market process functions. Behind the scenes, so to speak, individuals' needs determine strategies of action that are ultimately manifested in their supplies and demands. When, for example, an individual trading for necessaries meets one trading for luxuries, a focus upon equilibrium prices and quantities deflects attention from how relative to need uneven bargaining powers both lead to a minimal production of necessaries and generous production of luxuries and a comparatively high price for necessaries and a comparatively low one for luxuries. Moreover, though consequent market behavior can be explained in terms of market participants' allocation responses to changing prices, behind the scenes individuals with needs explained by their full character as human beings adopt strategies of survival and self-development that provide the real explanation of their future involvement in markets.

What is required to transform current thinking about market economics, then, is a fundamental change in vision. The very object of the science of economics has been misconceived since it has been things rather than persons that have preoccupied economists. Indeed, in their haste to become scientists on the model of such disciplines as physics, economists have been reluctant to include the human side of the economy in their theories. Less manageable theoretically, and deeply dependent upon the often complex realm of social value, economics with a human face has rarely been economists' chief object. Economists have sought concepts and notions such as "equilibrium" to explain market behavior, though the concept of "agreement" better characterizes the relationship between living, historical persons in the marketplace. Economists have made the mathematical model the paradigmatic representation of economic behavior, though the social value constituting framework of the marketplace cannot be represented in quantitative terms. Economics, in short, has long missed the real target of explanation, because its vision of its subject matter has been misconceived. The collections of essays here provides a path forward to better understanding of economics and economic life. Their common premise is that rethinking market economics first and foremost involves rethinking human nature, and that only in this way can modern societies and economies be understood.

The Dilemma

The authors of this collection are under no illusion regarding the difficulty of the task they contribute to in their respective essays. The very framework of mainstream economics makes a deeper investigation of the market economy a particularly awkward prospect. On the one hand, mainstream analysis of allocation and reallocation decisions is explained by market participants' responses to shortages and surpluses. On the other hand, market participants' responses to shortages in regard to fulfilling their needs and surpluses in regard to their resources operate in directions and patterns not always captured by supply-and-demand behavior. Thus, the mainstream theory of the market can well misdirect the search for better understanding of the market process because of its special focus. And indeed the appeal of a well-established theory with apparent professional prestige should not be underestimated.

Against this, however, are the implications of the fact that it is the market economy which the last years of the twentieth century have shown to be the dominant mode of economic organization for the future. This single fact necessitates that economists develop a workable and accurate theory of the market, irrespective of their limited success in the past. Though inertia, habit, and the desire for peer approval are likely to discourage many economists from going beyond their customary approaches to explanation, because the market will in large degree constitute the framework in which needs will either be met or go unmet, strong incentives exist for developing a better understanding of the market process. Indeed, not to seek this further understanding is to imperil future economic development, since whether or not needs are recognized in economic theory, individuals will pursue their fulfillment at all opportunities. Thus, as an indication of new directions economic analysis may travel given the foundations laid down in the essays here, we close with a brief investigation of how the market economy might be reformed through the reform of some of its most important institutions.

The Social Economy: A Reconstruction of the Market Economy

The reconstruction of the market economy requires remaking such socioeconomic institutions as business enterprises, government, labor organizations, trade associations, financial institutions, media, and educational institutions. In what follows, the necessary institutional reform is addressed at two venues— the workplace and the household—because it is there that unmet human material need is felt most acutely. The success of any reconstruction turns critically on whether it is able to provide additional economic security for both workers and consumers without interfering overly much in the economy's resource (re)-allocation process.

As to this reconstruction, innovations are required that strengthen cooperation and community without weakening competition and freedom. Reforms with these characteristics are of central importance in the reconstruction because renewed cooperation and stronger community are necessary for dealing more effectively with unmet human material need while vigorous competition and undiminished freedom are necessary for markets to allocate resources efficiently. Clearly, the reconstruction required is a demanding entrepreneurial task.

In the discussion that follows, four examples of specific, creative reforms in the private sector are presented. With regard to the unmet need of workers and the workplace, the innovations that are highlighted take place at the interfirm or suprafirm level (in chapter 6 Severyn Bruyn examined intrafirm innovations at great length). As to unmet need among consumers and in households, attention focuses on the reconstruction of the neighborhood spearheaded by persons acting collectively as a private group. At both venues, private-group action as opposed to public-group action is underscored (in chapter 4 Anthony Scaperlanda covered the role of government with regard to human material need). All four examples demonstrate that private-group decision making need not be cartel-like.

Helping Workers Achieve Greater Economic Security: The Workplace Venue

Dysfunction and Cooperation

In the product market especially, the organizing principles of competition and intervention appear to be sufficient to provision human physical need because the typical transaction involves buyers and sellers acting as individuals. If one party is systematically disadvantaged in an exchange, the state may intervene as in the case of government farm price supports to raise the incomes of farmers, making them more nearly sufficient to meet their own needs and more nearly the same as nonfarm incomes.

In the workplace, however, competition and intervention clearly are not sufficient to provide for human physical need because work is organized around not just individuals but groups as well—teams, crews, sections, and shifts, for example. At the intrafirm level, the group organization of work is critical and highly visible. At this level, the need for cooperation—a disposition on the part of the worker to perform certain tasks through collective action in order to produce a specific good or service that could not be produced by means of individual action—is virtually universal.

Without cooperation, the workplace disintegrates into envy, disorder, and inefficiency. Relationships between labor and management become adversarial. Conflicts are resolved in zero-sum or even negative-sum fashion. Quality deteriorates, productivity sags, costs escalate, and increasingly the firm finds itself at a competitive disadvantage. The workplace becomes a scene of absenteeism, accidents, slowdown, rework, jurisdictional disputes, strikes, vandalism, violence, and other dysfunctions—no place to provision either physical need or the need for work as such.[1]

Work is performed not just through individual action but collective action as well. That is, both competition and cooperation are necessary for organizing the workplace. Workplace dysfunction is not a matter of too much (too little) competition or too much (too little) cooperation. Rather, it is a failure to blend the two in a way that maximizes workplace performance and thereby provision human material need as well as humanly possible.

Workplace dysfunction attributable to some failure relative to contributive justice (a disposition on the part of the member of a group to contribute to the support of that group) may derive to some extent from a (mis)perception of humans as having only one aspect to their nature—the individual side. That is, extreme or rugged individualists might have no sense of obligation to the group because they deny being a member of any group or "mob."

More likely, the insufficiency of contributive justice stems from a lack of awareness of one's responsibilities to the group in the workplace. This ignorance follows from (1) continuous change occurring in the workplace that requires continuous redefining of specific individual responsibilities, (2) an economic ideology that persuades humans that they meet their obligation to the group by pursuing their own personal gains, (3) a political ideology, political customs, and legal practices that focus more on individual rights than on individual responsibilities, and (4) a vast welfare state that dulls the individual's sense of obligation to the group.

Over the past several years, major steps have been taken at the intrafirm level to deal with workplace dysfunction. Some of these initiatives have been promoted explicitly as efforts to foster cooperation in the workplace, including quality circles, participatory management, just-in-time scheduling, and incentive plans based on group performance (e.g., gain sharing). Given the tight linkage between cooperation and contributive justice, practices such as these that are initiated in the name of cooperation have the effect, whether explicitly intended or not, of dealing with an insufficiency of contributive justice.

Interfirm and Suprafirm Cooperation

In this section, dysfunction in the marketplace and the workplace is addressed in terms of interfirm cooperation or suprafirm cooperation. Suprafirm cooperation is private-group decision-making through a distinct, formal body that has a staff of employees or volunteers. Interfirm cooperation is private-group decision making that is not characterized by such arrangements. Reducing or eliminating such dysfunction makes possible the better provisioning of human material need.

Cooperation is identifiable by its positive-sum outcomes. Some if not all of the various parties involved in or affected by a specific cooperative arrangement at the suprafirm level or the interfirm level derive real economic gains from collective action that can be used to meet human material need and that are not available through individual action, while none of the parties experience any economic losses. The cartel, on the other hand, is identifiable by its zero-sum and, at times, negative-sum outcomes.

Private-group control of decision making in the workplace or the marketplace directs the individual members of the group to address the dysfunction(s) that they cannot resolve by means of individual action through voluntary agreement on the responsibilities of the various members of the group itself in collective action. The individual members are brought together because of some unsatisfactory performance or outcome in the workplace or the marketplace. They form into a group in order to deal with the dysfunction that each one, acting individually, is unable to resolve.

Both the common good and individual responsibility are clarified and specified in terms of reducing, eliminating, or preventing specific dysfunctions in the workplace or the marketplace that affect the various members of the group. Cooperation means a willingness on the part of the individual members to act collectively in a dysfunctional area without at the same time surrendering individual initiative in areas where there is no dysfunction. Cooperation may even mean acting collectively and therefore noncompetitively in one area all the while acting individually and competitively in others.[2]

Cartels are much different. The members of a cartel are especially mindful of opportunities to enhance personal gain. They are takers and exploiters; they are self-serving. The individual members of the cartel are encouraged to be irresponsible in that cheaters are rewarded because they are able to continue production without the help of other group members.

Private-group control of decision making based on cooperation that is identifiably positive-sum in nature means that the individual members are mindful of dysfunctions in the workplace or the marketplace: they see common problems and seek common solutions. They are givers and contributors; they are caring. The individual members are encouraged to be responsible in that cheaters are not rewarded since they cannot continue to operate as well without the help of the group.

The principle of subsidiarity—larger, more powerful groups in the socioeconomic order should not take away the functions of smaller, less powerful groups but should help the less powerful groups operate effectively—is instructive as to where control of decision making should be situated. In the case of workplace or marketplace dysfunction that contributes to unmet human material need or raises barriers to provisioning that need and that the private individual is not able to address satisfactorily alone, help is to be sought first through a private group and, only if that fails, from the state. To be a separate level of decision making, cooperation must be independent of the larger and more powerful public authority. Suprafirm cooperation and interfirm cooperation must be voluntary so as not to usurp control from a member of the group that is functioning satisfactorily. Additionally, cooperation of this kind should be representative of the various private-individual organizations that are linked in the workplace or the marketplace either directly through membership and participation or indirectly through competent spokespersons so as to know more precisely its own domain and to avoid zero-sum strategies.

The suprafirm level private group should be helpful in the sense that if an individual member encounters organization-specific dysfunction in the workplace or the marketplace and asks for assistance in managing a problem that other individual organizations do not have, the group should be ready and willing to provide whatever help it can to deal with the dysfunction in satisfactory fashion.

Private-group control does not diminish property rights. Rather, it actually protects those rights and enhances the net worth of the individual firm by helping it function more effectively through collective action and thereby contribute more effectively toward provisioning human material need.

Two Examples of Marketplace/Workplace Cooperation

IMAGE (Involvement and Management Advance Growth and Employment) is an independent association of private firms in the construction industry that was established in 1977 and that covers twenty-six counties in southern Illinois including the counties that form the Illinois part of the St. Louis metropolitan area. IMAGE is patterned after St. Louis's PRIDE, which is a suprafirm private group that was founded in 1972.[3]

IMAGE was organized to address the common and pervasive problem of bad labor relations in the construction industry on the East Side (of the Mississippi River). IMAGE operates through what are called "targeted projects." A targeted project is one on which the various parties involved are agreed to accept the assistance of IMAGE in working out solutions to whatever problems may occur on the job site. IMAGE provides assistance through a two-person team of volunteers, one representing the contractors in the area and the other representing the unionized craftsmen.

The superintendent on an IMAGE project receives an IMAGE "Super Kit," which includes an IMAGE job-site poster, a series of payroll-envelope stuffers that remind the workers of their responsibilities to the industry, IMAGE bumper stickers and hard-hat decals, along with copies of the Memorandum of Understanding[4] and an IMAGE newsletter. These materials are sent to the project superintendent by the IMAGE co-chairperson.

Establishing trust is critically important for IMAGE to be successful in changing labor relations from an adversarial basis to a cooperative basis. IMAGE is willing to work with contractors in the area to relax the conditions set forth in the collective bargaining agreement in order to make local contractors more competitive. Contractors that are competitive are especially important to area construction users that have comparable facilities located out of the area and that, on an intrafirm level, are competing with one another. The need for competitive contractors was strongly reinforced by A. O. Smith's decision to close its facility in the area because construction costs at the company's facilities elsewhere were more favorable. IMAGE makes a difference in the marketplace for the customers of area contractors by making a difference in the workplace with the various work crews that are brought together on a common task.

The East Side experienced significant economic deterioration during the recession of the early 1980s. Decline in economic well-being, however, is not a recent phenomenon in the area. Fully one-third of the total income in the two major metropolitan Illinois counties comes from transfer payments (Franke, 138). In East St. Louis, economic development problems are intertwined with severe social pathology. Contractors no longer bid on jobs in East St. Louis because the city is dangerous even in daytime.

IMAGE has been criticized for not having enough committed volunteers from the various trade unions and building contractors to cover targeted projects properly. Consequently, only a small number of projects are covered (the larger ones) and the quality of the coverage varies from project to project depending on the volunteers. IMAGE seems to rely too much on its co-chairperson to work on targeted projects.

In the absence of sufficient data to support firm conclusions, two impressions remain. First, IMAGE is not as successful in achieving its objectives as is PRIDE in St. Louis. This could follow from the fact that IMAGE is concerned about something intangible—the labor relations image of the East Side—whereas PRIDE sets more tangible objectives such as jurisdictional disputes and work rules. Second, IMAGE faces more difficult obstacles to the realization of its goals than does PRIDE. Indeed, Franke states that it is remarkable that IMAGE has survived (147).

Reed St. James is a licensing program for men's clothing

and accessory items that is geared especially for discount stores and the budget operations of department stores.[5] Sixteen manufacturers are included in this suprafirm cooperation: Arrow, Wembley, Haggar, Duofold, Jockey, Jantzen, Levi-Strauss, Cluett Hosiery, Aris Isotoner, Dumont Enterprises, Host Apparel, Hush Puppies, W. Shanhouse, Roytex, Resistol/Dobbs, and Swank. Haggar provided the leadership that resulted in this private collective action in the men's fashion industry.

Without compromising the quality for which they are known, the sixteen partners sell a comprehensive line of clothing and accessories under the Reed St. James label exclusively to mass merchandisers and budget stores. Advertising expenses are shared by the sixteen vendors at least in part through licensing royalties.

Reed St. James allows discounters and department store budget operations to feature clothing and accessories items that are coordinated and have a unified look because the manufacturers meet four times a year for that purpose. Before Reed St. James, these retailers typically sold casual sportswear and diverted brand-name merchandise. Reed St. James allows mass merchandisers to enter the market of fashion-conscious consumers who are willing to pay more for quality and style. This new label and cooperative marketing agreement allow consumers to buy at lower prices the equivalent quality available elsewhere due in part to efficiencies that mass merchandisers enjoy in receiving and shipping at their central warehouses. That is, the agreement makes possible a better provisioning of human physical need.

Finally, it allows the vendors to enter a rapidly growing market without offending their department store customer base that handles their well-known brand-name merchandise. Reed St. James is offered to discounters with the stipulation that the names of the parent brands not be connected with Reed St. James in any way.

Lessons for Mainstream Economics from the Workplace Venue

At the interfirm and suprafirm level, mainstream economics condemns out of hand all collective action without regard to outcome. This presumption has been a part of conventional economics for more than two hundred years. "People of the same trade seldom meet together, even for merriment and diversion, but the conversation ends in a conspiracy against the public, or in some contrivance to raise prices" (Smith, 128). Presumption, in other words, is taken for fact. Positive-sum solutions to pressing dysfunctions that complicate the provisioning of human material need are not uncovered precisely because all collective action is stereotyped as zero-sum or worse.

Three main conclusions follow from these and other cases of interfirm and suprafirm cooperation. First, greater cooperation, whether in the workplace, the marketplace, or both, commonly is a response to dysfunction in the marketplace relating to deliverability, quality, or service.

Second, because human beings are no less social beings than individual beings, collective action is as natural a remedy for dysfunction as is individual action. Put in terms of organizing principles, cooperation is as natural a remedy for dysfunction as is competition.

Third, collective action can be as entrepreneurial as individual action because, as indicated above, collective action is as much a part of human nature as is individual action. It follows that by dismissing collective action, mainstream economics misrepresents entrepreneurship and thereby misconstrues economic development.

A social economics based solidly on the twin activating principles of competition and cooperation, along with the limiting principle of intervention, provides a better representation of production, distribution, exchange, and consumption, because it derives from a more accurate understanding of human nature and insists that an entire class of human action that helps meet human material need cannot be written off by means of a presumption that has remained largely unchallenged for more than two centuries.

Helping Consumers Achieve Greater Security: The Household Venue

Neighborhoods and the Social Economy

Human need is at the very heart of any authentic neighborhood.[6] As with the workplace, neighborhoods help meet the need of human beings to belong. In addition, neighborhoods are marketplaces for the exchange of goods and services that satisfy human physical need. As long as there are unmet needs of these types, human beings will continue to build, maintain, and protect neighborhoods.

Mainstream economics, along with modern societies, largely ignores the centrality of neighborhoods to individual well-being and family life. As stated previously, conventional economists reduce the organization of economic affairs to competition and prize especially the social value of freedom.

In contrast, social economists recognize that competition and freedom are not sufficient for an orderly, tranquil, and efficient economic order. The organizing principle of cooperation and the social value of community are required for that purpose and the neighborhood is an expression of that organizing principle and its associated social value that is as old as city life itself. There is no social economy, no reconstruction of the market economy, without functioning neighborhoods.

If economic institutions are to be effective in responding to unmet human material need, they must be sensitive to that need and that means being close to human beings and their families and being accessible. The occasional practice of marching on Washington and the various state capitols underscores the problem of addressing a specific unmet human need in a group environment where the leaders with the necessary resources are distanced from the persons in need. Historically, the neighborhood has functioned as an intermediate body addressing unmet human material need with varying success. Chicago's "Back of the Yards," "The Hill" in St. Louis, and "Brighton Beach" in New York are examples of neighborhoods that, in the past at least, have been effective in helping men and women and their families achieve greater economic security. The reconstructed neighborhood offers considerable promise as a means for coping with the dilemma of the market economy—to meet human material need all the while using unmet need to (re)allocate economic resources—for several reasons. First, the neighborhood helps reduce the bewildering complexity of the modern U.S. society to proportions that are more understandable to those in need. The neighborhood is much better proportioned to humankind than is the city—the next larger organizational unit in the social order. For that reason, the neighborhood in principle is more likely than much larger institutions to be democratically governed.

Second, the natural communications networks of the neighborhood make it more difficult for needy persons, even those who are too proud to admit their unmet need, to remain unnoticed for long. These networks expedite the delivery of the goods and services that help satisfy human physical need.

Third, since the residents of different neighborhoods by definition hold different social values or assign different importance to otherwise common social values, reconstruction at the level of the neighborhood allows each one to customize its response to unmet human material need in such a way as to reflect its own unique blending of values and customs. Coercion and repression of individuals are reduced because those who are different have some freedom to leave and those who remain tend to become more alike.

Fourth, the initial and continuing organizational task is of manageable proportions. Therefore, the task of recruiting and retaining persons who are capable of designing and implementing a strategy to help meet human material need is much less demanding than it is for much larger units in the social order, such as the city or the state.

Fifth, from neighborhood to neighborhood different strategies can be tried and compared in order to help identify the ones that work best. Any mistakes in a neighborhood strategy for meeting human material need are limited to that neighborhood and therefore are confined to a relatively small population.

Sixth, even neighborhoods that have deteriorated badly commonly retain institutions, such as schools, churches, and associations for amateur team sports, that can serve as a foundation for reconstruction and revitalization. In the following section, we discuss briefly how a few families in a Chicago neighborhood established a boys club as one of the first steps in neighborhood revitalization.

Seventh, additional employment opportunities are a *sine qua non* of any strategy to help meet human material need effectively. Most new jobs are created in small-business enterprises and, given the physical dimensions of both, neighborhoods are well suited to fostering small-business development.

Eighth, and last, neighbors are much more likely to make the mutual commitments necessary to effectively address human material needs than are strangers. Commitment to neighbor, which we define as a willingness from time to time to voluntarily subordinate one's own interest to the need of one's neighbor, is a critical component of a neighborhood strategy because unsubordinated self-interest in effect deals with the dilemma of the market economy by ignoring it, by walking past it without taking notice.

The rhetoric of mainstream economics notwithstanding, there is no "invisible hand of the market" to help meet human material need. There are only the visible, human hands of caring, hard-working human beings for this task. People living next door to one another are not neighbors by virtue of their proximity to one another. They are neighbors only when they are committed to helping each other.

Because neighborhoods are defined in terms of boundaries, the problem of discrimination arises: How to prevent neighborhoods from becoming ghettos on the one hand or country clubs on the other? A person may encounter discrimination for who he or she is (e.g., black, immigrant) or what he or she does (e.g., speaks another language, practices an alien religion). Discrimination is community carried to extremes.

The solution to the problem of discrimination is not found in abolishing or bulldozing neighborhoods. What is needed is *Homo socioeconomicus*, the person who is aware of his or her social nature and social duties and is ever mindful of his or her own rights and the rights of others.

Respect for the rights of others and faithfulness in one's obligations to others are two principal deterrents to discrimination. Caring is another. Good neighborhoods, in other words, are a reflection of the virtues of the persons who live there.

Neighborhoods are vulnerable to another extreme: too much freedom. Street crime is one example of freedom carried to an extreme. Rioting is a more obvious threat to a neighborhood's viability. The remedies here are the same as for discrimination: good neighbors make good neighborhoods.

Two Examples of Neighborhoods That Work

Lincoln Park is a neighborhood on Chicago's North Side.[7] At the end of World War II, it was a blue-collar area with some light manufacturing enterprises. The population at that time was predominantly of German, Italian, and Eastern European origins. A small number of blacks lived in the southwest corner of Lincoln Park. During World War II, the housing stock deteriorated as larger buildings were divided into rooming houses or small apartments and maintenance was deferred for lack of resources that could be applied to such ends.

By 1950, one-fourth of the housing units in Lincoln Park were classified as substandard or dilapidated. Vacancies in commercial buildings climbed as residents took their retail trade to larger shopping areas with parking. More and more low-income families moved into Lincoln Park, the building stock deteriorated further, and it appeared that the area would become a ghetto. During the late 1960s, three major institutions—DePaul University, McCormick Seminary, and the area hospitals—decided to remain rather than relocate to the suburbs. Their decisions turned out to be crucial in the eventual renaissance of Lincoln Park. These three institutions were influential in steering a development course toward more community and less individualism. Community, in turn, is central to the quality of life in Lincoln Park.

Urban planning and renewal, along with various neighborhood organizations, also played an important role in bringing about what has been a truly remarkable rebirth of the area. The most significant factor, however, was the creative response of a small number of homeowners in the southeast corner of Lincoln Park known as Old Town who in the late 1940s decided to stay and restore their properties. Indeed, it was a few families on one block in Old Town that triggered the change. One of the first steps taken by their newly established neighborhood association was the opening of a boys club to provide recreational outlets for the troublesome youth in the area, many from Ozark and Appalachian families who migrated to Chicago during World War II. The club became a success not only for the boys but for other residents as well.

The early agents of neighborhood change experienced numerous problems along the way, including trash pickup and enforcement of the building and zoning codes. Financing was another. Lincoln Park at that time was red-lined by the savings and loan industry. Area savings and loan institutions were investing the shares of Lincoln Park residents in suburban housing. Commercial banks in the area were supportive of local businesses but applied only a small portion of their assets to home mortgages and improvement loans.

More funding became available through a few savings and loan institutions in the mid-1960s. The terms, however, were stiff: a 50 percent down payment was not unusual.

Lincoln Park began to attract high-income white professionals and middle-income black professionals, Hispanics, and Asians in the late 1960s and early 1970s. At the same time, low-income families were pushed out due importantly to large residential rental increases. Between 1964 and 1984, one single-family house in Lincoln Park appreciated in value from $25,000 to $475,000. Increases of that magnitude were commonplace. Retail businesses began to flourish, especially boutiques, bars, restaurants, book stores, and toy shops.

Violent resistance to change and to pushing out poor families surfaced in the late 1960s. The violence ended at the time of the U.S. withdrawal from Vietnam without bringing neighborhood change to a halt. The only effect was the revision of urban-renewal plans to include more housing for low- and moderate-income families.

Expelling poor or near-poor families through otherwise meritorious restoration and renewal efforts presents a particularly perplexing question for the social economist. If every human being by nature has a right to housing because shelter is necessary for human survival, how can persons of conscience approve such efforts?

One answer is that the right to shelter is not an absolute

204 / John B. Davis and Edward J. O'Boyle

right to a specific housing unit or parcel of land. The good of all is a telling consideration in such matters as is attested by the long-standing legal principle of eminent domain.

As suggested previously, the answer is that the restorers and the renewers have an obligation to the poor to offer some alternative housing that minimally is the equivalent of their former housing. Better yet, the restorers and renewers might deliberately develop better educational, training, and employment opportunities to improve the ability of the poor to extricate themselves from their often disabling unmet human material need.

A second example is not a specific neighborhood but a grassroots institution for revitalizing distressed urban neighborhoods and rural communities across the U.S.[8] The origins of the community development corporation (CDC) may be traced to the Bedford-Stuyvesant Restoration Corporation, in Brooklyn, New York. It was established in 1966 with the encouragement of Robert F. Kennedy and the support of the Ford Foundation. It was one year after the riots in the Watts neighborhood of Los Angeles. By 1970 there were fewer than a hundred CDCs in the entire U.S. By the mid-1980s, their numbers were estimated at three thousand to five thousand. From the beginning, CDCs have been based on the premise that even impoverished communities and neighborhoods have their own substantial resources and that, under the right circumstances, the residents have the desire and the will to solve their own problems, including unmet human material need.

CDCs are characterized by (1) community control, (2) economic development, and (3) targeting. Community control is achieved through a board of directors that is made up of mainly residents from the community. Economic development means that CDCs are involved directly in community economic development projects. Targeting is a focusing on a clearly defined geographic area with a large concentration of persons in need. The goal of every CDC is to relieve the severe economic, social, and physical distress of the community residents.

First-generation CDCs received considerable financial support from the federal government. Over the past ten years, however, that support has eroded both in nominal and in real terms as a result of the severe domestic budget cuts initiated by the Reagan White House. Some federal support remains, but more and more CDCs are forced to turn to state and local governments for funds and to private sources such as foundations, corporations, churches, and financial institutions. Most CDCs have few paid employees, operate from rented quarters, and rely on contributed services from professionals such as accountants and attorneys and from corporate enterprises.

One innovative source of financial backing is called "linkage." Linkage is a requirement that private developers contribute to low-income housing and other programs of assistance to the needy in return for zoning clearances or permits. The linkage strategy has been employed in several major cities including Boston, San Francisco, Miami, Seattle, Hartford, and Washington. CDCs have taken root most notably in the cities of the Northeast and Midwest and to a lesser extent in the Far West. Chicago and Boston are regarded as having the most highly developed CDC networks. CDCs have not taken hold in the Great Plains, the Pacific Northwest, in most cities in the South, or in rural areas west of the Mississippi River.

CDC activities may be classified as (1) advocacy of minority leadership and empowerment of the poor or (2) specific economic development projects. Over the years, community leaders have split over which of the two is the more appropriate and should receive the greater support. William Duncan, who heads a CDC in Kentucky, asserts that CDCs become more powerful when they are able to merge advocacy and specific development projects into one effort.

Results have been impressive. In many cases, the development projects have been entrepreneurial. In others, they have been visionary. For instance, in Boston in a recent two-year period, an estimated 80 percent of all new low-cost housing was CDC built. In South Bronx, herbs are raised for commercial purposes in the U.S.'s first hydroponic greenhouse—a CDC project. In Kentucky, a CDC enterprise buys, stockpiles, and resells hardwood products from several small lumber mills thereby helping protect them from a volatile marketplace. In Pittsburgh, a seven-step financial scheme with multiple partners allowed a CDC to refurbish an abandoned building for industrial use. Two years after its opening, the building was fully leased.

The CDC story is really the story of certain key persons who are committed, respected, and entrepreneurial, with the vision and the hope to see promise in the midst of the rubble of deteriorated and desolate urban tracts. These persons include Genevieve Brooks of the South Bronx, Charles Bannerman of the Mississippi Delta, Veronica Barela of Denver's Hispanic Westside, Sandra Phillips of Pittsburgh's Oakland section, and Mary Nelson of Chicago's West Garfield Park. Women, according to Pierce and Steinbach (51), are more effective in CDC leadership roles because they are better than men at conflict resolution, have a greater capacity for detailed work, and are not filled with braggadocio.

CDCs serve as intermediaries between residents in need and the larger and more powerful elements in the social order with the resources to meet that need. During the 1980s, a number of what might be called "second-tier" intermediaries emerged between the CDCs and the rest of the social order to help them serve their neighborhoods and communities more effectively. They include the Local Initiative Support Corporation, which makes loans and grants to support CDC projects, the Enterprise Foundation, which provides funds and technical assistance on CDC projects, and the Development Training Institute, which improves the skills of CDC directors and senior development managers.

Some CDCs have not been successful and some have been managed inefficiently and dishonestly. Even so, the growth in numbers especially in the face of substantially diminished federal support points to an institutional viability at precisely where it is most needed: among those persons who are the direct casualties of the market economy or its unfortunate collateral damage.

Lessons for Mainstream Economics from the Household Venue

First, in a market economy, change is inevitable and some change is destructive. For some persons and families, this destruction is too great to bear alone. Without help, some of the victims of this change may never recover.

Second, urban neighborhoods and rural communities, even those that are severely depressed and run down, can be reborn to provide the assistance required to help the needy lift themselves out of economic insecurity. An important aspect of rejuvenating a neighborhood or community is showing the needy how to develop and use their own skills and talents to address their own need.

Third, one person can make a difference in mobilizing a neighborhood or community toward collective action in response to unmet human material need. Typically, such persons do not have to be imported from outside the area. They already live in the neighborhood.

Fourth, the "invisible hand" does not assure the viability of neighborhood and community organizations that serve the needy. Without the visible hands of the more powerful elements in the social order, such as private business enterprises, city governments, state governments, and the federal government, neighborhood and community organizations will fail, leaving behind either ghettos or country clubs.

Final Remarks

Two vastly different but intertwined reconstructions are necessary to make economics a more effective tool for understanding economic affairs and to transform the market economy into a better means for provisioning human material need. For economics, this means reconstructing the discipline around the two dimensions of human material need: physical need and the need for work as such. For the economy, this means reconstructing the workplace and the neighborhood so that both become more effective in provisioning that need.

It would be a pity for economics itself if the first reconstruction fails. In addition, such a failure would further complicate the second reconstruction. Worse yet, any failure as to the second reconstruction would be a tragedy for many of the poor whose material future depends importantly on the help that should come from and through a reconstructed workplace and a revitalized neighborhood. The second reconstruction effort simply will not bend to the "invisible hand of the market." It requires flesh-and-blood human beings to make it happen.

Notes

1. Not all workplace dysfunction derives from some failure in cooperation. However, the specific dysfunctions cited have been selected as wholly or partially reflective of failed cooperation.

2. Von Hippel (76–92) in 1988 stated that ten of eleven surveyed steel minimill firms reported informal know-how trading with competitors.

3. For more information about PRIDE, see O'Boyle (140–41). See Lohman and Mayer (330–38) for information on Top-Notch, which operates in the construction industry in Indianapolis, and *Labor Relations Today* (3,7) regarding PALM, which operates in Philadelphia. Information about IMAGE derives from two sources: a 1984 study prepared by Southern Illinois University at Edwardsville and the writer's two-to-three-hour luncheon meeting with two IMAGE representatives.

4. The Memorandum of Understanding is a statement made by private parties in the industry in which each one voluntarily sets forth its obligations to the rest of the local industry. The Memorandum makes no reference to individual rights or the state. IMAGE operates as a private group without government fiat and without government funds.

5. Information from materials provided by Jantzen during a 1988 site visit to its (since relocated) facility in Eunice, Louisiana.

6. By "neighborhood" is meant a relatively small, clearly identifiable place where the residents generally know one another, share some common values—especially social values—and have some regard for one another. For our purposes, whole towns and places in rural areas may be regarded as neighborhoods.

7. An unpublished manuscript about Lincoln Park by William Waters and Maurice Forkert is the basis for our remarks about that North Side Chicago neighborhood.

8. Peirce and Steinbach's monograph is especially instructive regarding the origins, characteristics, and accomplishments of community development corporations.

References

Franke, Arnold G., and Paul E. Sultan. *IMAGE (Involvement and Management Advance Growth and Employment): A Study of Labor-Management Cooperation in the Construction Industry for Southwestern Illinois.* Edwardsville: Southern Illinois University, 1984. Mimeo.

Lohman, Jeff, and Henry C. Mayer. "Top-Notch Is More Than a Slogan." *Review of Social Economy* 42, no. 3 (1984): 330–38.

O'Boyle, Edward J. "Catholic Social Economics: A Response To Certain Problems, Errors, and Abuses of the Modern Age." In *Social Economics: Retrospect And Prospect*, edited by Mark A. Lutz. Boston: Kluwer Academic Publishers, 1990.

Peirce, Neal R., and Carol F. Steinbach. *Corrective Capitalism: The Rise of America's Community Development Corporations*. New York: Ford Foundation, 1987.

Smith, Adam. *An Inquiry into the Nature and Causes of the Wealth of Nations*. New York: The Modern Library, 1937.

U.S. Department of Labor. "Built-Rite for the First Time." *Labor Relations Today* 2, no. 5 (1987).

Von Hippel, Eric. *The Sources Of Information*. New York: Oxford University Press, 1988.

Waters, William R., and Maurice Forkert. "The Changing Economy of Lincoln Park after World War II to 1980." Unpublished manuscript, n.d.

Contributors
Index

Contributors

Severyn T. Bruyn is a professor of sociology at Boston College where he teaches graduate courses in social economy, the business corporation, economy, and society. He is the former director of the graduate program in social economy and social policy. He has helped organize several companies that consult in organizational development and has published books in the fields of social economy, community development, and social scientific methodology.

Peter L. Danner, emeritus professor of economics at Marquette University, in thirty-five years of college teaching offered a range of graduate and undergraduate courses with special concentrations in the history of economic thought and economics and ethics. His publications, particularly those in the *Review of Social Economy*, have been for the most part in the latter field as is his book, *An Ethics for the Affluent*, and his current work, *Getting and Spending: A Primer in Economic Morality*.

John B. Davis is an associate professor of economics at Marquette University where he teaches economics and ethics, labor economics, and history of economic thought. Among the journals in which he has published are *History of Political Economy*, *Journal of the History of Economic Thought*, *Economics and Philosophy*, *Economic Journal*, *Review of Social Economy*, *Cambridge Journal of Economics*, *Review of Political Economy*, and *Journal of Post-Keynesian Economics*. He has recently edited *The Economic Surplus in Advanced Economies* for Edward Elgar Publishing and completed *Keynes's Philosophical Development* for Cambridge University Press. He is currently the editor of the *Review of Social Economy*.

Edward J. O'Boyle is a research associate and associate professor of economics in the College of Administration and Business, Louisiana Tech University, where he teaches principles of economics, comparative economic systems, and ethics for the professions and the workplace. His primary research interests include human material need, and intrafirm productivity and innovation, along with interfirm partnerships and suprafirm alliances. His work has appeared in several professional journals and other publications.

Warren J. Samuels is a professor of economics at Michigan State University. He specializes in the history of economic thought, law and economics, and methodology. He is the coeditor of *Research in the History of Economic Thought and Methodology*, coauthor of *Economic Thought and Discourse in the Twentieth Century*, and author of numerous books, journal articles, and reviews. A five-volume collection of his work has been published by Macmillan Press and New York University Press.

Anthony E. Scaperlanda is a professor of economics at Northern Illinois University, DeKalb, Illinois, where he teaches international economics at both the undergraduate and graduate levels. His research interests have emphasized foreign direct investment and the social economics implications of multinational enterprises. Within the context of two monographs, one edited volume, and numerous articles and book chapters, his work directly connected to social economics is primarily found in the *Journal of Economic Issues*, the *International Journal of Social Economics*, and the *Review of Social Economy*.

Index